HIKING AND CYCLING IN
THE BLACK FOREST

HIKING AND CYCLING IN THE BLACK FOREST

WALKS, TREKS AND CYCLE RIDES IN SOUTHERN GERMANY

by Kat Morgenstern

JUNIPER HOUSE, MURLEY MOSS,
OXENHOLME ROAD, KENDAL, CUMBRIA LA9 7RL
www.cicerone.co.uk

© Kat Morgenstern 2019
Second edition 2019
ISBN: 978 1 78631 021 7
Reprinted in 2023 (with updates)
First edition 2014

Printed in Singapore by KHL Printing on responsibly sourced paper
A catalogue record for this book is available from the British Library.
All photographs are by the author unless otherwise stated.

Losshohlwege-Pfad and Neunlindenpfad and Katharinenpfad symbols
© Breisach-Touristik/Kaiserstuhl-Tuniberg Tourismus eV, Breisach am Rhein
Seensteig symbol © Baiersbronn Touristik

Route mapping by Lovell Johns www.lovelljohns.com.
Contains OpenStreetMap.org data © OpenStreetMap con-
tributors, CC-BY-SA. NASA relief data courtesy of ESRI

Front cover: Beautiful Münstertal with St. Trudperts Abbey

CONTENTS

Acknowledgements

Firstly, I wish to express my gratitude to the Schwarzwaldverein. Without its early efforts to preserve the culture and nature of the Black Forest and to make it accessible to visitors via a huge network of trails, the Black Forest would not be the wonderful walking destination that it is today. I am grateful for their tireless efforts to implement and maintain the thousands of kilometres of trails throughout the region and I am especially grateful to the chief trail warden Mr Schenk for his very helpful assistance and prompt responses to my questions.

I also wish to thank Frau Baur from Schwarzwald Tourismus GmbH and Frau Braun of Baiersbronn Touristik for their great support with this project.

Heartfelt thanks to my husband, Tino Gonzales, as well as to my sister and brother-in-law Christa and Rainer Klassen, who have accompanied me on many of these walks and offered valuable feedback and support.

Last, but by no means least, a sincere thank you to Jonathan Williams, Lois Sparling and the team at Cicerone for their ever-helpful and quick responses, and of course, for taking on the project in the first place.

Updates to this Guide

While every effort is made by our authors to ensure the accuracy of guidebooks as they go to print, changes can occur during the lifetime of an edition. Any updates that we know of for this guide will be on the Cicerone website (www.cicerone.co.uk/1021/updates), so please check before planning your trip. We also advise that you check information about such things as transport, accommodation and shops locally. Even rights of way can be altered over time. We are always grateful for information about any discrepancies between a guidebook and the facts on the ground, sent by email to updates@cicerone.co.uk or by post to Cicerone, Juniper House, Murley Moss, Oxenholme Road, Kendal LA9 7RL.

Register your book: To sign up to receive free updates, special offers and GPX files where available, create a Cicerone account and register your purchase via the 'My Account' tab at www.cicerone.co.uk.

Map key

———	walk route	🏃 finish	
———	cycle route		
———	alternative route	🏃 start	
🍴	picnic spot	🏃 start/finish	
🍽	restaurant	A5	Autobahn (motorway)
✝	chapel/church	B500	Bundesstraßen (=UK A roads)
▲	peak	L123	Landstraßen (=UK B roads)
P	car park	═══	minor country roads
◯	lake	• •	geological/water feature
——	river	➤	route direction
⬤	town/village		
▮	urban area	-----	track
✦	landmark	🔺	serviced hut
——	ski lift	⌂	unserviced hut
⊓SP⊓SP	signpost		
⚡	wind turbines		

Map scales

The maps for the walks are at 1:50,000 (2cm to 1km), as indicated on the first map in each route description.

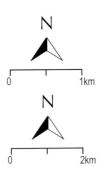

N
0 — 1km

The maps for the rides are at 1:100,000 (1cm to 1km), as indicated on the first map in each route description.

N
0 — 2km

Allerheiligen Falls (Walk 9)

A long view of Münstertal (Walk 3)

INTRODUCTION

The Black Forest could well be described as the epitome of picture-book Germany: ancient castles perched high above small towns with quaint old timber-frame buildings, ancient wooden farmhouses sat on the side of forest-clad hills, flower-strewn mountain meadows that make cows happy and fat, tiny wayfarers' chapels inviting the weary traveller to linger for a while and take in the views, hidden gorges and impressive waterfalls, serene forests with raspberries and blueberries galore, and bald, subalpine mountain tops with panoramic views stretching as far as the Alps and the Vosges. An extensive trail network covers 24,000km of well-marked routes providing endless possibilities for exploring this beautiful region.

As a medium-sized mountain range, or *Mittelgebirge* as Germans call it, the Black Forest is not a destination for peak-baggers, but the perfect place for romantics. Instead of trying to impress with superlative landscapes it seduces the visitor with its unpretentious charm and authenticity rooted in age-old traditions and colourful heritage.

There are few places that manage to blend so well an old-world charm, which lets you forget the troubles of the modern world, with a superb and well-maintained infrastructure providing all the conveniences to which we have grown accustomed.

And yet, the Black Forest has a lot more to offer than just pastoral peace and quiet. Blessed with an abundance

A flower-strewn Black Forest meadow in spring

Karlsruher Grat – volcanic fissure (Walk 8)

of curative hot springs it has been an oasis for 'wellness' seekers since pre-Roman times. Spa tourism culminated during the 18th and 19th century. Back then only the rich could afford such luxuries, but today they are affordable for anyone. What could be more restorative than to relax in a pool of hot soothing waters after a long day's walk?

If you like walking for pleasure, enjoy the harmonious interplay between nature and culture, appreciate fresh produce and regional specialities, and value a good night's sleep in a comfortable bed, you will love the Black Forest.

Last, but not least, the Black Forest is a budget-friendly destination. Contrary to popular belief, Germany is one of the least expensive countries in Western Europe, yet offers some of the highest standards of infrastructure, quality and service.

GEOLOGY

The Black Forest lies deep in the southwestern corner of Germany. It stretches from Pforzheim in the north down to the Swiss border, between Lake Constance and Basle. As mountain ranges go, it is quite old, with its bedrock of granite and gneiss originating more than 200 million years ago from volcanic activity. When the region was submerged under a shallow and warm inland sea it became covered with sedimentary deposits. Countless generations of corals and crustaceans lived and died in these waters, forming thick layers of calciferous deposits. The best place to see these layers is Wutach Gorge, in the southeastern corner of the region, where the River Wutach has carved a geological timeline into the rock (Walk 6).

Up until the Eocene era (56–34 million years ago), the Black Forest and the Vosges were still part of the same tectonic plate. Eventually, volcanic activity caused the plate to crack, resulting in rifting and the creation of the Rhine Valley. The small mountain range of Kaiserstuhl, situated between the Vosges and the Black Forest, was formed during the Miocene period (23–5 million years ago) at the climax of volcanic

activity in that region. After the tectonic break, the plates on either side lifted along their Rhine-bound edges, which accounts for the steep hills that border the Rhine Valley.

Glaciers that covered the entire Black Forest during the last ice age have left their unmistakable mark on the topography. Today's Black Forest is characterised by softly contoured hills and valleys, dotted with near circular tarns that lie at the base of the hills. As the glaciers retreated, the land, freed of their weight, started to rise. It is still rising today, but at a rate that is offset by the forces of erosion.

Geographically, the Black Forest is generally divided into a southern and a northern/central part, although the dividing lines are a little arbitrary.

The source of the Danube (Walk 10)

SPAS: THE HEALING POWER OF WATER

The Black Forest's position on the edge of a fault line that runs through the rift valley of the Rhine has endowed the region with an abundance of hot springs. The Celts revered the springs as sacred, but the Romans turned them into 'bath temples' at Baden-Baden, Badenweiler, and Augusta Raurica, where the remains of these complexes can still be seen.

Remains of a Roman bath temple (Ride 1)

Mineral-rich hot springs have always been deemed to possess curative powers and have long been used therapeutically for conditions ranging from arthritis and rheumatism to heart disease and respiratory problems, depending on their mineral composition.

Balneology (water therapy) experienced its heyday in the 18th and 19th centuries, when spa towns such as Baden-Baden, Badenweiler or Bad Wildbad became Meccas for well-heeled health tourists from all over Europe and Russia. The rich and famous flocked to the Black Forest with their families and entourages of attendants, often spending many weeks or months 'taking the waters' and bathing in the soothing pools. Today, 'wellness tourism' is less exclusive. Although there are clinics and recuperation homes for patients who have been prescribed a therapeutic stay (*Kur*) by their physicians, the spas are affordable and open to anyone who simply wants to relax and enjoy the rejuvenating waters.

A typical thermal spa usually has several pools with water temperatures ranging from 28 to 36°C and most have outside pools with powerful jets for water massage, as well as saunas and steam baths. Massages and other wellness treatments are available at an extra charge.

A listing of spa towns in Baden-Württemberg can be found at www.heilbaeder-bw.de. Not all of these are in the Black Forest, but you can check their location on the map.

In the north the mountains rarely reach much more than 1000m, with Hornisgrinde at 1164m being the highest peak. The mountains here are deeply incised by fast-flowing rivers that have cut steep and narrow valleys into the hills. The southern part is known as Hochschwarzwald (High Black Forest), and it is here that the highest peaks are found, several of which reach almost 1500m. Here, near the headwaters of the Danube, runs another important geological dividing line – the European watershed that determines the flow of water either into the Atlantic via the Rhine or into the Black Sea via the Danube.

The Black Forest can further be bisected into an eastern and western side divided by its main crest. While the mountains along the western edge erupt quite abruptly from the Rhine Valley, the eastern part rises gradually, forming an extensive high plateau characterised by gently rolling hills.

Thanks to this varied topography, the Black Forest offers a surprising range of different landscapes and habitats, which are best explored by foot.

HISTORY

Celts, Romans, Alemanni and Benedictine monks

The history of human activity in Baden-Württemberg dates back to the dawn of humankind. In 1907, a jawbone was found near Heidelberg, which has been dated to between 600,000 and 500,000 years old and belonged to a pre-Neanderthal hominid known as *Homo heidelbergensis*. Most archaeological discoveries have been made on the eastern side of the Black Forest and in the Danube Valley in the Swabian Jura. In the Rhine Valley there is evidence of hunter-gatherers dating back to 40,000–35,000BC. In Neolithic times, the fertile soils along the river were used by the earliest farming communities who established themselves on prominent hilltops, especially on the edges of Kaiserstuhl at Breisach and Burkheim.

From about 750BC, Central Europe north of the Alps was predominantly Celtic, and this was the first significant civilisation to inhabit the area of the Black Forest. Remains of Celtic settlements in the region have been dated to about 650BC. Among the most significant archaeological sites from that period are the huge Magdalenenberg burial mounds near Villingen-Schwenningen and a hill-fort settlement on Münsterberg in Breisach. Other traces of Celtic civilisation are dotted throughout the area, but are often poorly preserved or documented.

When Caesar conquered Gaul between 58 and 50BC, the Celtic territories were absorbed into the Roman Empire. At first, the Rhine formed the natural limit of the empire, but with their eyes set on expansion, the Romans gradually pushed their borders further east and north. Soon the Danube became the border

Roman theatre at Augusta Raurica (Ride 1)

demarcation and the line was extended north from Rottweil to what is now Mainz, on the Rhine. The Celtic population became assimilated or withdrew further into the hills, while the Romans settled along the Rhine and controlled certain trade routes at strategic points. As early as AD75, they had built a road along the River Kinzig to cut through the Black Forest from Offenburg to Rottweil. To control their borders and ward off ambushes from barbaric tribes the Romans constructed a defence wall known as the Raetian Limes, which stretched some 550km from Koblenz to Regensburg and was guarded by approximately 900 watchtowers and 120 'castells' or military outposts.

In the long run, however, the Romans were unable to defend the extensive borders of their empire. Continued attacks, not only along the Raetian Limes but also along their borders in the east, significantly weakened their position. By the middle of the 3rd century the empire had began to crumble. Military posts along the Raetian Limes were abandoned in order to attend to crises that were escalating elsewhere. Meanwhile, Germanic barbarians (Alemanni) seized the opportunity to invade and settle in hitherto Roman-occupied territories, forcing the Romans to withdraw back to their former borderline along the Rhine.

The Alemanni were not a homogenous group, but rather a loose alliance of various tribes without a common leader. There is some debate as to where they came from. Some authorities suggest that they originated in northern regions (Elbe/Saale), others believe that they were Suebians. Whatever their origin, they were fierce and determined, and quickly spread throughout the Upper Rhine region, populating not only the Black Forest, but also what is now Alsace and the German-speaking parts of Switzerland. Even though Alemanni cannot be defined by a common ethnic identity, their former strongholds share a common cultural heritage and language that has persisted to the present time.

In a decisive battle at Zülpich in AD507 the Franks defeated the Alemanni, a key event in the history of Europe. The Frankish leader Clovis, who had just converted to Christianity (allegedly to please his wife, a devout Christian), had only a few years earlier defeated Syagius, the last Roman official to rule over Gaul. Thus, Clovis inherited almost all of the previously Roman-controlled territories north of the Alps.

At that time the Black Forest was still a sparsely inhabited wilderness, populated mostly by heathen Alemanni. At first, they were largely left alone and free to continue their pagan ways. But by around the 7th century, the region had become a target for Christian missionaries, many of them hailing from Ireland, who fervently began to 'civilise' the area. Missionary hermitages soon grew into powerful monasteries, making the Church the most influential and wealthy economic power

St Trudpert Abbey, Münstertal (Walk 3)

in the region. The remnants of these once powerful abbeys and their pervading influence are still seen today.

Most monasteries in the Black Forest belonged to the order of St Benedict. In the 9th and 10th centuries many of them joined the Cluniac reform movement, which demanded stricter adherence to spiritual values and independence from the influence of worldly powers in the affairs of the monasteries. In effect, they became a power unto themselves, as they were now directly subordinate only to the Pope, many hundreds of miles away. The reforms significantly changed the political power structures in the region. The fragmentary distribution of territorial rights between different worldly and religious entities gave rise to continuous power struggles, which were really only settled during secularisation in the late 18th century. Even today, the religious affiliations of individual communities largely follow their former political allegiance.

The green gold of the Black Forest
In Celtic times the Black Forest was still a dangerous, uninhabited and almost impenetrable wilderness. Agrarian settlements developed mainly on the edges of the mountains, especially along the eastern plateau, where 'islands' of forest were cleared around central settlements. Yet, there is clear evidence that the first inroads into the forest

A charcoal-maker's hut

18

This kind of raft was used in logging until the 19th century

were made as early as 500BC, mostly in the northeastern regions.

The Celts were metalworkers and familiar with the process of making iron tools. What drove them into the mountains was not the trees – there were plenty of them all over – but the search for iron ore. A number of Celtic iron furnaces have been found in Neuenbürg, evidence that this was a highly organised place of manufacture. Celtic society was already segregated, with specialists carrying out specific tasks such as working in mines or at the smelting furnaces. Making iron is a wood-intensive industry as it requires large amounts of charcoal to fire the ovens, and these early activities were the first to change the face of the Black Forest.

The Romans also dug for metal and cut down trees to build their defence posts and towns along the Limes, but it was during the Middle Ages, when monastic culture flourished, that mining really took off. At that time, the population of the Black Forest swelled as monasteries grew up around small settlements. Great wealth was excavated from the mountains, notably in the form of silver. The revenue was invested in the construction of some of the great medieval castles and cathedrals, and the forest provided much of the building material. The demand for wood was enormous and the forest was ruthlessly decimated for timber, charcoal, tar and potash (needed in glass manufacture). Between AD900 and 1350 fully two-thirds of the forest was cleared and turned into fields and

Deciduous trees in the Black Forest in autumn colour

pasture. If it hadn't been for calamities such as the outbreak of the Black Death or the Thirty Years War in the 17th century, which temporarily halted the destruction, the entire region might long since have been turned into a wasteland.

The last great assault on the forest came during the 17th and 18th centuries, by which time the supply of wood was no longer restricted to local markets, but it was exported as far as the Netherlands, where it was used to build the Dutch war and merchant fleet. The construction of a single war ship required 700 oaks – the equivalent of about 2.5 hectares (ha) of forest.

Once more, vast areas of forest were cleared, but transport was still a problem. There were no usable roads, so the only way to move the large numbers of trees was by water. Chutes were built to send logs from remote mountainsides sliding down into the valleys. Some logs were milled for local use, but others were tied together into rafts up to 40m long, which raftsmen then had to navigate down to the mouths of the rivers. Those that were bound for the Netherlands were tied into enormous rafts, up to 400m long, to travel down the Rhine. These gigantic rafts had room for 800 people, and carried cooks and butchers as well as livestock, provisions, trading goods and passengers.

Glass manufacture was another wood-hungry industry. To produce one kilogram of glass, two cubic metres of wood were needed, 97 per cent of which was burnt to obtain potash, an essential ingredient in the glass making process. Glass makers usually settled in remote areas until all the nearby forest was cleared, before moving on to virgin ground elsewhere.

By the beginning of the 19th century the situation was truly dire. The forest ecosystem was on the brink of collapse and something had to be done. Remarkably, the virtual destruction of the Black Forest led to what was perhaps the first piece of environmental legislation to be passed. It stipulated that in any given year no more wood was to be cut than could grow back naturally within 12 months.

A monumental reforestation effort was also undertaken. This, however, was somewhat misguided: while the original forest was a mixture of conifers and deciduous species such as beech and oak, the reforestation effort consisted almost exclusively of fast growing and economically valuable conifer trees, planted on a massive scale. Although they provided a 'quick-fix' by restoring tree cover and replenishing wood resources in as little as 60 years, a monoculture of conifers is prone to insect pests and diseases; what is more, it is vulnerable to adverse weather conditions – especially high winds, as was demonstrated by Hurricane Lothar, which devastated thousands of acres of forest in December of 1999.

By the 1980s the folly of this 'quick growth' policy was finally realised. Since then the Forestry Commission has made a shift towards sustainability and has started to reintroduce as broad a spectrum of native deciduous trees as possible. Trees are still continuously harvested, but instead of clear felling, usually only individual trees are taken out. Some rare and endangered species are even planted for no economic reason at all, but simply to conserve them. Gradually the forest is changing into a healthy mixture of conifers and deciduous trees.

Thanks to these new sustainable practices, the forest has been able to recover from the brink of almost total destruction. While at the end of the 19th century only 32 per cent of the area was forested, today trees cover almost 80 per cent of the total area.

'Naturpark Schwarzwald' – a new model for conservation

By the middle of the 19th century the winds of change, unleashed by the Industrial Revolution, started to blow in and affected even the backwaters of the Black Forest – but not quite as one might expect. As the world entered an era dominated by industry and machinery, an ideological backlash against industrialisation began to develop, characterised by the idealisation of nature and a longing for old ways and traditions: Romanticism was the new vogue.

Although the Black Forest was by no means 'an untouched wilderness', the blend of cultivated lands, forest and wilderness tended by human hands seemed to exemplify the Romantic vision of 'the simple life' in harmony with nature. At about the same time the first railway lines opened up the Black Forest and rapidly turned it into an accessible tourist destination. Its appeal was not only what was left of its nature, but also the numerous thermal springs, with their curative powers.

By the late 19th century the Schwarzwaldverein, or Black Forest Association, had been set up and began to establish dedicated walking routes through the Black Forest, the first of which was the famous West Way (inaugurated in 1900), a route of 260km from Pforzheim to Basle. Next were the Middle and East Ways, and many others have followed since. The broader aim of the Schwarzwaldverein has always been to promote and preserve the unique heritage of the Black Forest, to protect its many fragile habitats and to educate the public on both its nature and culture.

Fast forward to early 1999: after many months of negotiation 'Naturpark Südschwarzwald' was launched, and by the end of 2000 'Naturpark Schwarzwald Mitte/Nord' followed. The naturpark concept is based on the ideas of bioregionalism and sustainable development – very similar aims to those originally pursued by the Schwarzwaldverein, but now with much broader support, as it is administered by the communities as well as the county of Baden-Württemberg. The Schwarzwaldverein still works closely with the naturpark administration.

A view up to the weather station at Feldberg (Walk 1)

LEHRPFADE: NATURE INTERPRETATION TRAILS

Germans have a thing about interpretation trails (*Lehrpfade*); they are everywhere. They are intended to stimulate interaction with the places one walks through by providing information boards on various themes. There are *Weinlehrpfade* about the grapes and viticulture of the region, *Geologische Lehrpfade*, about the geology, *Natur-* or *Waldlehrpfade* about the natural history, and many more. The information is often quite interesting, but the boards can feel a little intrusive.

A naturpark is not a national park or a nature reserve as such, although there are many protected areas, as well as strict forest reserves (*Bannwald*) within the naturparks. Instead, the aim is to regulate development and tourism in a sustainable manner that is sensitive to the environment in which it takes place. The task is to balance the needs of the many different interest groups in the Black Forest – particularly those of tourism, industry and traditional farming, the latter of which plays a vital role in maintaining the character of the landscape. In practice, this means making the landscape accessible to walkers, skiers, mountain bikers and others, while managing the flow of visitor traffic. An important aspect of this work entails restrictions. In order to protect fragile habitats some areas have been declared off-limits, walkways are sometimes fenced to minimise erosion, car access may be restricted, and making wildfires and wild camping are prohibited.

Thanks to measures such as these, previously degraded areas have been able to recover and several rare endemic species have once again returned to the Black Forest. Protective regulations not only benefit nature, but also enhance visitors' enjoyment. To help these efforts, please respect the rules and keep to the designated paths.

Germany's newest national park, National Park Schwarzwald, was inaugurated in January 2014 to protect parts of the northern Black Forest and to re-establish safe habitats for various endangered native species. It will take time for the forest to regenerate into a fully functioning ecosystem, but it's a start.

PLANTS AND WILDLIFE

The very name 'Black Forest' is deeply evocative, conjuring up images of dark, thick pine and fir tree forest stretching monotonously into the distance. Nothing could be further from the truth. In Germany the term 'forest' is frequently applied to medium-sized forested mountain ranges. In the Black Forest the landscape is a harmonious

Black Forest flowers (clockwise from top left): Bee orchid; Marsh Cinquefoil; Masterwort; and Sundew

blend of large tracts of forest interspersed with pastures, orchards and, along the western foothills, with vineyards. To be sure, conifers are the dominant species, especially in the north. However, the region comprises a surprising variety of habitats and species, especially considering its relatively small size.

Plant communities vary with the different climatic conditions. The warmest regions are found along the southern and western edges, facing the Rhine. The foothills, from Ortenau to Kaiserstuhl and Markgräflerland, are famous fruit and wine growing terroirs. This sun-blessed region

of Germany is home to many Mediterranean species that are not found elsewhere in the country. Sweet chestnuts and walnut trees flourish, along with oak, hazel, beech and hornbeam. There are even good stands of wild holly. Well-established orchards of cherry, apple and plum burst into flower in April, draping the countryside in a festive cloak of pink and white.

In the southern Black Forest there are numerous highland meadows that are not intensively farmed, but instead used as summer pastures or cut for hay. These are rich habitats for wildflowers and butterflies. Highland meadows with brooks meandering down through the valley provide refuge for wet meadow species, such as bistort, marsh marigold and meadowsweet, that have disappeared from marshes on flatter ground, much of which has fallen victim to drainage. A surprising number of orchids, including rare lady's slipper and bee orchids, can also be found, and not just in protected areas.

In the northern Black Forest, firs predominate and bilberries cover much of the forest floor. Upland moors known as *Grinden* top many of the northern peaks; these are not natural habitats, but have developed over several hundred years of use as pasture for goats and sheep. Today they are considered precious habitats with a unique moorland flora, where rare mosses and plants such as sundew, cotton grasses and marsh cinquefoil flourish.

The wide variety of habitats provides a home to numerous animal species. Common species such as deer, wild boar and fox inhabit the forest. More excitingly, lynx has recently been making a comeback. A true rarity is the highly endangered Bechstein's bat, which finds sanctuary in the extensive forest ranges.

Among the more notable bird species are capercaillie, peregrine falcons, kestrels and hawks, as well as storks, ravens and cuckoos. There are no dangerous animals in the Black Forest, except for a couple of species of poisonous snakes (adder and asp viper), but you would be very lucky to catch even a glimpse of them.

Bannwald

On some of the walks described in this book you will come across signs warning that you are about to enter a Bannwald (strict forest reserve). These areas are minimally managed forest reserves, which have been created as part of a Europe-wide programme to study the regeneration process of different ecosystems. Here, the forestry service does not interfere with nature's cycles and it is hoped that in 100 years or so these oases will have transformed into primordial forest. The reserves have a particularly natural and wild appearance, but they also require walkers to be more aware of falling branches or of trees obstructing the way. These reserve zones should be avoided in high winds or poor weather conditions and extra caution is advised at all times.

GETTING THERE

By plane
Getting to the Black Forest is quite easy. The nearest international airport hub is Frankfurt, Germany's largest airport. Unfortunately, it is also extremely busy and it may be more convenient to fly into one of the smaller, regional airports located nearer to the Black Forest.

Karlsruhe/Baden-Baden serves the northern and northwestern

Waldkirch (Walk 12, Stage 1)

Black Forest, although only Ryanair flies there directly from the UK. Shuttle buses connect the airport with Baden-Baden, Karlsruhe (Hahn-Express) and Rastatt. More information is available at www.badenairpark.de.

Stuttgart is the most convenient international airport for access to the eastern and northeastern Black Forest. BA and Eurowings fly there direct from the UK. Local city-trains (S-Bahn) transfer passengers to Stuttgart main station for onward travel. More information is available at www.flughafen-stuttgart.de.

Friedrichshafen, on Lake Constance (Bodensee), provides easy access to the southeastern Black For-est. Easyjet offers flights from Gatwick during the winter. Regional trains leave from the train station right outside the airport. For most destinations you'll have to switch at the main station in town. For more information see www.bodensee-airport.eu.

Basle/Euroairport serves Basle/Freiburg and Mulhouse. It is ideal for access to the southwestern Black Forest. Served by BA and Easyjet, the airport has direct exits into both Switzerland and France. It is a good idea to decide on your onward transport before you arrive, as that will determine which exit to take. On the Swiss side there is a regular shuttle bus to Basle main station (Basel SBB). From here a limited number of trains continue directly on to Germany. There are more frequent services from Basel (Bad), where you can catch a regional train to your final destination. (Confusingly, Basel has three train stations, Basel SBB is the Swiss terminal,

Basel Bad is the German station and Gare de Bâle SNCF is the French station.)

A direct shuttle bus to Freiburg leaves from outside the French exit (with a request stop in Neuenburg, which, however, is not very useful as it stops a long way out of town). There is also a French shuttle bus to Mulhouse from where a regional train crosses over the border to Germany. More information is available at www.euroairport.com.

Be sure to note which terminal (French or Swiss) your return flight will be departing from.

As major international hubs, Frankfurt and Zurich airports can be accessed from just about anywhere. They are reasonably convenient for access to the Black Forest. By train, Freiburg can be reached in approximately 2 hours from either city. For more information see www.zurich-airport.com and www.frankfurt-airport.com/en.html.

By car

It is also possible to drive to the Black Forest, but it is a long journey from anywhere in Britain. You can follow the Rhine from Hook van Holland (about 7hr without stopping) or cross over to Dunkerque or Calais, which is a slightly shorter route. However, traffic conditions in the Netherlands and on the A5 motorway down to Baden-Württemberg are terrible. Expect congestion at any time.

By train

The journey planner on the Deutsche Bahn (DB) website is a very useful tool for planning your journey as it integrates local bus connections into its system where a train service is not available. See www.bahn.de. The DB app is a useful tool for planning the journey and getting last minute updates and notifications in case of delay. Deutsche Bahn is currently undertaking a major infrastructure update on the Rheintalbahn. Check schedules carefully and be prepared for delays on this route.

Thanks to high-speed railway services that connect the major hubs of Europe, taking the train to the Black Forest need not take much longer than getting there by plane. Eurostar services to Lille, Paris or Brussels connect with fast TGVs and ICEs that service the main stations in Germany. The train journey from Paris to Freiburg takes only about 3 hours.

GETTING AROUND

Local transport

Local transport infrastructure is excellent throughout the region. Even the smallest villages are serviced several times a day and what is more, buses are usually on time. In remote areas they do not run as frequently and the last bus may pass through at 5pm or earlier. At train stations there are always also buses available that will take people to more remote villages.

Since May 2023, Germany has implemented a subsidised ticket that covers local transport throughout Germany. The ticket, known as the Deutschland Ticket, is available as a subscription service that can be cancelled at any time. It covers local and regional (slow) trains and buses but not the fast long-distance train services (ICE, EC or IC, Flix Trains) or touristic trains (e.g. Säuschwänzlebahn).

The ticket is valid from the first of the month and renews automatically every month until cancelled. The frustrating business of making sense of local transport systems in different parts of Germany has finally become a thing of the past. The ticket can be purchased via the DB app, but don't forget to cancel it at the end of your trip.

Konus Card

If you are only visiting the Black Forest, you may not need the Deutschland ticket, depending on where you stay. Local tourist authorities have a scheme that provides free transport if you are staying in one of the participating villages or towns.

The Konus Card scheme, was devised to encourage rural tourism. When guests arrive, their host will issue them with a special guest card that entitles them to free public transport (local trains and buses only) throughout the Black Forest for the duration of their stay. Many, but not all, communities participate. Unfortunately, the larger towns

such Freiburg, Offenburg, Karlsruhe, Pforzheim or Baden-Baden currently do not, but some nearby villages do.

More information and a map showing the towns that are part of the scheme is available at www. schwarzwald-tourismus.info/planen-buchen/konus-gaestekarte/. (Please note that youth hostels and similar establishments do not participate in the scheme and can't issue the card. Ask your host at the time of booking.)

Baden-Württemberg Ticket

If you are not staying long enough to make the Deutschland ticket worthwhile, but wish to travel to other parts of Baden-Württemberg, beyond the geographic region of the Black Forest, a 'Baden-Württemberg Ticket' may be the best solution, especially if you are travelling as a small group.

This is a day-ticket that allows you to travel on all buses (except airport shuttles) and regional (IRE, RE, RB and S) trains throughout Baden-Württemberg (fast services, ICE, IC and D trains are excluded). It can be purchased for up to five people travelling together. On weekdays it is valid from 9am to 3am the following day and on weekends (Saturdays, Sundays and public holidays) from midnight to 3am the following day. More information is available at www.bahn.com.

Buying tickets at the machines (an English interface is available) is a little cheaper than buying them at the ticket counter. Tickets must be purchased before boarding the train.

Day passes
Day tickets cover only the service area of the local transport authority where the ticket is purchased. Unfortunately, at the time of writing, none of these companies have made their websites available in English. Enquire at the local tourist office or train station.

During the walking season, from May to October, special bus services provide easy access to remote sections of a trail (for example *Wanderbus Schluchtensteig*), but such services are often limited to weekends.

Bicycles and local transport
Regional trains (RE, RB and S) transport bicycles, sometimes even free of charge. However, every transport authority has its own regulations and restrictions may apply, especially during peak travel times (6am–9am). Enquire before boarding. Trains are often packed with bicycles, even though special compartments are provided (on RE and RB trains usually the last and/or first compartment).

Regular buses don't usually allow bicycles on board, but velobuses (Radbus) fitted with special trailers for bicycles operate along routes that are popular with cyclists. However, they are usually available during the summer season, on weekends and public holidays between May and October only. If you are travelling as a group, it is advisable to make reservations in advance at www.schwarzwald-tourismus.info/erleben/radfahren/radbusse.

Cycling has become hugely popular in the Black Forest, especially since Covid. E-bikes are now the norm, making it a lot easier to cover greater distances by bike. There are numerous rental stations and it is easy to recharge the battery at public charge points or at your hotel. Some hotels even offer their own e-bike rentals. Local tourist offices also often rent them by the hour, day, or for a weekend. Multi-day tours such as the Südschwarzwald Radweg can be booked with a regular touring bike or e-bike, if you don't want the hassle of bringing your own. You can find more information at www.schwarzwald-tourismus.info/erleben/radfahren.

Checking connections
Figuring out local transport connections can be a challenge. An electronic timetable is available at www.efa-bw.de and an English interface is offered.

An electronic app 'Bus&Bahn' is available from the iTune and Android marketplace, but it preferentially shows fast connections that include ICE service (where applicable), which cannot be used with a Konus Card, Baden-Württemberg Tickets or other local transport tickets. To use the Bus&Bahn app enter the information that is given for public transport in the information box at the beginning of each route **exactly** as it is written and check NAHVERKEHR in the options below, the app should find the correct place and give you the best connections using local transport. If it offers you different stops to choose from a dropdown menu, use the one that most closely reflects the information given in this guidebook followed by (*Haltestelle*) or (stop) if you use the English interface.

Another useful app is Öffi, which shows both fast and slow alternatives, but you have to select the relevant transport network in the settings. The good thing is, it works for other regions and countries as well. All you have to do is switch networks.

Rental cars
Rental cars are available in all larger towns and cities and, of course, at the airports.

When driving be extra aware of motorbikes, cyclists and walkers. Bikers love the winding roads and sadly, often ride recklessly. Dedicated cycle paths usually accompany busy roads, but occasionally they don't, forcing cyclists into the flow of traffic. Walking trails sometimes cross busy roads, or a trail may run on a road for a short distance, forcing walkers to walk along the edge of the road. Expect the unexpected!

ACCOMMODATION

The Black Forest is one of Germany's top holiday destinations. Tourism has been developing there for over a hundred years but the area has tried to stay in keeping with the traditional way of life and, for the most part, aims

to be sustainable. A wide range of accommodation is available in every class and budget range, from simple private rooms (bed and breakfast) and walkers' hostels to family-run inns and guesthouses, self-catering holiday flats and farmstays, or sophisticated country lodges, luxurious five-star hotels and romantic castle hotels.

Many hotels offer special package deals, which in the spa towns may include free access to the local thermal baths. Such packages provide exceptional value. They can be found under the accommodation section of a town's website or on individual hotel websites (look for *Pauschal Angebote* or *Pauschale*).

Holiday flats are usually rented for a minimum of three nights and often incur extra cleaning fees. They are still a great deal, especially for families, as they provide far more space and privacy than hotel rooms and are usually less expensive.

Walkers' hostels offer very basic, inexpensive youth hostel style accommodation. It is always best to book in advance as they are usually packed with small groups or school children, especially during peak walking season in spring and autumn.

The only website you need for finding accommodation or package deals in the Black Forest is the excellent www.schwarzwald-tourismus. info website. This site is very comprehensive and provides direct links to all the communities of the Black Forest. You can search for accommodation

Grünhütte (Walk 16)

on the main site or follow the links to specific towns or regions to search their listings. There is also a good overview of available packages and links to agencies where they can be booked. For the long-distance trails it is best to book 'Wandern-ohne-Gepäck' (hiking without luggage) or 'Radeln-ohne-Gepäck' (cycling without luggage) packages as it takes the headache out of making all the arrangements directly, especially for non-German speakers.

'Wanderbar' label

Some hotels are certified by the 'Wanderbar' label, a scheme that appraises particularly walker-friendly hotels according to a specific set of criteria, such as availability of staff with knowledge of local trails and routes, availability of maps, pick-up or drop-off service to the local station and/or trailhead, proximity to a marked trail network or route, walk-in bookings even just for one night, tolerance towards walkers coming in all wet or muddy after a long day's walk, and availability of a first aid kit.

Check the website of the town or village you are interested in. They all provide an accommodation search facility.

Walking (or cycling) without luggage

Luggage-forwarding packages are a very popular option for those who do not want to be burdened with a heavy pack during a multi-day itinerary. These packages usually include accommodation with breakfast, luggage-forwarding service and a

QUALITÄTSGASTGEBER

(c) Deutscher Wanderverband

WANDERBARES
DEUTSCHLAND

hiking map. They are usually offered on long-distance trails like the West Way, Wiiwegli or Schluchtensteig. Luggage-forwarding services can also be booked separately from accommodation: ask at the local tourist office. Packages are also offered for some multi-day cycle tours such as the Southern Black Forest Cycle Trail. For more information on walking and cycling packages see www.schwarzwald-tourismus.info.

FOOD AND DRINK

Southwest Germany is blessed with an abundance of fresh local produce, much of it organic. It is hardly surprising that chefs of all categories take pride in their regional and seasonal specialities.

Regional and seasonal produce are widely incorporated into the menu. Spring features asparagus (*Spargel*) and wild garlic (*Bärlauch*) dishes, while in summer anything goes – huge, colourful salads or an array of more hearty dishes, eat as you please. Berries are popular, not just fresh or as fillings for delicious cakes, but also as a kind of jelly-like dessert known as *Rote Grütze* composed of fruits such as strawberries, bilberries, raspberries, redcurrants and cherries. It is served cold with vanilla sauce or ice cream, or sometimes over waffles and pancakes.

In late summer wild mushrooms are the stars of the seasonal menu. They may be served on *Rösti* (potato pancake), with *Knödel* (dumpling), omelette or, more traditionally, in sauces to accompany meats.

Autumn's seasonal special is *Zwiebelkuchen* (onion pie) and *Neuer Süsser* (very young, barely fermented wine – caution: it tastes like juice, but due to the high sugar content you can be sure of a headache the next day if you drink more than a couple of glasses). Meat and game dishes also feature strongly. Increasingly, grass-fed, free-range and organic meats are served at the better restaurants. Look for the 'Bioland' label (certified organic) and 'Freiland', which means 'free range'. *Schwarzwälder Schinken* (smoked ham, thinly sliced) is a regional speciality that is famous throughout Germany.

Flammkuchen, originally from Alsace, is another speciality of the region. It is similar to pizza, but the crust is extremely thin and crispy. It is spread with crème fraîche and

A restaurant menu

toppings such as spinach and salmon, leeks and bacon bits or tomatoes and feta cheese – there are many permutations on the theme.

Vegetarians will be pleased to know that their chances of finding a delicious meal are better here than in most places in Germany. Although meat is prevalent, almost every restaurant and eatery will have some vegetarian options, and even those that do not are usually happy to accommodate vegetarian requests.

Bioregionalism is thriving in this area and it is well worth visiting some of the colourful farmers' markets to sample the local specialities. Many items cannot be found anywhere else – not even at the local supermarkets

or groceries. Freiburg's excellent market is located around the cathedral (*Münster*) and is open every day until about noon, except Sundays).

Cakes

Baden-Württemberg is a paradise for cake lovers. Every bakery offers a good selection of the standard varieties, but cafés and patisseries are the true temples of gooey delights! Avoid these places if you were hoping to walk off some weight!

Schwarzwälderkirschtorte, or Black Forest Gateau, is a rich, creamy chocolate-cherry gateau that has gained fame far beyond the borders of Germany. Most cafés serve homemade versions. Careful though – they

33

often come in monstrously sized slices and are frequently heavily laced with alcohol (Kirsch).

Drinks

According to the stereotype, Germany is a country for beer enthusiasts. Indeed, there are innumerable varieties of beer, and micro-breweries abound. However, the rolling hills facing the Rhine are among Germany's premier wine regions. Contrary to popular belief, Liebfrauenmilch is not the only German wine. Kaiserstuhl, Markgräflerland and Ortenau all produce excellent wines, especially whites, such as Pinot Blanc (Weissburgunder), Chablis, Cabernet Sauvignon, Müller-Thurgau and Chasselas (Gutedel), Chardonnay, Gewürztraminer and more. Gutedel

is the regional speciality of the Markgräflerland and is not produced anywhere else in Germany. The Ortenau (central Black Forest) also produces reds, but none with any claim to fame. They are okay, but lack body. Most wineries offer wine tastings. Enquire at the local tourist information office for guided tours, tastings and wine festivals.

The western rim of the Black Forest is an important fruit growing region. A surplus of fruit calls for creative ways of utilising the excess – such as preserving their essence by distillation to create fruit brandies (similar to 'eau de vie'). Best known of these is *Kirschwasser*, one of the essential ingredients of Black Forest Gateau. But there are many others to choose from: yellow plum

Winter wonderland in the Black Forest

(*Mirabellen*), plum (*Pflaume*), pear (*Birne*), apple (*Apfel*), raspberry (*Himbeere*), cherry (*Kirsche*) and more. Mixed fruit brandy is known as *Obstler*. Many small producers sell direct from the farm and even offer tastings, but beware – these brandies are high-octane stuff!

Where to eat

An *Almgasthof* or *Almgaststätte* is a mountain café or restaurant (also often referred to as *Hütte*). These popular rustic restaurants are often located in stunning locations along the trail, up on the saddle of a mountain overlooking rolling hills, valleys and mountain meadows. Originally these were farms that offered simple, hearty fare to passers-by. Essentially that is what they still are, except that by now, feeding hungry hikers has become their main source of income. They are usually good places to stop for refreshments and to take in the views, but don't expect gourmet fare.

Besenwirtschaft/Straussen-wirtschaft (*Straußi*) are mostly found in the Markgräflerland and Kaiserstuhl. These are rustic farmhouse restaurants, which are usually only open seasonally. A large decorated broom hung above the sign indicates that the Straußi is open for business. Most Straußis also operate a farm shop where farm produce and homemade goodies are sold.

Vesper is a colloquial term for 'a small meal', often reminiscent of ploughman's lunches, served in a *Vesperstube*, an informal eatery. However, not all items on the Vesper menu are necessarily light. Sausages and potatoes abound. As does cake. And beer, of course.

WHEN TO GO

The southwestern corner of Germany is known as the warmest and sunniest part of the country. However, the mountain climate is always changeable and actual conditions can vary widely between different regions. Generally speaking, the north and east are quite a bit colder and wetter than central or southern parts of the Black Forest. The warmest regions are the western fringes facing the Rhine, and Kaiserstuhl, which during the summer can get oppressively hot and humid.

Spring and especially autumn are delightful times for a walking holiday in the Black Forest. Temperatures are pleasant and rainfall is generally very low. October is the driest month and late warm weather with golden foliage can transform the Black Forest into a truly idyllic rambler's delight. Furthermore, so-called 'inversions' are prevalent in autumn: while fog blankets the lower valleys, the sun may be shining up in the mountains.

Summer weather tends to be a bit more ambiguous. In the lower altitudes it can be oppressively humid and hot. Walking through the forest at higher elevations is refreshing, but thunderstorms (which can be ferocious) often build up in the afternoons.

In winter the Black Forest turns into a winter wonderland and a heaven for cross-country skiers. Miles of grooved and signposted cross-country routes make it easy to explore the region on skis. The latest trends in winter sports are snowshoeing and winter walking and there are miles of marked trails for both. Winter walking trails are not cleared completely – rather, the snow is flattened to make it easier to walk on – while snowshoe-trails are not cleared at all. Snowshoes can be rented at many local tourist offices or sports shops. Special winter sports maps show both prepared walking routes and cross-country trails.

Walking in winter is not without risks. Sudden snowstorms can be disorientating and even those who are familiar with the terrain can easily lose their way. Add to that inadequate clothing or insufficient provisions and you get a disaster waiting to happen. Most routes in this guide are not suitable for winter walking.

WHAT TO TAKE
- Day pack or cycle pannier
- Water bottle
- Weatherproof jacket
- Lightweight, quick-drying trousers
- Map, compass and/or GPS (a signal may not always be available)
- Sunscreen

- Insect repellent (must be effective against ticks) and tick removal tool
- Binoculars (optional)

For walking
- Walking boots with good grip
- Walking poles (optional)
- Hat

For cycling
- Cycle shoes or trainers
- Helmet
- Reflective vest/jacket/wrist or ankle bands (optional but a good safety measure)
- Cycle gloves (optional)

As walking regions go, the Black Forest probably ranks as one of the safest and most 'civilised'. Villages are never far away and even in the middle of nowhere restaurants with wonderful panoramic views offer snacks, cakes or beer – just the thing after a few hours of walking. Still, it is always a good idea to bring along a few energy bars or some fruit and nuts, just in case that restaurant with the wonderful view is closed (most likely on Mondays and Tuesdays).

What type of bike
The routes described in this book are suitable for regular touring bikes, with at least seven gears. Most cycle paths are paved and in good condition. Occasionally, sections will run on gravel or dirt roads for a few kilometres. Trails marked as 'scenic' (with a

Not the biggest cuckoo clock, but close!

little stylised tree and hill symbol next to the destination) are more likely to run through this type of terrain.

There are also plenty of mountain bike routes in the Black Forest, but they are not covered by this book.

If you don't want to bother taking your bike over to the Black Forest, there are many places where you can rent bikes for a day or more. Ask at the local tourist information office (or see Appendix C). Some hotels have bikes available for rent or even let you use them for free. Lately E-bikes, fitted with a small electro-engine, have become fashionable. They may be useful if you want to cycle more demanding, hilly routes. They give you a bit of a boost for tackling the hills, but you still have to pedal. These are also available for rent at many tourist offices and some

bicycle shops. Rentals usually include a helmet and lock, as a minimum. Some also provide a basket, pump, or bicycle repair kit and some may also have children's seats or trailers available at an extra charge.

The multi-stage Southern Black Forest Cycle Trail can be booked as a 'luggage-forwarding' package at https://original-landreisen.de/radreisen-im-schwarzwald/suedschwarzwald-radweg/. If you book through this website you can also rent a bike through them (not included in the package price). Bicycle rental includes helmet, lock and repair kit.

If you book your accommodation independently you might like to check for the 'bett & bike' label, a certification scheme for cyclist-friendly accommodations, devised by the

German bicycle association (www. bettundbike.de).

Beasties

These days there are few real dangers lurking in the forest. There are a couple of species of poisonous snake, the common adder (*Vipera berus*) and the asp viper (*Vipera aspis*), which occur in the southern Black Forest. But one would have to be extremely lucky to catch even a glimpse of either, as they are both very rare and highly endangered. Potentially more hazardous is the risk of coming across wild boar, which can be quite vicious, especially in early summer, when females are out foraging with their young. However, they are mostly active at dawn and dusk and generally try to avoid encounters with humans.

The smallest creatures pose the greatest danger: beware of ticks. Ticks can carry a multitude of diseases, the most serious of which are Lyme disease (present in about 5 per cent of ticks) and tick-borne encephalitis (TBE). TBE can result in symptoms ranging from a mild headache to fever and joint pain, and in the most severe cases can even be fatal. A vaccine is available, but there is no effective treatment once TBE is contracted. For more information see www.nhs.uk. Lyme disease affects the neuro-muscular system and can become chronic. There is no vaccine

Charming old street sign

for it. Treatment consists of antibiotics – however, these are only really effective when administered during the early stages of the disease. Symptoms include a 'bulls-eye' rash around the bite site, fever and flu-like symptoms, including muscle pain. For more information see www.lymediseaseaction.org.uk.

The best strategy is to avoid getting bitten. Using an effective insect repellent containing DEET is a must. Light-coloured clothes make it easier to spot ticks. Long-sleeved shirts and long trousers are recommended, especially when walking through undergrowth or tall grass (tuck your trousers into your socks). Check clothes and exposed skin frequently and thoroughly (especially after returning to your base). Carry a tick removal tool in your daypack. Ticks can be present anywhere – whether you are in the woods, fields, campsite, or picnic area (and even in London city parks). Not all carry Lyme or TBE, but vigilance is your best defence. If you do get bitten you can remove the tick and take it to a pharmacy (*Apotheke*) to determine whether or not it was infected with any dangerous viruses.

NAVIGATION AND SIGNAGE

The trails

The Schwarzwaldverein has made an amazing job of establishing a comprehensive trail network throughout the region. To date it comprises about 24,000km of marked and maintained trails, using small footpaths, farm tracks, access and forestry roads, and even guiding walkers through villages and urban areas right from the train station or bus stop into the hills.

In the past, each municipality devised its own routes in co-operation with the local chapter of the Schwarzwaldverein and designed the signs and symbols according to their fancy. A century later, a plethora of markers had sprouted on tree trunks everywhere, becoming a source of confusion.

Eventually this led to a thorough reform. A coherent and easy-to-follow trail system now integrates the myriad of local paths into a web of interconnecting trails with just a couple of basic markers: the yellow rhombus for local paths and the blue rhombus for longer, trans-regional routes. Long-distance routes and certain special trails have preserved their individual symbols. The enormous task, which started in 2000, took about six years to complete. Admittedly, the old-style signs had more charm, but for practical purposes the new system is far superior. In some regions old-style signs still co-exist for the sake of sentiment and often provide an additional aid to navigation. In other areas, new local trails with their own trail marker designs have begun to creep back in. But even the new trails are better integrated with the new system, making it easier to find the right way.

Interpreting the signs

The trail network is well marked with dedicated walkers' signposts. Cyclists have their own signposts.

At first, signposts may seem a little confusing, as there are often many blades pointing in different directions, sometimes even to the same destination. Study the signs carefully. One of the blades, usually featuring a yellow or blue marker, will bear the name of the current location and altitude on one side. On the main part of the sign various places and distances are listed. The uppermost listing always indicates the closest destination, which will also be the name of the next signpost that will be encountered in that direction.

Bus stops, train stations, restaurants or viewpoints are also noted next to the destinations, each with a different symbol. (The bus stop symbol, for instance, is a yellow circle with a green H.) This is particularly helpful if you want to shorten the route and find the next nearest bus stop or train station. The last entry is always a distant destination in that general direction.

The regional or long-distance route signs do not always show the name of the current location, especially if a yellow-marked, local trail also intersects. Always check the yellow trail sign to determine your position.

Location marking signposts are strategically placed at trail intersections. In between signposts the route is marked only with small plaques showing the appropriate trail symbol, which are pinned on trees or some other convenient surface.

In general, routes are clearly marked and well maintained. But sometimes markers are not in the most obvious places, or may have faded; or, if two routes run parallel for a while, the symbol of one route may be present, but not the other. Some municipalities seem to be more sparing with their signage, while elsewhere markers proliferate. Occasionally, signs may have been damaged or bent and thus become unintelligible. For this reason it is still important to carry a map and to familiarise yourself with the route and territory.

Because there are so many paths and forestry roads, it can sometimes be confusing when there are no obvious markers at crossings or forks. The rule of thumb is to keep on walking straight (in line with your direction) unless a marker specifically indicates otherwise. Sometimes markers appear 10m or more after the junction, or can

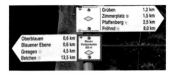

One square panel on a busy signpost shows the name of the sign's location (as well as the altitude and trail symbol). This name is the one cited in the route descriptions in blue italic text.

be obscured by foliage and may be hard to see without actually starting to go down that path.

Markers may also unexpectedly take you off a broad forest road and lead you up or down steep little trails on the side of a hill. In recent years walkers have developed a preference for unmade, rough paths through the forest rather than monotonous forestry access roads. (These are sometimes known as 'Wurzelpfade' or 'roots trail'. I use the term 'sticks and stones' paths in this guide.) Accordingly, trails have been rerouted and now often only intersect with forest roads for short distances before leading off again on a small path through the undergrowth. Thus, always be alert for arrows and markers that point straight into the woods on some narrow little trail.

Following the markers is a bit like a treasure hunt, but once you get used to the system, trails are quite easy to follow. Even if you lose your intended trail, following any trail symbol will sooner or later lead you to another signpost with detailed directions. In the route descriptions in this guidebook key named signposts are indicated in *blue italic* type (but not every one is mentioned).

Long-distance routes

Long-distance trails were invented in the Black Forest – at least so the locals say. Of course, long-distance routes have existed all over the world for many centuries. But the first purpose-designed long-distance walking route for leisure, the now legendary West Way, was inaugurated by the Schwarzwaldverein in 1900. Long-distance routes usually cover 50–270km and utilise mostly local trails, but have their own symbols. There are three main north–south routes: the West, Middle and East Way. Several more routes cross from east to west, such as Querweg Schwarzwald-Kaiserstuhl-Rhein or Querweg Freiburg-Bodensee. There are also themed routes such as the Wiiwegli or Ortenau Wine Trail, which mostly run through the vineyards and wine villages along the western edge of the Black Forest, or Schluchtensteig, which explores an extensive gorge system in the far southeast of the region. Of course, you do not have to go the full length of these trails, but can sample any section as a day walk.

'Quality Trails'

Germany has a certification scheme for long-distance trails that assesses the 'quality' of a trail according to a certain set of criteria. In order to qualify, a trail must comply with nine essential and up to 23 optional criteria, such as utilising predominantly small 'sticks and stones' paths, only a small percentage of the trail can be on tarmacked surfaces, the route should pass sites of cultural or other interest, and should be accessible by public transport. In the Black Forest, Schluchtensteig, Zweitälersteig and West Way (which had to be re-routed to comply) have all been certified.

Resting beside a field on the way to Kirchzarten (Ride 1, Stage 5)

CYCLING

Germany has a huge cycle trail network that covers the entire country. It consists mostly of tarmacked lanes, dirt roads, or regular quiet roads that are used for cycle traffic. Long-distance trails are routed for maximum scenic appeal and many of them follow rivers, which makes for easy cycling on mostly flat paths. In the Black Forest there are several such river trails: Enztal Radweg, Nagold Radweg and Kinzigtal Radweg to name just three (*Radweg* means cycle route). There are also more demanding routes (not covered in this guide) for mountain bikers or sports cyclists, such as the Schwarzwald Panorama Radweg, which traverses the whole of the Black Forest, north to south, much of it at high altitude, with beautiful panoramic views.

Cycle trails have their own signposts. Long-distance route markers are tagged at the bottom of these signs. In between they follow the regular cycle route markings. If in doubt, stick to the trail you are on until directed otherwise. A small tree symbol next to a destination on a signpost indicates a scenic route, which may not be paved all the way and may be hillier than the alternative (if there is one), which may run alongside a busy traffic road.

MAPS

Many companies publish good maps of the region. Kompass publishes laminated maps that do not tear or disintegrate in bad weather. The maps are at scales of 1:50000, 1:35000 and 1:25000, but not for all regions. The 1:50000 and 1:35000 are best for cycling. Kompass also offers an online subscription service similar to Outdooractive.

The Schwarzwaldverein maps are produced in cooperation with the LGL (Ordnance Survey equivalent). They have recently been updated and their 1:25000 map range has been expanded. At the time of writing they now cover the entire Black Forest. A very helpful feature of the Schwarzwaldverein/LGL maps is the fact that they actually mark the names and positions of signposts (little yellow flags), making it easy to identify your location on a map. The Schwarzwaldverein also has an online map portal that can be used for planning tours.

Many tourist offices publish their own maps, which are also based on the LGL data and show the location markers. These are not as sturdy, but should survive a few weeks of use. They are cheaper than other maps and in some cases cover the entire length of a particular route (such as Zweitälersteig), where otherwise several maps would be needed. They also provide useful information about other recommended routes, or accommodation and restaurants along the way.

LGL maps show walking and cycling routes in different colours, with their symbols if they are long-distance trails.

ETIQUETTE

German walkers tend to be friendly and greet one another on the trail. If someone greets you with 'Guten Tag' or 'Grüß Gott' it is good manners to return the gesture, even if you only mumble 'hello'.

Some trails are shared between walkers and cyclists. Walkers have the right of way, but be aware that mountain bikers sometimes come tearing down those forest roads at high speed. Luckily they make a lot of noise. To avoid accidents, it is best to get out of the way. Unfortunately, many mountain bikers do not respect the rules when it comes to the smaller footpaths, which technically are off limits to them. Confrontations do happen, as many walkers get extremely upset about this sort of thing.

For their part, cyclists should always be considerate towards pedestrians. In towns and along roads trails are often shared cycle lanes and footpaths. Pedestrians have the right of way. Sometimes cycle lanes are bidirectional. Keep to the **right** to avoid accidents.

USING THIS GUIDE

The Black Forest is a hillwalker's dream. The terrain is so varied that walkers of all ages and abilities can find a suitable tour to enjoy. The walks described in this book range from easy to hard, although, of course, such terms are relative.

Belchen above the clouds (Walk 2)

Walkers with some hillwalking experience will have no difficulty completing the routes. Some routes are quite long and require stamina, for others sure-footedness is needed. Maximum height gain on any route is about 1000m, but most are much less demanding – anyone of average fitness should be able to do these walks and enjoy them. If you do find them too long or too hard, the nearest bus stop or train station is never far away, making it easy to shorten the routes, if need be.

The route description for each walk or ride is preceded by an information box containing the following essential data: start; finish; distance in kilometres (km); height gain/loss; difficulty; estimated time to complete the route (this does not include pauses for picnics, photos and nature stops, so allow extra time when planning your day); maps required; refreshments available; public transport links (see notes under 'Getting around'); access at the start and end of the walk; parking; and trail markings used. Other information such as websites or webcams is given where appropriate.

Within the walking and cycling route descriptions, text in *blue italic* indicates a named signpost (generally not named on the route map) that is important for navigation. There are many signposts along the routes and they are a key aspect of finding your way around the Black Forest (see 'Interpreting the signs', above). In the walks, text in **bold** also indicates a feature which is passed on the route and marked on the route map.

Each route or route stage is accompanied by a contoured map showing the route line, significant roads and landmarks, parking areas

THE BLACK FOREST: KEY FACTS

Language: The official language is German, but the local dialect bears little resemblance to what you might have learned at school. It is more like Swiss or Austrian German. Most younger people speak at least some English.

Currency: Germany uses the Euro (€).

Banks/ATMs: Most small towns have banks and ATM machines that accept Cirrus, MasterCard and Visa. However, many shops and even some restaurant only accept Eurocard or cash.

Healthcare: Germany has excellent healthcare. Inoculations are not required, but the TBE vaccine may be useful (see 'Dangers and annoyances'), especially if you are planning on camping. Carry the Global Health Insurance Card (GHIC) to gain access to local healthcare.

Electricity: Germany uses 220–240 Volts. Adaptor plugs (two-pronged) will be needed for appliances.

International phone calls: The international country code for Germany is 49. To call Germany from the UK dial 00 49, then drop the initial 0 from the local dialling code. To call the UK from Germany dial 00 44. Newsagents and internet cafés often sell pre-paid phone cards that have a long number code that must be entered before dialling the phone number you wish to reach. These cards offer great discounted rates. Your mobile phone carrier might also offer special deals for calling to or from abroad.

Emergency: In case of emergency dial 112, or the police 110.

and refreshment stops. The maps that accompany the walking routes are at 1:50,000 (2cm to 1km) and the maps that accompany the rides are at 1:100,000 (1cm to 1km), as shown by the scale bar on the first map in each route. GPX files are also available for every route at www.cicerone.co.uk/1021/GPX. See the back of this guide for full details.

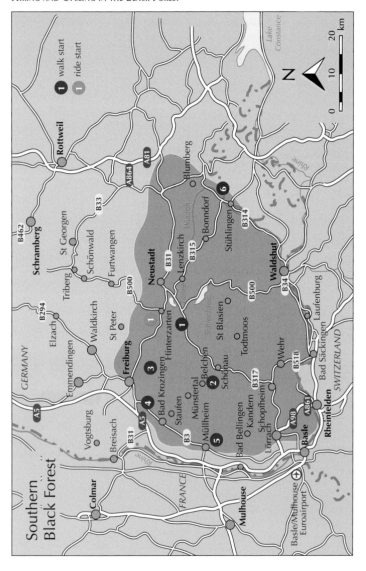

SOUTHERN
BLACK FOREST

Wutach River (Walk 6, Stage 3)

INTRODUCTION

The sparsely populated southern region is often thought of as the most beautiful part of the Black Forest. It has the highest mountains (Walk 1), deepest gorges and biggest lakes (Walk 6). Open valleys, dotted with rustic old mountain farms create a romantic scene of rural idyll. It is perfect hillwalking terrain, with trails varying from forestry roads to field tracks and little 'sticks and stones' paths, far off the beaten track. The highest hilltops and southernmost slopes offer magnificent views of the Alps, the Jura and the Vosges.

The biggest principal city of the region is the lively university town of Freiburg (Walk 4), situated between the western edge of the Black Forest and the Kaiserstuhl. South of Freiburg the rolling vineyards and orchards of Margrave's Land (Markgräflerland) are dotted with pretty little wine villages and small towns (Walk 5). Comeliest of them all is Staufen, set at the entrance of Münstertal, a beautiful valley cradled between Belchen (Walk 2) and Schauinsland (Walk 3).

The spa towns of Bad Krozingen, Bad Bellingen and Badenweiler attract mostly 'wellness' tourists and convalescents, who benefit from the therapeutic thermal hot springs. Along the Swiss border a string of picturesque historic towns like Bad Säckingen, Laufenburg or Waldshut-Tiengen line the shores of the Rhine (see Ride 1), while Hotzenwald, the southernmost range of hills rising up from the river valley, is almost entirely devoid of urban settlements. The most significant towns of the southern hills are St Blasien with its oversized dome and Todtmoos at the top end of Wehraschlucht, both of which are on the route of Schluchtensteig (see Walk 6). This southernmost part of the Black Forest is perfect for those seeking solitude and peace.

The interior to the east of Freiburg comprises a region known as Hochschwarzwald (High Black Forest), where the highest peaks are found. Some villages, such as Hinterzarten or Titisee, offer excellent year-round infrastructure as well as a delightful setting. A little further south Todtnau, Todtnauberg and Schönau also make great rural bases, but getting around beyond the immediate vicinity is much harder without a car – and even with a car, always involving many miles of twisting roads.

WALK 1

Feldbergsteig – Black Forest's highest peak

Start/finish	Haus der Natur, Feldberger Hof
Distance	12km
Difficulty	Medium
Time	4–5hr
Height gain/loss	570m
Maps	Schwarzwaldverein Wanderkarte Hochschwarzwald 1:35,000; Schwarzwaldverein Wanderkarte Titisee-Neustadt 1:25,000; Kompass Feldberg–Todtnau 1:25,000
Refreshments	St Wilhelmer Hütte, Zastler Hütte, Baldenweger Hütte, Raimartihof, Seebuck Hütte (see www.hochschwarzwald.de/Feldberg); numerous snack places at Feldberger Hof www.liftverbund-feldberg.de
Public transport	Bus to Feldbergerhof (1250m), Feldberg (Schwarzw)
Access	By car, B317 via Todtnau or Titisee, turn off at Feldbergerhof. Haus der Natur is the big building right in front of the car park, opposite Feldberger Hof Hotel.
Parking	Haus der Natur car park, or the huge new parking garage.
Trail markings	Feldbergsteig symbol (pictured)
Website/webcam	www.feldberg-erlebnis.de/aktuelles/webcam
Note	Firm footwear is essential and walkers must be surefooted and vertigo-free. In parts the trail is very narrow and may be rather slippery. It is not a good choice in bad weather or snow/icy conditions. Beware of capercaillie on the northern slopes, especially during mating season, as males can be a bit forward and intimidating. Avoid visiting during St. Laurentius feast day, an annual event on or around 10 August.

At 1493m Feldberg is the highest peak of the Black Forest. On a clear, crisp day the views from the top are simply wonderful: the southern hills of the Black Forest roll into the distance towards the Rhine, the jagged snow-capped peaks of the Alps paint a craggy line into the southern sky and the blue ridge of the Vosges defines the western horizon. Beyond the touristy bustle at the top a delightful trail awaits those that venture further.

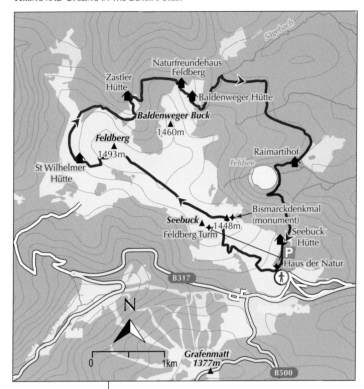

The Feldbergsteig trail is well marked and easy to follow. It starts at Feldberger Hof, by the Stonehenge-like gateway to the left of **Haus der Natur** (Nature Interpretation Centre) on the paved path marked towards Feldberg-Gipfel and Bismarckdenkmal. You can also access the trail through the back exit of Haus der Natur: cross the alpine garden and re-join the paved trail via a small path at the top right corner. After about 900m, at *Herzogenhornblick*, the trail abruptly heads off through the bushes to the right on a small, steep footpath and about 10min later emerges just below the hill station of the cable car.

Passing underneath the cable car trusses head for the stone pyramid, the **Bismarckdenkmal**. Feldberg peak is further over to the left, near the weather station. Cross this open expanse on any trail you like. Feldbergsteig continues left of the Bismarck monument, just below the ridge, while the upper trail passes by **Feldberg Turm**, the observation tower that marks the top of Seebuck, Feldberg's twin peak.

By the first buildings, you reach *Feldberg Gipfel*. For the actual summit continue straight on, to the viewing platform opposite the weather station. Return to signpost *Feldberg Gipfel* to continue on Feldbergsteig and follow the broad path towards St Wilhelmer Hütte. At a sharp bend ignore a steep, serpentine path that leads down to Todtnauer Hütte and continue on the broad main trail to **St Wilhelmer Hütte**. ▸ The trail continues just below the terrace to the right, towards Zastler Hütte.

After about 400m (*St. Wilhelm Weide*) cross the field and follow the narrow path through the trees and blueberry bushes. At a trail junction continue straight on, down along the edge of the hill, crossing a highland watershed meadow.

Pass **Zastler Hütte** and continue on the gravel road to the right towards Naturfreundehaus Feldberg and Baldenweger Hütte. The dirt road gradually turns into a forest trail, which soon reaches the playground of **Naturfreundehaus Feldberg**. Continue on the paved road to the right. Just a few metres past **Baldenweger Hütte** (*Abzw.Sägebachschlag-Steig*), the trail heads off into the woods to the right. The next section ambles through the forest on a 'sticks and stones' trail, passing several streams and ravines. This is a lovely passage, but can be slippery as this area forms part of the Feldberg watershed.

The path eventually joins a forest road to the right, towards Raimartihof. Ignore the first fork (which is a mountain-bike trail), but at the second fork take the

Stone pyramid of the Bismarck monument

On a clear day the views from the terrace of the hut are gorgeous.

This trail is badly marked, but if you miss it the forest road will also lead to Raimartihof.

right-hand track. A little further on ignore the West Way (red marker) at Seewald, but a few metres further on follow the right fork of a trail that starts off quite broad, but soon narrows to a skinny path leading down the hill through the woods. ◄

At *Raimartihof/Koppel* follow the dirt road to the right and at the bend continue straight on the forest path towards **Feldsee**, a tarn formed by the glaciers that once covered Feldberg during the last ice age. Swimming is prohibited to protect a rare water fern, which is only found here and at Titisee, the largest natural lake in the Black Forest, just a little bit to the east.

You can circle around the lake, but Feldbergsteig continues to the left across a little bridge and quickly starts to climb back up the hill via a steep and narrow path towards Seebuck and Feldberger Hof. After about 1km turn left on the gravel path and continue uphill. Soon **Seebuck Hütte** and the ski-lift base station come into view. Pass the restaurants and shops and you are back at Feldberger Hof bus stop and car park.

Feldsee was formed by glaciers during the last ice age

WALK 2

Belchen – Sacred mountain of the Celts

Start/finish	Haldenhof (inn), Neuenweg
Distance	15km
Difficulty	Medium
Time	5hr
Height gain/loss	630m
Maps	Schwarzwaldverein Wanderkarte Nördliches Markgräflerland 1:35,000; Scharzwaldverein Wanderkarte Schönau im Schwarzwald 1:25,000 (W257)
Refreshments	Haldenhof www.haldenhofberggasthofschwarzwald.de (open every day during the summer, closed Nov–Mar, depending on weather), Belchenhaus (open daily, depending on weather and cable car schedule)
Public transport	Bus to Haldenhof, Neuenweg (Kr LÖ)
Access	By car, L131 from Müllheim/Badenweiler or Schönau or L130 from Münstertal
Parking	At Haldenhof or at Im Mond car park, 1km from Haldenhof (towards Schönau)
Trail markings	Red, blue, yellow
Website	https://schwarzwaldregion-belchen.de
Webcam	www.belchen-seilbahn.de/webcam.html

This walk offers panoramic views across Wiesental, the entire alpine chain, the French Jura, the Rhine Valley and the Vosges. Much of the route follows an old border demarcation, partially on broad farm or forestry access roads, partially on narrow trails through gnarly mountain beech forest. The first section, from Haldenhof to the summit, forms part of the famous West Way.

Belchen is one of the most popular mountains in the southern Black Forest, and at the top it is always busy, especially on weekends and during holidays. Most people get to the top by cable car (from Multen) or walk the short distance from the cable car base station. The trails around the mountain remain fairly quiet.

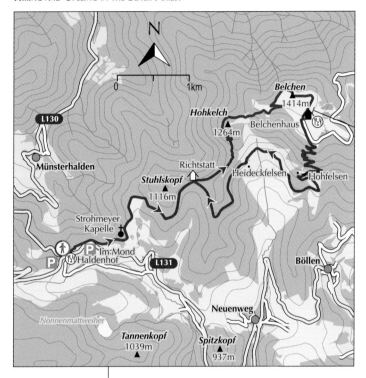

According to local legend the Celts considered Belchen as sacred to the **Sun-God Bel**. Together with four other mountains of the same name (the Swiss Belchen, Belchenfluh near Eptingen and Ballon d'Alsace, Grand Ballon and Petit Ballon in France), it formed part of a giant astronomic mountaintop observatory that marked the equinoxes and solstices. Modern sun worshippers and neo-Celts gather to celebrate the midsummer sunrise on the top of the Black Forest Belchen.

The trail starts opposite **Gasthaus Haldenhof**, next to the bus stop at *Haldenhof*. The red marker of the West Way shows the way up to the summit (Belchengipfel).

After passing a couple of private homes the trail leads down to a hikers' car park called **Im Mond**. Cross the car park and continue on Unterer Stuhlskopfweg, towards **Dekan Strohmeyer Kapelle** (Deacon Strohmeyer Chapel).

A small chapel up on the ridge commemorates **Deacon Strohmeyer**, who served at Trudpert Abbey in Münstertal during World War II. On 22 April 1945, just days before Germany surrendered, Nazi thugs abducted the Deacon from his office, brought him up to Haldenhof and brutally murdered him. The chapel is a serene place to reflect on peace and war and the cruelty and injustice committed by human beings against their fellow men and women.

The trail continues as a beautiful panorama path towards Spänplatz, Metzg and Richtstatt (shelter hut). At

Belchen's southern slopes

55

Richtstatt keep following the red marker uphill. Just after passing the remains of the old border wall on the right, the trail splits. Both paths lead up to the mountain saddle at Hohkelch. The left-hand trail, marked 'Belchen über Gemarkung Münstertal', is the more adventurous path. It clambers through a magical forest strewn with moss-covered boulders and rocks. This trail can be dangerous in wet, muddy or icy conditions, however. The other path continues up the hill on the broad forest road with scenic views across the valley.

Hohkelch is a great place for a short rest before tackling the final ascent. Several trails meet here. Continue on West Way, past Rapsfelsen to *Wiesentalblick*, where the trail meets *Belchen Rundweg* (a circuit around the summit).

Take a sharp left on Belchen Rundweg to *Franz-Schlageter Rundweg*, where a small gravel path leads up to the top towards the summit (*Belchengipfel 200m*). The trail emerges by the summit cross

Back in the 1970s Belchen was close to becoming an environmental disaster area: a never-ending motorcade made its way up to the top and tourists swarmed all over the hill, paying little attention to the sensitive eco-system. Eroded paths marred the summit. Finally, in 2001, Belchen was declared a **car-free zone** and the road to the summit was closed. Instead, a cable car was built to give easy access for families and disabled visitors. Paths were laid and sensitive areas were fenced off to protect them from further erosion. Since then the summit area has made a remarkable recovery. Please help these conservation efforts by sticking to the marked trails.

Note The sign looks as though it is pointing straight down the paved road, but in fact, the narrow, fenced trail goes off to the left and soon dips down below the level of the road.

A broad path crosses the summit and joins Belchen Rundweg. Take either path down to Belchenhaus (restaurant, toilet and cable car hill station). At **Belchenhaus**, by a big wooden information board, follow the blue marker towards Böllener Eck. ◄

Hohfelsen

Within minutes the bustle at the top is left behind. A path snakes down the hill through ancient mountain beech forest. There are not many markers, but there is really only one way to go. Pass the rocky outcrop at **Hohfelsen** on the way down to *Böllener Eck*. Here leave the blue-marked trail and continue to the right, now following the yellow marker towards Haldenhof.

After 200m, at *Wasserweg*, the trail splits. Take the right fork towards Heideckfelsen/Haldenhof on a beautiful panoramic path across Belchen's southern slope. At **Heideckfelsen** take the left fork towards Richtstatt and Haldenhof. At a junction about 1km further along turn right. Soon you are back at **Richtstatt**. Retrace your steps down to Haldenhof via West Way (red marker).

WALK 3
High above Münstertal

Start	Schauinsland Bergstation (hill station) car park
Finish	Münstertal station, Untermünstertal
Distance	19km
Difficulty	Easy, but long, with some steep downhill sections
Time	5hr30min
Height gain/loss	150m/1000m
Maps	Schwarzwaldverein Wanderkarte Nördliches Markgräflerland 1:35,000
Refreshments	Café Restaurant Bergstation Schauinsland www.diebergstation.de (open every day, but often fully booked well in advance), Gasthaus Gießhübel www.gasthof-giesshuebel.de (closed Weds and Thurs), Wirthschaft zum Kohler www.wirthschaft-zum-kohler.de (closed Mon and Tues), Historic Gasthaus zur Linde www.landgasthaus.de (closed Mon and Tues); Café Kreuz am Kloster www.cafezumkreuz.de (closed Mon and Tues), various cafés and restaurants in Münstertal www.muenstertal-staufen.de/
Public transport	Bus to Schauinslandbahn Bergstation, Freiburg im Breisgau (weekends and public holidays only). Or take the cable car from Freiburg/Horben Schauinsland Talstation www.schauinslandbahn.de/en. Return by bus or train from Bahnhof, Münstertal. (The train station is called Münstertal Bahnhof but it is located in Untermünstertal, the lower end of Münstertal, which is how it is marked on signposts.)
Access	It is possible to drive up to Schauinsland, but not practical for this walk. On week days, take the cable car from Horben (L124 Freiburg–Todtnau) www.bergwelt-schauinsland.de
Parking	At the cable car base station in Horben, or at the station in Kirchzarten (it will be easier to get back there after the walk than to return to Schauinsland to retrieve your car). It is only practical to use the car park at the hill station if you just want to do the short circuit around the top.
Trail markings	Blue, yellow
Note	This route can be divided into a short walk around the top of Schauinsland (about 3km) and a long, downhill ridge walk to Münstertal. If you want to shorten it, there is a bus that runs through Münstertal, but check timetables in advance.

This scenic route explores the top of Schauinsland before ambling along a lovely ridge trail above Münstertal down to St Trudpert Abbey. On clear days views from Schauinsland stretch as far as the Bernese Oberland. Closer by, Feldberg, Belchen and Kandel stand guard, while across the Rhine Valley the Vosges paint a blue silhouette against the western horizon. Pastoral panoramas create a picture-perfect scene all the way down into the valley.

Look for the signpost *Parkplatz Bergstation* at the top car park of Schauinsland hill station. The yellow marker leads up some wooden stairs towards the observation tower, Schauinsland Turm. (If you took the cable car, walk up the steps to the right of the playground and at the top join the broader path to the left towards **Schauinsland Turm**). Both trails meet at *Naturwiesen* and jointly continue to the right. At the fork, follow the blue marker uphill to the left, to reach the peak.

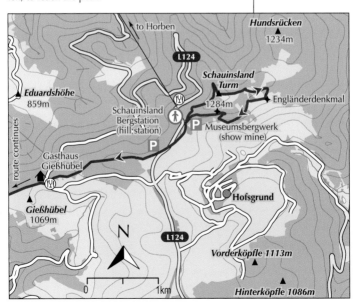

After taking in the views, follow the yellow marker down the steps to the left. Cross the paved lane at *Sonnenobservatorium* and follow the yellow markers down through a field on a small footpath to **Engländerdenkmal**, a large memorial that faces Feldberg across the valley.

> The **Engländerdenkmal** commemorates a tragic event that took place on 17 April 1936, when a group of English boy-scouts and their guardian lost their way in a freak snowstorm. Being woefully ill equipped (many only wearing shorts and shirts), five of the boys died of hypothermia and exhaustion. The other boys were saved, thanks to some local villagers who came to their rescue. Although the Black Forest seems quite 'safe', these are mountains nevertheless and should never be underestimated.

Facing the wooded slope, look for the sign pointing towards the **Museumsbergwerk** (a show mine) and follow the small path across the wooded slope. After about

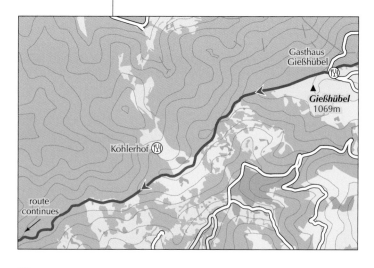

1km turn right and follow the zigzag trail up the hill on a steep, gravelly path, then turn left to reach the mine.

Engländerdenkmal with Feldberg across the valley

> **Schauinsland** may seem like a solid mountain, but in fact, it resembles Swiss cheese. This is the oldest and most extensive ore mine in Germany, more than 800 years old and with over 100km of shafts and tunnels. It now serves as a museum. For more information see **www.schauinsland.de/museums-bergwerk/en/the-museum-mine-museums-berg-werk-schauinsland/**.

Cross the yard and continue straight to the access road. Turn left to reach the car park.

At *Parkplatz Bergstation* follow the blue marker towards Staufen. The path starts by the wooden information hut (*Rothlache*) and runs parallel to the road past picnic tables and a ski-lift. Cross the road at *Sailenmatte* and head towards the left-hand corner of the car park to *Sailendobelkar*. From here follow the yellow marker

61

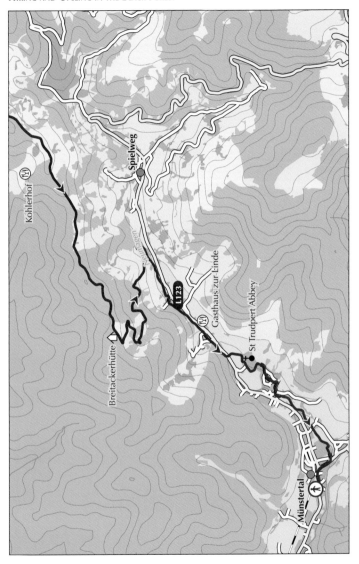

through the forest, straight past *Burggraf* towards **Gießhübel**.

After about 1km the trail reaches some buildings. Continue straight on down the hill through the forest. When you reach the building compound look for a path that crosses a field to the left and leads to the road below, where you will find Gasthaus Gießhübel with lovely views from the terrace.

Follow signs for Staufen, not for Münstertal. The Staufen trail runs along the ridge, offering panoramic views almost all the way to Breitacker.

From Gasthaus Gießhübel turn left to *Am Gießhübel* where the trail continues on the left fork. Thereafter the route is pretty straightforward. Just follow the ridge trail past *Stutz*, *Sonnhaldenkreuzle* and *Sonnhaldeberg*. At *Sonnhaldeeck* bear left to *Gstihlberg* (or take a detour down to the right to Kohlerhof if you are feeling hungry) and continue to **Breitackerhütte**. The trail dips in and out of the forest or runs along the forest edge, offering beautiful views of Belchen and Münstertal below. Ignore any signs pointing left towards Untermünstertal until you reach Breitacker.

Just after Breitacker hut, at *Breitacker* (somewhat awkwardly placed up on a rock to the right), turn left, down a farm track towards St Trudpert. After about 1km at a T-junction without markings continue down the hill to the left. Soon the forest road turns into a paved lane. At a small crossing (Maisstollenweg), take the lower left-hand fork down into the valley. Cross the car park at *Wolfgarten* and follow Talweg to the right along the stream. At *Vogtshalde*, by a rather fanciful looking crucifix, Talweg makes a little jink to the right, then continues down the valley on an unlikely looking footpath that passes right behind someone's house, and passes **Gasthaus zur Linde** to reach *Mühlenmatten*. Here take the left fork to reach **St Trudpert Abbey**.

St Trudpert was an Irish monk, who came to this region around 600AD on a mission to bring Christianity to the heathens of the Black Forest.

Ridgeway above Münstertal

Only six years later he died a martyr's death at the hands of some local peasants. According to the legend, a spring gushed forth at the spot where he died. Despite the short duration of his mission, his legacy lives on.

At *Sandmatte* head up towards the back end of the church. You will find St Trudpert's Crypt and the sacred spring opposite the cemetery. Circle around the church and head up the hill to *St Trudpert/Ökonomie*. Turn right and follow the yellow marker towards Untermünstertal station. At the end of Kirchweg turn right towards *Prestenberg* and continue on Talweg along the stream. After passing the school and playing fields, cross the car park and turn right towards the junction. Follow the main road to the left to find the little station at **Münstertal** (*Untermünstertal/Bahnhof*).

WALK 4

Panorama trail around Schönberg

Start/finish	Merzhausen village centre
Distance	13km
Difficulty	Medium
Time	4hr
Height gain/loss	510m
Maps	Schwarzwaldverein Wanderkarte Nördliches Markgräflerland 1:35,000; Kompass Freiburg und Umgebung 1:25,000
Refreshments	Unterer Schönberger Hof (closed Mon, Tues, Wed) www.gasthaus-schoenberghof.de, Café VIKREGo Jesuitenschloss www.vikrego-cafe-jesuitenschloss.de
Public transport	Bus to Gasthaus Grüner Baum, Merzhausen (Brsg) (stops on the main road), return from Ortsmitte/Merzhausen
Access	From Freiburg take L122 towards Merzhausen/Hexental
Parking	Car park by the swimming pool (Bürgerbad) by the cemetery, or at Jesuitenschloss (turn off L122 on Schlossweg and follow the signs up the hill to Jesuitenschloss)
Trail markings	Yellow (two short sections have no markings at all but are easy to find)
Note	A new trail has been created around Schönberg called NatURWALDpfad, which intertwines with this route. Its symbol is a stag beetle. Just after Hedwigsbrunnen (now part of NatURWALDpfad), a big tree lies across the path, which may prove to be a bit of an obstacle for less agile walkers.

This lovely circuit covers varied terrain: amble through fields and fruit orchards on the lower slopes of Schönberg and the nature reserve around Berghauser Kapelle before climbing up to the castle ruins of Schneeburg and from there to the top of Schönberg. The plateau offers some of the best views of Kaiserstuhl and the Vosges to the west, and the chain of southern Black Forest peaks, stretching from Kandel to Schauinsland, Belchen and even Hochblauen, far to the south.

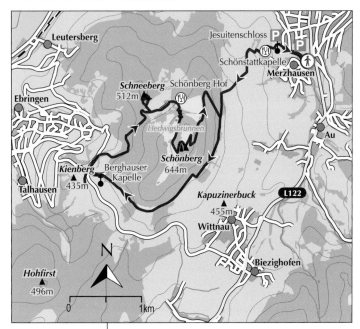

Geologically, **Schönberg** is not actually part of the Black Forest massif. Together with the hill to the south (Hohfirst), it forms a short range of foot-hills on the edge of the Rhine Valley that broke off when the earth's crust between the Vosges and the Black Forest collapsed some 35 million years ago. Thanks to its many different types of mineral and soil deposits Schönberg is known for its unusually varied plantlife, which is protected by several nature reserves around its slopes. Archaeological remains indicate that Schönberg was once the site of a Neolithic village and later a Celtic settlement.

From the centre of Merzhausen by the new Forum follow Friedhofweg, past the public pool (*Bürgerbad*). At the end of the car park continue on the field track up the hill into the vineyards. Halfway up the track head towards the little chapel to the left, on the broad, grassy path through the vines (no marker).

From **Schönstattkapelle** a short, steep trail behind the chapel leads up the hill to the back of Jesuitenschloss. At the top turn left and at *Bei der Schönstattkapelle* cross the courtyard of the old Jesuit castle. At **Jesuitenschloss** circle around the back of the building to the left, towards Gaisberg and Berghauser Kapelle. After about 100m, at *Am Drescherkopf*, follow the farm track up towards the edge of the forest. At the top (*Gaisberg*), turn left on the broad track through the forest, pass *Kopfacker* and ignore any trails to the right or left. Just after *Dürrstein* follow the yellow marker to the right and then continue on the field track towards Berghauser Kapelle to the left. The track circles around the hill past *Obere Englematt*, with excellent panoramic views to the south. After passing a barrier the trail ends on a little lane at *Untere Langhard*. Turn left towards the road and you will see **Berghauser Kapelle**,

Schneeburg ruins

amid old fruit orchards – a lovely spot for a picnic before tackling the next leg of the walk.

Retrace your steps to signpost *Berghauser Kapelle* and continue on the small, unmarked lane next to the one you came down on. This section has no markers. Just after the wayside cross, by the water fountain, follow the field track to the right, into the forest. Immediately behind the tree line continue on the track to the left. At the end pass the barrier and turn right, up the hill along the dirt road to *An der Schneeburg Ruine*. Follow the footpath to the **castle ruins**. (Where the trail splits you can take either fork). After enjoying the views from the top retrace your steps to *An der Schneeburg Ruine* and continue to the left, to **Gasthaus Schönberg Hof**.

Opposite the restaurant, take the footpath across the field and up through the trees to *Ladhöfle*. Cross the lane and continue uphill on the narrow footpath towards the water fountain Hedwigsbrunnen. At *Hedwigsbrunnen* cross the forestry road and continue up towards Schönberg on the stony path along the edge of the forest to a paved lane at *Oberer Schönberg*. Follow the lane to the left to reach the clearing on the top. At the top of Schönberg you'll see a transmitter mast to the right. ◀

Walking around the transmitter, there are some benches facing south, the perfect spot to enjoy the views.

To get back down to Merzhausen, turn around so you are facing towards Freiburg (north). Follow the footpath across the grassy top close to the right-hand edge of the clearing and head towards a prominent tree that displays a small summit sign (Schönberg Gipfel 646m). About 20m after this tree there is a narrow, unmarked path on the right (slightly obscured by the bushes) that snakes down the hill. At the bottom the trail meets another track (NatURWALDpfad). Follow this track to the left on a stony trail, crossing a couple of forestry roads. The trail finally leads along the edge of the hill, with quite a steep drop to the right, and reaches a trail junction. Turn right towards Jesuitenschloss and Merzhausen. At *Am Felsele* turn left to *Am Kopfacker*. Follow the forestry track to the left, back to *Gaisberg*, and retrace your steps to **Merzhausen** via Jesuitenschloss.

WALK 5

In the heart of Margrave's Land –
Wiiwegli and Bettlerpfad

Start	Badenweiler Sportbad (outdoor swimming pool)
Finish	Staufen
Distance	16km
Difficulty	Easy
Time	4hr30min
Height gain/loss	380m/460m
Maps	Schwarzwaldverein Wanderkarte Nördliches Markgräflerland 1:35,000; Kompass Münstertal, Nördliches Markgräflerland 1:25,000
Refreshments	Numerous places in Sulzburg and Staufen; Straussenwirtschaft Probst www.schleifsteinhof.de/strausse.html (closed Mon)
Public transport	Bus to Sportbad, Badenweiler. Return by bus or train from Bahnhof/Staufen im Breisgau or Süd Bahnhof/Staufen im Breisgau
Access	Take B378 towards Badenweiler
Parking	Next to the outdoor swimming pool
Trail markings	'Bettlerpfad' (yellow markers) and Wiiwegli (yellow bunch of grapes on red rhombus)
Note	This trail can be walked at any time of the year, but is especially idyllic in spring and in late autumn. During the summer it may be rather hot as there is little shade. The full 84km Wiiwegli trail is available as a 'walking without luggage' package www.schwarzwald-tourismus.info

This is a lovely route through the rolling vineyards and wine villages of Margraves' Land with almost constant views of the Vosges. This walk combines the best parts of two long-distance trails in one route, from the historic spa town of Badenweiler to the charming village of Staufen.

Bettlerpfad runs from Merzhausen, on the outskirts of Freiburg, to Badenweiler following an ancient route that Benedictine mendicant monks used during

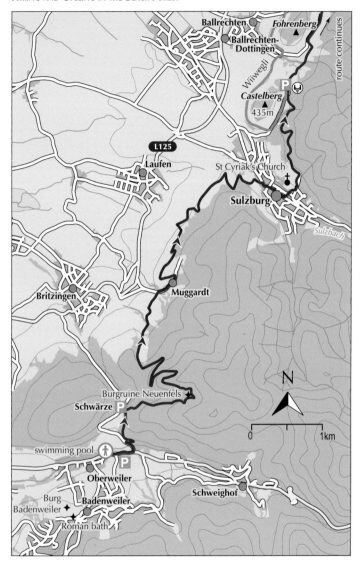

the Middle Ages, begging for alms at the farms along the way. **Wiiwegli** is an 84km wine trail that runs from Basle to Freiburg and introduces walkers to some of the best terroirs of Margraveland. Parts of the route are conceptualised as interpretive trails for those interested in learning more about viticulture.

Wiiwegli waymark

Starting at the bus stop in front of the **outdoor pool**, follow the main road past the car park to the next junction. Turn left along the road towards Britzingen and Römerberg Klinik for about 100m. At *Köhlerpromenade* turn right on Köhlerweg. Almost immediately climb up the hill on the small trail towards Schwärze, a trailhead car park where many trails intersect.

At **Schwärze** take the narrow, yellow-marked footpath towards Burgruine Neuenfels (not the forestry road Tannwaldweg). Eventually the trail joins a forestry road to the left. Cross another forestry road and continue straight up the hill to the old castle ruin of **Neuenfels**.

After enjoying the views across the Rhine Valley and the Vosges, retrace your steps to signpost *Ruine Neuenfels*. Turn right down the hill and join *Theodor-Braus-Weg* to the left, towards Muggardt. At the T-junction turn right on Eichenbergweg and follow it around the tight bend. Continue straight to *Tannwaldweg* and follow Buchmattweg to the right, out of the forest. Soon the trail forks to the right through a field, crosses a brook and emerges in the vineyards. Continue to the lane and turn left to a little junction at Muggardterweg. Cross Muggardterweg and follow the narrow, fenced trail down through a field to *Muggardt/ Kleematt*. Turn right to pass through the village.

At **Muggardt** follow Wiiwegli markers in an almost straight line through the vineyards to Sulzburg. Keep a sharp eye out for markers as the trail makes a couple of unexpected jinks! At the end of the first terrace it passes through some trees to the vineyard below and continues to the right. At *Im Ennwegen* walk down the lane to *Auf der Wurmisholen* and continue across another vineyard. At the next lane turn right and just before the lane runs into the forest, continue to the left. Finally, turn right

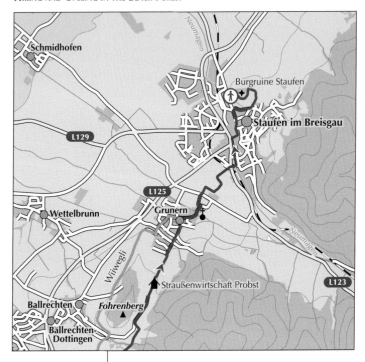

up to *Freusig*. Here a narrow trail leads down towards **Sulzburg** along the edge of the field. By the old barn turn right, towards the main road.

From *Sulzburg/Fliederbachbrücke* follow yellow markers to Grunern. Turn right through the city gates and pass the market square. At *Sulzburg/Klostergasse* turn left to reach the ancient church of **St Cyriak**. ◀

Originally a Benedictine monastery, this is one of the oldest churches in the region, with some parts dating back to the 10th century.

Cross the churchyard and follow the lane to the left to Kosakenwäldele and continue up the hill along the edge of the forest towards Castellberg and Staufen. After about 400m watch out for two narrow trails right next to each other, on the right. Ignore Arthur-Feisst Wegele but follow the left-hand trail to the end, where it re-joins the forestry road to the right to reach Bierenstiel Rank. Continue to the left towards Castellberg.

> Castellberg, the site of a **Bronze Age hill fort**, is now a nature reserve. At the top there is a modern observation tower built at the site of an old 'castell' (some ruins can still be seen). Drystone walling has been restored around the vineyard terraces, offering a special habitat for some rare plants and animals normally found in more Mediterranean climates.

At *Castellberg* Wiiwegli goes around **Castellberg** and **Fohrenberg** on the western side to reach Grunern (in wet weather conditions this is the better alternative).

Bettlerpfad continues down the lane to the right and then takes an unexpected shortcut across an orchard to the right. After crossing a brook the trail climbs up to *Brunnenmatt*. Follow the track opposite, straight through the field and around to the left past the benches by the walnut trees to join a vineyard lane. Turn right at *Etzmatten*. Pass **Straußenwirtschaft Probst** and head straight down through the vineyards to the outskirts of **Grunern**. At the bottom bear left to the corner, then follow Altenbergstraße to the right to *Grunern/Altes Rathaus*.

St Cyriak's Church, Sulzburg

Staufen castle ruins

Here Bettlerpfad and Wiiwegli meet again. Follow Wiiwegli markers to the right, along the main road (Dorfstraße) to the church. Just before the bend turn left on a little lane (Karweg) and follow it around to the country road. Cross and follow Wiiwegli through the fields and gardens, first to the right, then bending around to the left. Just before the school follow the small footpath to the right to *Staufen/Krichelnweg*, by the tiny (now defunct) train stop of Staufen Süd (the new station is just down the tracks, by the school).

According to local legend and historic records, the events that inspired the story of **Dr Faustus** took place in Staufen. Like many medieval alchemists, Dr Faustus aspired to make gold for bankrupt aristocrats. Working for the Lord of Staufen, Dr Faustus was in pursuit of this aim when one night his experiments went badly wrong. He was found the next day 'in a badly mutilated state' in his chambers at the local inn (Gasthaus Löwen). The townsfolk blamed the devil for his demise and it was rumoured that Mephistopheles himself had come to get the doctor's soul.

Cross the main road and continue straight on to *Schießrain Steg*, then follow the stream to the left, to *Fichter Steg*. If you still have the energy you can climb up to the castle ruins of Staufen (**Burgruine Staufen**): turn right to the market square and follow Hauptstraße to the left to *Staufen/Post*. Follow the yellow marker up to *Burgruine*, via *Staufen/Krautäcker*.

To reach the station turn left at *Staufen/Post* along Bahnhofstraße.

WALK 6
Schluchtensteig

Start	Stühlingen
Finish	Wehr
Distance	120km
Time	6 days
Terrain	Schluchtensteig means 'gorge trail' and much of the route leads through gorges, often on very narrow ledges but there are also climbs. The highest point of the route is Bildstein (1134m) in Stage 3. Stages 4 and 5 only briefly pass through small creeks and otherwise run through fields and forest on small paths or forestry tracks.
Refreshments	Take plenty of food and especially water with you, as there are not many opportunities to fill up water bottles or buy food along the way.
Website	There is a very informative website at www.schluchtensteig. de (in German). Check under: Wanderservice > Aktuelle Weginfos for current information (they use Google Translate to translate the very useful pages into cringeworthy English). If sections of the trail are closed or altered it will be mentioned here. Route alterations are usually well marked at the site – look for *Umleitung* signs.
Trail markings	Stylised S for Schluchtensteig (pictured) symbolising the Wutach. It also says 'Schluchtensteig' on the signposts.
Note	This trail is best from May to the end of October, as long as there is no snow or ice. For Stages 1, 2, 3 and 6 sure-footedness and firm footwear is **essential** as trails can be narrow, steep and sometimes slippery. Walkers should be vertigo-free. These sections should not be attempted in poor weather (high winds, after heavy rain or snowmelt, or while there is snow or ice on the ground). Make a note of the rescue sector signs (*Rettungssektor*) as you pass through. In case of emergency dial 112 and state the rescue sector where the accident occurred in order to help rescuers find you quickly. Bear in mind that a phone signal is not always available in the gorge.

One of Germany's top ten long-distance routes, this gorgeous gorge trail leads through some of the most scenic and adventurous terrain of the Black Forest. Over a distance of 120km, Schluchtensteig explores the gorges of the Rivers Wutach and Wehra, from Stühlingen to Wehr.

Schluchtensteig is a certified 'Quality Trail' and was voted 'Germany's Best Long-Distance Trail' in 2011. From the end of April to the end of October the trail is easily accessible by public transport and each section can be done as an individual day tour. For those who want to walk the entire length of the route, 'Walking without luggage' packages are available.

Some sections of the route are on narrow trails along the edges of almost vertical cliffs and hillsides. Other sections traverse highland meadows with views of the Alps, or pass through the forest. Individual stages are not too long and are technically not difficult, as long as the weather is good and your shoes have good grip.

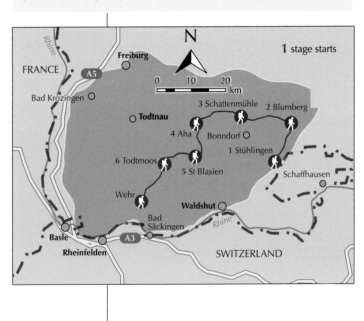

STAGE 1
Stühlingen to Blumberg

Start	Stühlingen catholic church, Kronplatz
Finish	Blumberg town centre
Distance	19.5km
Difficulty	Medium
Time	5–6hr
Height gain/loss	580m/340m
Maps	Publicpress Fernwanderwege (Leporello) Schluchtensteig 1:25,000
Refreshments	Various cafés and restaurants in Stühlingen and Blumberg; Gasthaus Wutachschlucht, Lausheim (closed Mon and Tues)
Public transport	Bus to Kath. Kirche, Stühlingen. Return by bus from Hauptstraße, Blumberg (Baden)
Access	Take B314 between Waldshut and Blumberg to Stühlingen
Parking	At the town hall (Stadthalle). From the parking follow Am Bahndamm, Eichwiesenweg, then turn right on Hallauer Straße to reach the starting point.
Note	There are some fairly steep sections. The passage through the gorge can be dangerous and mudslides and rock falls can occur, but a new, bad-weather alternative through the Flühen has been signposted ('Bei Schlechtwetter' with an arrow pointing the way). You can shorten this stage by taking the bus (or train) to Lausheim/Blumegg and starting from there.

This stage offers an adventurous and at times challenging walk through the Wutachflühen. *Flühen* is an old word denoting a cliff. The path climbs up through the gorge and along the edge of the rock face – an exciting introduction to Wutach Gorge.

Starting at the orientation board by the catholic church in the centre of Stühlingen follow Hauptstraße through town towards Weizen and Blumberg. At the roundabout turn left on Bahnhofstraße and at the end cross the big road via the subway. Before reaching the playing fields

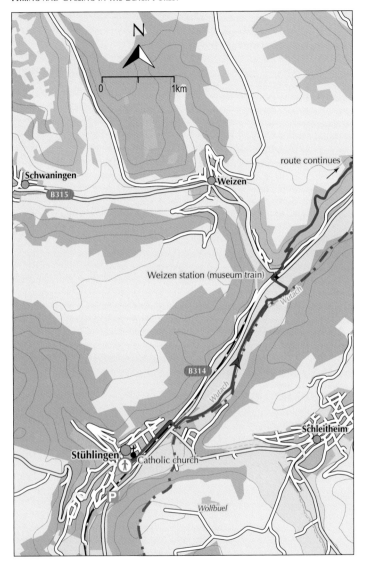

(*Sportplatz*), the trail takes an unexpected turn and heads through the bushes on a small footpath to the right. For the next 2.5km it follows the river, sometimes on the broad cycle path, sometimes on a little footpath close to the river. At *Weizener Steg* cross the footbridge across the B314 and turn right, towards **Weizen station**.

> The railway line is no longer in use except for the **historic steam engine** known as Sauschwänzlebahn, which means 'pigtail train', an allusion to the tight turns it has to make to overcome the 231m of height difference between Blumberg and Weizen, over a distance of only 9.6km. This was accomplished by extending the distance to 25km with a combination of viaducts and tight switchback tunnels. At the time of construction, in 1887, the project was considered a daring feat of engineering. The steam engine runs during the summer months Thurs-Sun, and in Sept-Oct on Sat and Sun only (must be booked in advance at **www.sauschwaenzlebahn.de**).

At *Bahnhof/Weizen* the trail starts to climb the hill on a steep and narrow path behind the station. It soon joins a broader forest road to the left. After about 1.5km, by the power lines, Schluchtensteig starts climbing up the side of the hill on a smaller footpath. After crossing a lane and passing *Alter Salzweg*, the trail reaches a large trail junction. Turn right and follow the winding path down to reach **Gasthaus Wutachschlucht**.

Cross the road and railway tracks to the right. At *Bahnhof Lausheim-Blumegg* follow the small footpath to the left, along the river. By the **viaduct** at *Eisenbahnbrücke* bear right, pass underneath the bridge and cross the river via the footbridge. Continue to the right to a little picnic area. This is the last opportunity for a picnic before the most demanding part of the trail starts. There are no places to stop and rest until you reach the top of the gorge. ▶

The trail starts to climb on a narrow path across a boulder-strewn slope. Close to the top it levels out and

The trail crosses a couple of waterfalls along the way, and after heavy rain or snowmelt these sections can be treacherous. (In this case, follow the bad weather route, marked 'Bei Schlechtwetter', which follows the river and climbs the slope more gradually on a more comfortable path.)

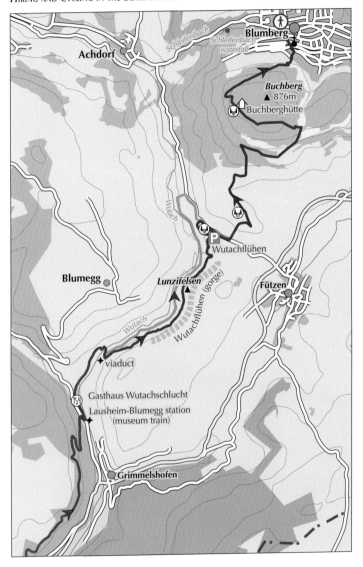

Achdorf

Blumberg

Schleifenbach

Schleifenbach
waterfall

Buchberg
▲ 876m

Buchberghütte

Wutach

P
Wutachflühen

Blumegg

Lunzifelsen
▲

Wutachflühen (gorge)

Fützen

Wutach

◆ viaduct

Gasthaus Wutachschlucht
Lausheim-Blumegg station
(museum train)

Grimmelshofen

edges along the rock face as a narrow ledge (rescue sector X2). At *Wutachflühen/Bei der Mutter Gottes* continue straight on towards **Parkplatz Wutachflühen**. At the fork take the right-hand trail. A couple of vantage points offer great views before the trail leaves the gorge and emerges at a car park and picnic area.

Cross the car park and follow the lane to the right. After passing underneath the railway bridge take the grassy path up through the field at *Hintere Reutenen*. At the top, bear right to reach *Bei der Bielwasenhütte* and just past the layby turn sharply to the left on the gravel track. Cross the little crossroads and continue up the hill. Follow the track to the right, and after 150m to the left. The broad track soon turns into a steep footpath through the trees. After crossing a clearing continue to the right and follow the trail up the hill at *Buchberg*.

At the trail junction take the small footpath just to the left of the broad gravel track and continue steeply uphill to *Ottilienhöhe*. At the top the trail continues to the left to

The trail through the 'Flühen'

A view across the gorge and 'Flühen'

Buchberghütte, a scenic picnic spot with sweeping views across the rolling hills.

Follow the small trail down the hill in tight zigzags. Near the bottom continue to the right, to the junction with Rupreuteweg. Bear right, and a few metres further follow Schluchtensteig to the left, down a grassy path to a small lane and car park. Pass the car park to the left and continue down the steps, past the cemetery. Turn left, and at *Blumberg/Evang. Kirche* follow Friedhofstraße to Hauptstraße to reach the centre of town (*Blumberg/ Gänseliesel*). There is a bus stop just past Gasthaus Hirschen.

STAGE 2
Blumberg to Schattenmühle

Start	Hauptstraße, Blumberg (hiking signpost Gänseliesel)
Finish	Schattenmühle
Distance	20km
Difficulty	Easy
Time	6hr30min
Height gain/loss	330m/380m
Maps	Publicpress Fernwanderwege (Leporello) Schluchtensteig 1:25,000
Refreshments	Options in Blumberg, Achdorf and at Schattenmühle; carry plenty of water
Public transport	Bus to Hauptstraße, Blumberg (Baden). Return by bus from Wanderparkplatz, Schattenmühle (complicated) or by taxi.
Access	Take B27, between Stühlingen and Hüfingen
Parking	There is no central car park in Blumberg, but parking is free anywhere in town.
Note	This is an easy walk, but stamina is needed and it can be dangerous in poor weather conditions. Rock fall and mudslides are possible. Walkers must be sure-footed and vertigo-free.

Many consider this the most exciting part of Wutach Gorge – which makes it a popular place. It is a walk through a geological timeline and a very special ecosystem with many rare plants. Due to the sloping terrain the river's path gradually reveals deposits that date back some 225 million years. The trail often runs on mere ledges along sheer rock faces, giving a very tangible feel for the passage of time, carved into stone, as it were.

Starting at Blumberg Hauptstraße (*Blumberg/Gänseliesel*) follow Schluchtensteig markings towards **Schleifenbach waterfall**, through a residential area. By the last buildings there are some information boards and the trail continues on a grassy footpath down into the gorge. A steep

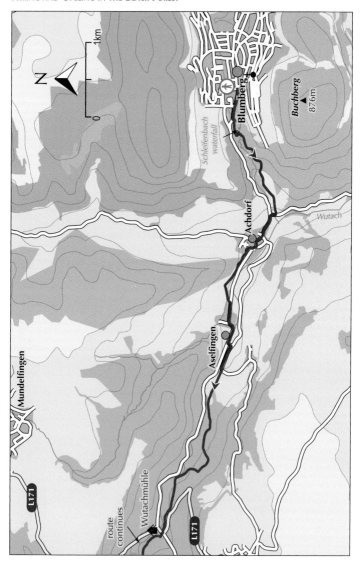

ladder leads down to the bridge across the falls. On the other side continue along the stream out of the forest and through the fields to **Achdorf**. At *Achdorf/Kalenäcker* turn right and head into the village along the main road.

By the orientation boards (*Achdorf/Ortsmitte*) turn left on Lindenstraße. Cross through the yard of Gasthaus Scheffellinde to the right and turn left, past Haus des Gastes. The trail continues on the left-hand side of the little stream through the park, passes the car park and heads up into the fields. At *Beim Kreuz* follow the farm road towards **Aselfingen** to the left and pass through the village along the road. By a bus shelter at *Abzw. Überachen* turn left across the bridge and follow the track that starts off next to the river towards Wutachmühle to the right. At a clearing it joins another forest road and continues straight for about 100m, then abruptly turns downhill to the right. It emerges by the road and continues to the right behind

Wutachschlucht

85

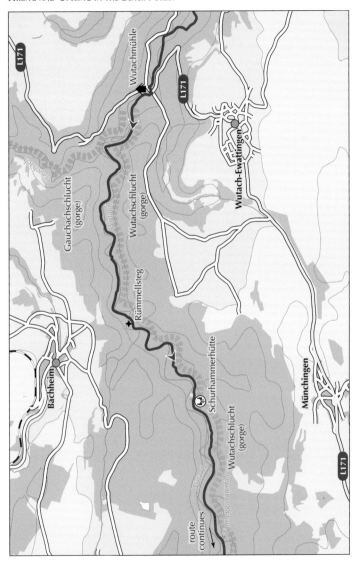

the guardrail. Cross the road and head through the yard of Wutachmühle sawmill. At the far end a broad forest track (Bühlertälerweg) leads down to *Kanadiersteg*, the beginning of the gorge passage.

From here the path is easy to follow. Just pay attention to the markers through the gorge towards Schattenmühle guesthouse/restaurant at the other end. The trail some-times runs on a broad forest trail, sometimes on a narrow rocky ledge along the cliff and crossing the river back and forth. Caution is advised, especially if the ground is wet and slippery.

At **Rümmelesteg** you can see the remains of the orig-inal bridge, one end still firmly anchored and the other hanging in mid-air, which clearly demonstrates that the gorge is still widening. Soon the trail reaches a rocky 'beach' facing a limestone cliff.

> For a stretch of about 1.5km the **Wutach disappears** into an underground cave system, but as the granite bedrock does not allow for an alternative way to the Rhine the water is forced to re-emerge near the imposing Muschelkalk cliff. During hot summers the water may subside completely leaving this part of the riverbed dry.

After passing the picnic area at **Schurhammerhütte** the trail passes **Tannegg waterfall** at *Sinternase*. The sign is named after the calciferous volcanic rock behind the flow of water that continues to grow as calcium-rich waters run over it. Continue to the site of the former spa at *ehem. Bad Boll*, where now only a **chapel** remains.

> At the end of the 19th century **Bad Boll** was among the most illustrious spas of the Black Forest and it was partially owned by the Fishing Club of London (1894–1913). Its more prominent guests included Churchill and Nietzsche. Like many spas of the region, Bad Boll went into decline during the war years. When the main building burnt down some years ago the spa was never reconstructed.

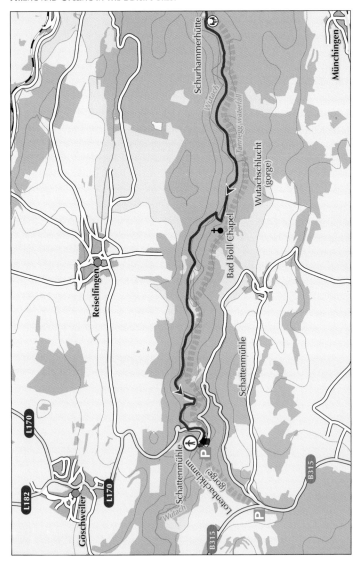

Sinternase at Tannegg waterfall

Due to a landslide that occurred in 2017 just up the track, the trail now continues on the other side of the river. Cross the river on Fritz-Hockenjos Steg (Bad Boll) and turn left on Münzlochweg to the picnic area. ▶

Soon the trail reaches **Schattenmühle**. The bus stop is to the left, at the trailhead car park by the road.

In Roman times this was the site of a major thoroughfare along a trade route that connected the Rhine with the Neckar River.

STAGE 3
Schattenmühle to Aha

Start	Schattenmühle
Finish	Aha station
Distance	22km
Difficulty	Hard
Time	7hr
Height gain/loss	780m/520m
Maps	Publicpress Fernwanderwege (Leporello) Schluchtensteig 1:25,000
Refreshments	Schattenmühle www.schattenmuehle.de (open from Easter to mid-October, closed Thurs); various cafés and restaurants in Lenzkirch; Hotel-Gasthof Hirschen in Fischbach www.hirschen-fischbach.de, Aha
Public transport	Bus to Wanderparkplatz, Schattenmühle (limited, seasonal service May–Nov); or bus to Lotenbachklamm, Gündelwangen (year-round service) and walk to Schattenmühle through the beautiful Lotenbachklamm – adds about 1.5km/30min). Return by bus or train from Bahnhof, Aha (Schluchsee)
Access	B315; for day trips, car access is best from Gündelwangen/Lotenbachklamm
Parking	There is a car park at Schattenmühle, but Gündelwangen/Lotenbachklamm trailhead car park is much easier to get back to at the end of the day.
Note	The walk can be shortened to Lenzkirch (14km) or Fischbach (19km). Overnight accommodation is available in Oberfischbach or Schluchsee (one train stop or about 5km from Aha). The gorge section can be dangerous.

This is a scenic walk through varied terrain – but not without challenges. The 'official' end of this section is the tiny hamlet of Fischbach, but it is worth continuing to Aha on the shore of Lake Schluchsee. It is not much further in terms of distance, but there is another ascent to tackle, up to Bildstein, before the trail reaches Aha. The actual peak is just off the trail to the right, but the extra 200m are well worth the effort, as you will be rewarded with fine views across Schluchsee and the peaks of the Hochschwarzwald.

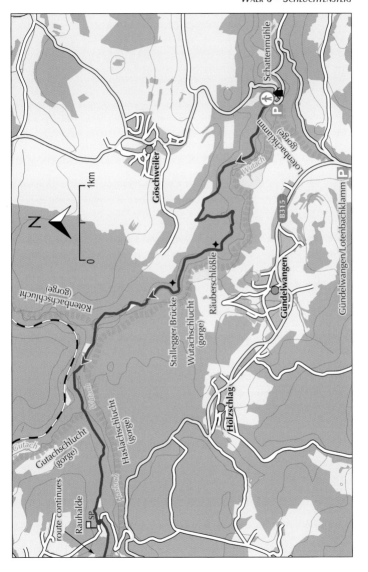

If you start from *Abzw. Gündelwangen/Lotenbachklamm* bus stop or car park, follow the yellow marker through Lotenbachklamm Gorge to Schattenmühle.

At Schattenmühle car park cross the bridge and follow Schluchtensteig markings steeply up the side of the hill towards Räuberschlößle via Glöcklerhalde and Eichwäldle. The little footpath soon joins a broader track to the left and after passing a picnic area follows a field track to the left. Circle halfway around the field and follow the small footpath through the bushes to the left. The trail now enters a nature reserve. Continue along the rim of the gorge to **Räuberschlößle** (*Räuber* means 'highwayman', *Schlößle* means 'little castle'), where a tiny path leads past the huge boulder to a spacious, but precariously positioned hideout that once gave cover to waylaying highwaymen.

The trail continues towards Ruine Stallegg, where it joins a broader access road to the left and passes a covered bridge (**Stallegger Brücke**). ◄

Continue along the river to the picnic area at the confluence of Rötenbach and Wutach at *Rötenbachmündung*. Cross the bridge and continue to *Wutachhalde*. Follow the left fork to *Haslachmündung* where the rivers Gutach and Haslach join to become the Wutach. Cross only the first bridge and continue straight, on a rough, steep track towards Rauhalde. Just before the top the trail branches off to the left and continues on a path, which after passing a narrow rock crevice at Rechenfelsen starts to climb up the side of the gorge. ◄

After passing a rocky precipice at Höllochfelsen the trail emerges on a forest road, which is also part of the Southern Black Forest Cycle Trail. Continue to the left and follow the bend around to **Rauhalde**. Due to storm damage the path has been re-routed here indefinitely and continues for a short section on Südschwarzwaldradweg to Mühlenweg, where it continues on its regular path, to the left, down into the valley next to a cascading little stream. At the bottom turn right, along the Haslach. At *An der Schleifensäge* take the small footpath to the left

There has been a passage across the river here since at least 1500BC, when it formed part of a major trade route between the Neckar and Upper Rhine regions.

Note There are old wooden signs here and there, saying 'Kein Wanderweg' ('not a trail'). Stay off those paths – they are dangerous.

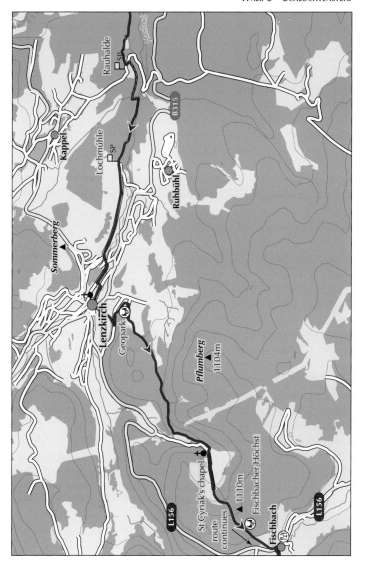

St Cyriak's Chapel | towards **Lochmühle**. The trail emerges from the forest and follows the paved lane down to **Lenzkirch**.

At the corner of Kapplerstraße bear left. Halfway down Ludwig-Kegel-Straße the trail turns left, across the stream and into the park. Turn right, past the Kurhaus towards the church (*Lenzkirch/Rathaus*). Follow the main road to the left to *Lenzkirch/Bühl*, by the bus station and head up Bühlstraße. At the end pass the small car park and continue up the hill on a grassy footpath behind the last house and into the forest. The trail reaches a paved lane and joins it to the left for about 100m. Just before the bend follow the path to the right signed to 'Geopark'.

A scenic picnic spot overlooking Lenzkirch, **Geopark** marks the 50km point of Schluchtensteig. The boulder display serves as an educational exhibit about the geology of the area.

Pass through the rock gallery and bear left to *Am Geo-Park*. Turn right down the residential street to the way cross and then turn left, past the playing fields. The trail continues uphill through the forest (keep to the left). Where the track levels out follow the left fork down to *Am Pflumberg* and continue to the left towards **St Cyriak's Chapel**. Pass the chapel and head straight up the hill through the tiny hamlet. Continue up on a long, steep track to **Fischbacher**

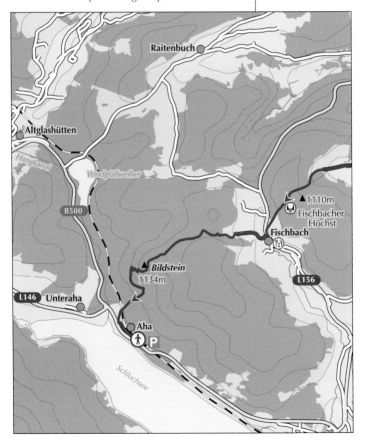

View of Schluchsee from Bildstein

Höchst by a picnic area and playground. From here the trail leads straight down the hill to **Fischbach** (at the bend continue straight, down the smaller track).

Cross the road and follow the lane opposite up into the forest to *Kohlplatz*. Continue straight on and join the crossing forest road to the left, to *Am Zwerisberg*. From here the trail continues straight on to **Bildstein**. The actual peak is just off the trail, to the right. The extra 200m are well worth the effort.

Follow the trail down the hill on the steep, winding path. After crossing a forest road, the trail immediately forks to the right, next to a stream. At the bottom, pass underneath the railway tracks (*Unterer Bildsteinweg*) and turn left after the barrier to find the station in **Aha**.

STAGE 4
Aha to St Blasien

Start	Aha station
Finish	St Blasien bus station
Distance	17km
Difficulty	Easy
Time	4–5hr
Height gain/loss	330m/490m
Maps	Publicpress Fernwanderwege (Leporello) Schluchtensteig 1:25,000
Refreshments	Unterkrummenhof www.unterkrummenhof.info; various cafés and restaurants in St Blasien
Public transport	Train or bus to Bahnhof, Aha (Schluchsee). Return by bus from Busbahnhof, St. Blasien (bus station)
Access	Via B500
Parking	Aha station
Note	In bad weather or icy conditions the section through the creek at the end should be bypassed using the access road that runs next to it.

A very scenic and easy section of Schluchtensteig – almost entirely gorge-free. The trail meanders partly through the forest and partly across open pastures, revealing sweeping views across the rolling hills and an alpine skyline across the southern horizon. The stage ends in St Blasien, once considered one of the most powerful clerical centres of the region.

From the train station turn right and just after the hotel cross the large road via the subway. Schluchtensteig joins the lakefront path (Seerundweg) to the right, towards Unterkrummen. Pass the marina to the right and after crossing the little bridge bear left. At first the trail follows a small footpath along the lake, but soon bears right to join a forest road to circle halfway around the lake to **Unterkrummenhof**. At *Unterkrummen* follow the farm track up the hill towards Krummensäge. At

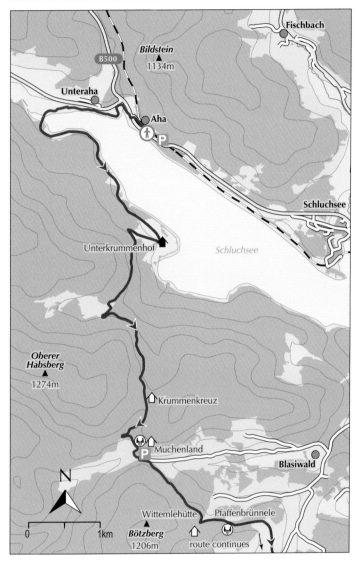

Dome of St Blasien

Kirschbaumweg turn left along the forest road to the junction of Muchenländerweg and Oberkrummenweg. Follow Muchenländerweg to the left, across a little bridge to *ehemalige Krummensäge* and up the hill past *Oberkrummen* towards Krummenkreuz.

Pass the water fountain (Krummenkreuzbrunnen) and **hut** (Krummenkreuzhütte) and follow the right fork at the end of the field. At the T-junction with Kohlbuchweg (*Muchenländer Brunnen*) continue to the left and head towards Blasiwald-Althütte. Follow the lane around the rim of the valley to the picnic area and car park at **Muchenland**. Turn left on Wittemleweg, towards **Wittemlehütte**. At *Wittemle* turn left on Pfaffenbrünnleweg, to a little picnic area and historic water fountain (**Pfaffenbrünnele**). Here follow the right-hand fork up across a lovely mountain pasture (make sure to close all gates) to **Blasiwald-Althütte**, a former glassmaker's settlement. On a clear day there is a superb panoramic view across the Alps from here. The trail runs down to the village and follows the lane to the right towards the **church**. ▸

The little church dates from the 17th century and the days of the glassblowers.

99

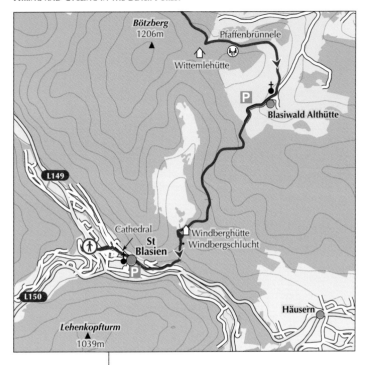

Follow the lane around the bend to the car park at *Blasiwald Althütte*. Schluchtensteig continues straight across, on an old forestry road called Alter Blasiwalderweg. Cross Rotrütteweg at *Sandgrube* and continue down the hill. At *Blasiwalderweg* cross another forest road and continue down the hill, past a 250-year-old silver fir, to **Windberghütte**.

Cross Kohlerbrückenweg and go straight across the bridge (*Windbergbrücke*). Turn left to *Obere Windbergschlucht*, where the trail leaves the broad forestry road to sneak off to the left and ambles down through the little creek of **Windbergschlucht**. After crossing the little bridge at *Klosterweg* you suddenly find yourself on the outskirts of St Blasien. Follow the path down to the street and continue to the right past *Friedrichstraße*, towards the centre of **St Blasien** along the river. To find the bus station cross the bridge by the Rathaus and follow Todtmooser Straße up the hill (approximately 150m).

STAGE 5
St Blasien to Todtmoos

Start	St Blasien town hall
Finish	Todtmoos bus station
Distance	18km
Difficulty	Easy
Time	5hr30min–6hr
Height gain/loss	580m/540m
Maps	Publicpress Fernwanderwege (Leporello) Schluchtensteig 1:25,000
Refreshments	Various places in St Blasien or Todtmoos; Klosterweiherhof www.klosterweiherhof.com, Dachsberger Hof in Wittenschwand (detour required) www.dachsberger-hof.de
Public transport	Bus to Rathaus, St. Blasien. Return by bus from Busbahnhof, Todtmoos (infrequent service at weekends)
Access	From B500 turn off on L149 to St Blasien
Parking	Just off the bypass (follow P signs)
Webcam	www.stblasien.de/stadt-handel/webcams

This is an easy and delightful panoramic section of Schluchtensteig across the 'southern balcony' of the Black Forest. Open pastures offer sweeping views towards Feldberg and Hochschwarzwald on one side and the southern foothills of Hotzenwald on the other, against a backdrop of snow-capped peaks. This section is almost devoid of gorges except for the last kilometre before reaching Todtmoos, where the trail runs through a narrow ravine formed by the headwaters of the River Wehra (Hohwehraschlucht).

In the centre of St Blasien (*Rathaus*), Schluchtensteig passes through the archway of the town hall and crosses the park, heading towards Lehenkopf and Klosterweiher.

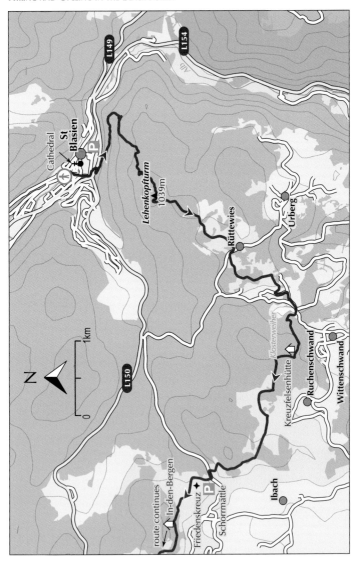

After passing a small parking area and some buildings (Alte Mühle) at the back of the monastic complex, follow the paved footpath to the right to a subway to cross under the busy road. On the other side continue to *Holzberg*. Follow Alfred-Weissenbergerweg to the left to *Weissenbergweg* and start climbing up the side of the hill on the right-hand trail. At *Luisenruhe* turn right on the forestry road. By an old water fountain called *Schwandbrünnele* Schluchtensteig continues up the hill on the steep trail. At the fork keep to the right, cross another forest road and continue up the hill to Lehenkopf with its **wooden tower**.

The path continues to the left of the tower (*Lehenkopfturm*) down a steep slope. At a trail junction/clearing continue straight towards Rüttewies and Urberg (old wooden signs). Keep to the right at the next fork to reach *Lehenrütte*. Turn right along the lane to the hamlet of **Rüttewies**. At the T-junction cross the main road and continue to the right for about 50m, then follow the track to the left across the field. After passing the stile continue

Klosterweiher, the former abbey fishpond

103

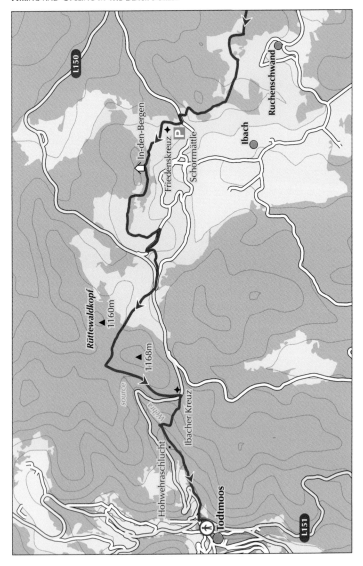

on the small footpath to Hoheck and turn left past the fields to *Horbach*. Bear right to a little vantage point. The trail continues down the hill via some tall steps to reach a farm road. Turn left (Auf der Breite), and at the T-junction (zum Bürgle), turn right. Cross the main road and head towards the pond (**Klosterweiher**). ▶

The trail passes between the buildings of Landgasthof Klosterweiher and continues to the right towards Ibacher Kreuz and Todtmoos. At a Y-junction take the left fork to reach an information board.

Klosterweiher used to be the fishpond for St Blasien Abbey.

> During the 19th century the **mine**, Friedrich-August Grube, was exploited for pyrite and nickel. One of the shafts has been reopened and converted into an exploratory trail for children. The area has been turned into a nature reserve. Some parts still have not recovered, as is indicated by the presence of certain rare mosses, fungi and lichen that thrive only on heavy metals.

Continue up the hill to the left. At *Friedrich August Grube*, turn left towards **Kreuzfelsenhütte**, a shelter hut above Wittenschwand, and a nice place for a picnic, especially on clear days, when the whole alpine chain stretches across the horizon. At *Am Kreuzfelsen* turn right, steeply up the hill. Continue to the left at *Auf den Köpfen*. After about 50m take the path to the left, to *Bruchhalden*, and carry on straight on along the edge of the field.

The path joins a lane to the right, turns left across a field and finally merges with another dirt road to the right. At *Hohrütte* continue to the right along the edge of the pastures, passing *Schorrmättle* on the way down to the road. Walk along the road to the left for about 100m and cross over to the trailhead car park at **Schorrmättle Parkplatz**. Cross the car park, past **Friedenskreuz** (viewpoint) and turn left on a track across a pasture. At the T-junction bear left again and then head up the hill to the right at *Beifang* to reach a shelter hut (**In-den-Bergen**). Pass the hut and continue to the left to *Langwinkel* and *Wachtbühl*, where the track joins a paved lane and

Kreuzfelsenhütte, above Wittenschwand – on a clear day the alpine panorama is fabulous

To visit the source of the River Wehra follow Wehraerlebnisweg, just after passing the Wehraquelle signpost.

continues to the right. At a bend, before reaching the main road, the trail suddenly sneaks off to the left and runs across the meadow down towards a minor road. Continue to the right towards the junction and cross the main road. On the other side (*Großbühl*), Schluchtensteig follows the farm road up into the forest, straight past **Rüttewaldkopf**, to *Schwarzer Stock*. Turn left on Schwarzerstockweg to reach **Ibacher Kreuz**. ◀

At Ibacher Kreuz, cross the road and bear to the right to find a trail that quickly turns into a stony path leading steeply downhill. Cross the forest road at *Unterm Berglewald* and continue on Wehratalweg on the other side. The trail meanders through the ravine of the young **Wehra** river down to *Todtmoos* (do not cross the first bridge). In Todtmoos follow the big road to the left to find the bus terminal.

STAGE 6
Todtmoos to Wehr

Start	Todtmoos bus station
Finish	Wehr bus station (at disused train station)
Distance	23.5km
Difficulty	Medium/hard
Time	7hr
Height gain/loss	430m/900m
Maps	Publicpress Fernwanderwege (Leporello) Schluchtensteig 1:25000
Refreshments	Various cafés and restaurants in Todtmoos and Wehr
Public transport	Bus to Busbahnhof, Todtmoos. Return by bus from Busbahnhof, Wehr (Baden)
Access	Todtmoos lies at a crossroads and can be reached via B518/L148 from Bad Säckingen/Wehr, via L150 from St Blasien, via B317/L149/L151 from Schönau or Todtnau, via L146 from Schluchsee/Aha
Parking	Todtmoos bus station
Note	The section through the gorge can be dangerous in bad weather. You can shorten the walk as the trail passes a couple of bus stops (Todtmoos Au, Am Schluchtensteig)

A great finale for this six-day walk, the trail gets wild and exciting again as it edges its way along the almost vertical walls of Wehraschlucht and crosses boulder-strewn slopes on narrow trails. If you are lucky you may spot chamois, or catch a glimpse of peregrine falcons overhead.

Behind the bus shelter follow the trail across the footbridge and through the car park of a private clinic to the main street of Todtmoos. Follow Hauptstraße to the left to the entrance of the small park (*Todtmoos/Löwenplatz*). Turn right up the hill on Kurparkweg and straight past *Todtmoos/kath. Pfarrhaus,* now on a forest road that leads to a **clinic**. At the T-junction by the car

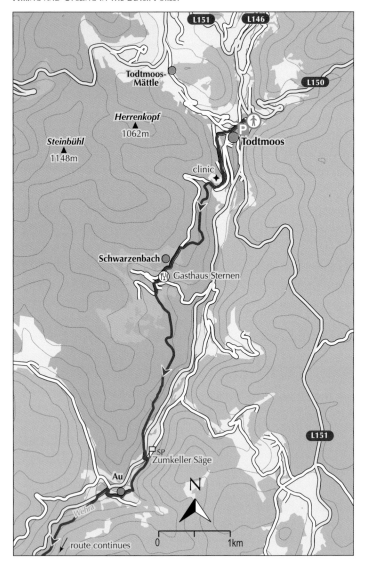

park turn right towards the end of the building and look for Schluchtensteig markers pointing to the left, down a gravel path (there is also a sign for Landgasthaus Sternen). At a trail crossing continue straight, on the upper trail, (Weiherweg), towards Gasthaus Sternen.

At the entrance to Schwarzenbach turn left and continue straight to the main part of the village. At the corner of Alter Kirchweg and Hangstraße turn left down the hill and pass **Gasthaus Sternen**. Head for the little crossroads (Gatterweg/Hangstraße). Cross the bridge at *Schwarzenbach* and continue straight. At the bend at *Unter der Sternwarte* Schluchtensteig leaves the lane and continues on a gravel path to the left and at the end follows the left fork on Neuer Hornweg into the forest. After about 2km on a broad forest road, at an odd junction in a tight bend, take the second track off to the right, (essentially continuing straight on) down the hill towards the sawmill by the main road.

The baroque pilgrims' church of Todtmoos

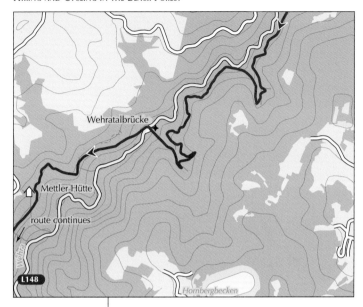

Cross the road to the right and turn left across the bridge to **Zumkeller Säge**. Take the steep forest track to the right, past the wildlife enclosure. Cross the stream and follow the lane through the village of Au, past *St Josefskapelle* and down to the main road to the right. Turn left along the road for about 170m, to a lay-by and information board.

Here the trail continues up the hill on a broad forest track to the left (Schwandhaldenweg). By the second bench take the right-hand fork. At a tight bend turn sharply right and follow the grassy forest track down the coombe, next to a stream. Before reaching the bottom the path suddenly goes off to the left on a small footpath and starts edging its way along the steep hillside. By a precipice it looks as though the trail continues straight to the point, but this only leads to a vantage point. Continue to the left.

The path soon joins a regular forest road to the right, but almost immediately leaves it again on another track to the right. At *Am Sägebach* follow the rocky trail down through the ravine next to the stream to an old bridge (**Wehratalbrücke**, bus stop 'Am Schluchtensteig').

Cross the road and continue on the steep and narrow footpath on the other side. Soon after passing *Wehratal/Brandhalde* the trail enters a Bannwald (see Introduction 'Plants and wildlife') and the terrain takes on a much wilder appearance. A badly placed marker points straight to the left, where there is no trail. Go left at the next fork, a few metres further on, and left again at *An der Mettlerhalde/Mettler Hütte* (**Mettler Hütte** is just 200m off to the right). After crossing the bridge at *Mettlen Graben* the trail leaves the forest reserve. After about 500m Schluchtensteig follows a narrow footpath to the left to a timber landing. ▶ Turn right to *Jockles Ebene Weg* and follow the left fork (Stolles Graben Weg) down to the **reservoir**.

Cross the dam and just after the barrier take the steps on the right, down to a lane (*Wehrastausee*). Continue to the left and at the bend follow the footpath straight along the Wehra to the chapel at *Wehr/St Wolfgang*. Turn right, cross the bridge and turn left past *Wehr/Schwimmbad*, before crossing over to the left side of the Wehra again and following it to the centre of **Wehr** (passing a mini-golf and tennis courts and a covered bridge at *Storchensteg*). At *Am Schloss* cross the bridge to the right and turn left along the main road to reach the bus station.

Timber landings where logs are gathered for loading onto trucks for transport are a common sight in the Black Forest.

High up in the gorge

111

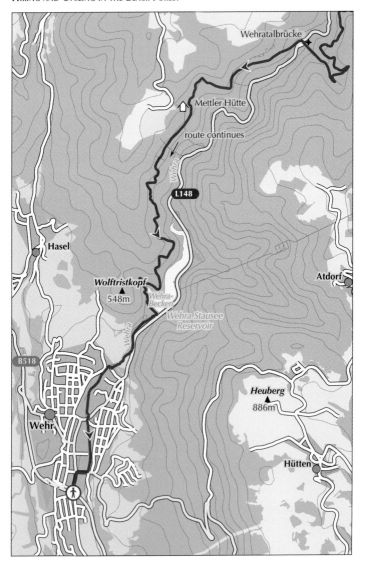

RIDE 1
Southern Black Forest Cycle Trail

Start/finish	Hinterzarten
Distance	Option 1 (via Basle): 246.5km; Option 2 (via Kandern) 242km
Time	4–5 days
Terrain	Option 1: flat, mostly on quiet roads without too much traffic, but through very urban terrain. It is best to time your trip so you will be riding the Basle section on a Sunday; Option 2: more challenging through the hills, but avoids heavy traffic
Maps	The only map that shows the trail through Switzerland and France in full is LGL Landkreiskarte LLÖ Landkreis Lörrach 1:50,000 (2011). Older versions do not mark the Südschwarzwald Radweg. Freizeitkarte Lörrach does not cover the Swiss parts fully.
Warning	Although there is rarely anybody on guard at these small border crossings, you must always carry your passport with you when you cross international borders.
Website	www.suedschwarzwald-radweg.de Luggage-forwarding packages available. See Appendix C for more information.
Trail markings	Südschwarzwald Radweg waymark (pictured)

The Southern Black Forest Cycle Trail (Südschwarzwald Radweg) makes a circuit of the southern Black Forest, and without too much effort. Although you can start the route anywhere and do it in either direction, the way it is described here is recommended, as the section that leads down from the plateau to the Rhine (between Bonndorf and Waldshut-Tiengen) would not be as effortless in reverse.

Starting in Hinterzarten, a small mountain resort at 900m, the trail meanders to nearby Titisee, and on to Neustadt, where it starts to climb up to the high plateau on a disused railway track. Via Lenzkirch and Bonndorf the trail reaches the eastern edge of the Black Forest and finally whizzes down

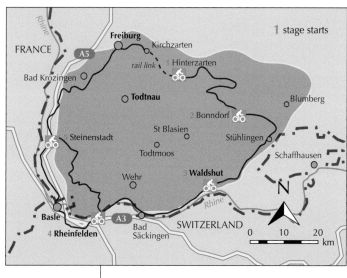

1 stage starts

FRANCE

Rhine

Freiburg

Kirchzarten

rail link

1 Hinterzarten

Bad Krozingen

Todtnau

Blumberg

2 Bonndorf

5 Steinenstadt

St Blasien

Stühlingen

Todtmoos

Schaffhausen

Wehr

3 Waldshut

N

Basle

4 Rheinfelden

A3

Bad Säckingen

SWITZERLAND

Rhine

0   10   20
km

Schloss Beuggen

from the plateau to the Rhine. Leisurely following the river, it passes through a string of charming old towns such as Waldshut-Tiengen, Laufenburg and Bad Säckingen.

In Rheinfelden, 20km before Basle, you can choose between two alternative routes.

- **Stage 4A** In Rheinfelden the trail crosses the Rhine into Switzerland and passes near the old Roman city of Augusta Raurica (www.augustaraurica.ch) and the old town of Basle. It then enters France via small back roads and follows the Rhine to Weil-am-Rhein, where it returns to Germany. After bypassing the industrial port of Weil the trail follows the Rhine to Steinenstadt. Unfortunately, the waymarking in both Switzerland and France is not very good.

- **Stage 4B** This route ambles through the hills via a series of small villages to the market town of Kandern. From there it turns west to re-join the main route in Steinenstadt.

From Steinenstadt the trail continues first along the Rhine, then through the fields to Neuenburg before heading through wine villages and vineyards of Margrave's Land to Freiburg. The section from Freiburg to Kirchzarten follows the River Dreisam. The last part back to Hinterzarten is by train.

To make the most of your tour add some extra days, for instance in Lenzkirch or Bonndorf to explore Wutach Gorge (see Schluchtensteig Stages 2 and 3), or in Rheinfelden to visit Augusta Raurica and Basle's numerous interesting sights. There are also several spa towns along the way where you can soothe your tired muscles and enjoy a relaxing break. During the main tourist season it is advisable to book accommodation in advance.

The trail is well marked and easy to follow. It utilises existing bike routes through quiet back streets or farm roads as well as dedicated cycle lanes that run alongside bigger roads. There are, however, some sections through traffic without a separate cycle lane, so caution is advised.

It is also possible to do individual sections as day trips. With the exception of the part between Neustadt and Waldshut-Tiengen, the route is accompanied by railway lines, making it easy to return to your starting point.

STAGE 1
Hinterzarten to Bonndorf

Start	Hinterzarten station
Finish	Junction of Philosophenweg and Lindenstraße, Bonndorf
Distance	38.5km
Difficulty	Easy
Time	4hr
Height gain/loss	330m/340m
Maps	LGL Freizeitkarte Blatt F509 Waldshut-Tiengen 1:50,000; LGL Landkreiskarte LBH Breisgau–Hochschwarzwald 1:50,000
Refreshments	Many possibilities along the way in Hinterzarten, Titisee, Neustadt, Lenzkirch and Holzschlag
Public transport	Train to Bahnhof, Hinterzarten. For day trips return to Hinterzarten via the same route, or take the train back from Bahnhof/Neustadt – return from Bonndorf with bike is not possible by public transport.
Access	Via B31 (between Freiburg and Donaueschingen)
Parking	Hinterzarten station
Webcam	https://bonndorf.fotonetz.com
Note	This stage is best suited for those who want to do a multiday bike tour and spend the night along the way. To do it as a day trip with public transport, start in Neustadt and continue to Waldshut-Tiengen (end of Stage 2). Not recommended between October and May when there may be snow and ice in the Hochschwarzwald.

This is a pleasant and easy ride through the high mountains of the Black Forest and along the edge of Haslach Gorge (part of the Wutachschlucht gorge system, see Schluchtensteig). Except for a couple of short steep bits the route is easy and almost level, because it utilises a disued railway track, known locally as Bähnleradweg, almost all the way from Neustadt to Bonndorf.

Hinterzarten–Titisee (4.5km)
With the station behind you turn left and follow the cycle route to Titisee-Neustadt, past the car park and up Winterhaldenweg. Pass the houses and continue through

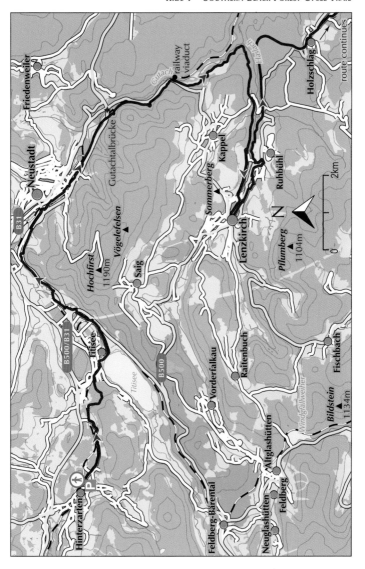

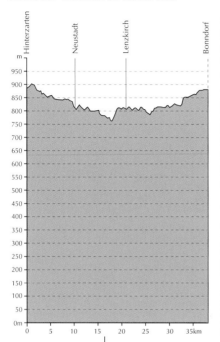

the fields. Turn right on a dirt track just before the railway crossing. After about 400m, take the right fork into the woods. At a clearing (*Beim Eisweiher*) turn left, past a pond, to the outskirts of Titisee. Follow Alte Poststraße down into the village and turn left on Strandbadstraße. Turn right on Seestraße and push your bike through the pedestrian zone to the lakefront.

Titisee–Neustadt (6km)

At the other end of the promenade (by the cuckoo clock shop) turn left on Seebachstraße. After passing beneath a railway bridge continue on Seebachstraße to the left, across a little bridge. Bear right (do not go under the railway tracks again) past some farms. Pass underneath the main road and after 350m cross the road again via a small bridge. Continue to the right on Scheuerebene, between the railway tracks and the road. At the junction turn right (Im Bildstöckle) and immediately right again onto a dirt track. Pass through a subway then continue to the left, parallel to the big road. At *Unterführung B31* turn left and pass underneath the B31 again. Continue to the right, parallel to the road, bypassing the roundabout and crossing the railway tracks to reach a T-junction at Gutachtalstraße.

Neustadt–Lenzkirch (12.5km)

Turn right on Gutachtalstraße and pass through town. Fork right on Schützenstraße towards Lenzkirch and Bähnleradweg. Pass underneath the railway bridge and

The Titisee

continue to the left, quite steeply uphill. At the corner of Auf der Riese and Kapfweg follow Kapfweg between the train tracks and the road. After the last houses the trail turns into a dirt track. Climbing steadily next to the train tracks the trail passes underneath a huge bridge (Gutachtalbrücke). Immediately afterwards take the left fork downhill.

Cross the road and continue on the other side on a paved track (Bähnleradweg). Ignore all trails forking off to the right or left. At a compound called Rekultivierungsareal continue straight on, past the barrier and follow the dirt track into the forest. There are no cycle trail markings, but the route follows the broad forest road, which is also shared with several hiking routes. By the old station house of Kappel-Grünwald pass through the barrier and continue straight on. After about 1.5km the trail emerges from the forest in the fields above Lenzkirch. Follow the little right-left wriggle and head straight down into the village. Take the left fork on Ludwig-Kegel Straße to the corner of Schwarzwaldstraße and turn left towards the town hall (Rathaus) and the church.

Lenzkirch–Holzschlag (7.5km)

By the town hall turn left past the church and the Kurhaus on Am Kurpark towards Bonndorf/Holzschlag. At the T-junction cross the road to the left, then immediately fork off to the right on Trenschelweg. At the fork follow Trenschelweg to the right (uphill) through a residential area, then turn left on Jägerweg. At the next corner follow the field track Am Trenschelbuck to the right. At the fork continue straight on the gravel path (Hasenhofweg). At the junction turn left towards the main road. Continue along the road to the right, cross the wooden bridge. Follow the sidewalk to the next corner at Bräuerei Ausschank Rogg. Cross the road and turn left on Lochmühleweg, steeply downhill. In the bend take a sharp right, uphill. Continue on Bähnleradweg on a fairly level and straight path through the forest, crossing a metal bridge on the way. After about 3.5km, cross the road via the little wooden

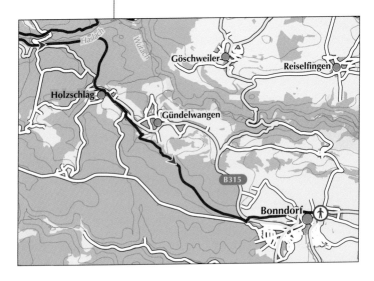

bridge. Bear left towards Gasthaus Krone in the village of Holzschlag.

Trail by Holzschlag

Holzschlag–Bonndorf (8km)

Turn right by the car park of Gasthaus Krone. Follow the bike path through the fields on a paved farm track towards Bonndorf/Gündelwangen (Südschwarzwald Radweg not marked). At the T-junction turn left, then right. Shortly afterwards, at an odd junction, take the second turn to the right, passing the old station house of Gundelwangen. At the fork take the left trail and 20m further on turn right on a gravel path (Mittlemattweg) through the forest. At the T-junction turn right uphill on a paved lane and pass underneath the little bridge and follow the bicycle trail straight on through the forest. At a junction by another railway house cross the dirt road and continue straight on to a big car park by a main road. Cross the road and immediately turn left on a narrow paved path next to the road to the big junction and cross via the subway. On the other side, at *Schleierweg* turn right. Go around the cemetery to the left, and follow the bend to the right. Cross Bergstraße and continue straight on Philosophenweg to the end, where it meets Lindenstraße. ▶

Bonndorf has seen better days, but it is conveniently located for access to Wutachschlucht (Walk 6, Stage 2).

STAGE 2
Bonndorf to Waldshut

Start	Junction of Philosophenweg and Lindenstraße, Bonndorf
Finish	Zollweg, Waldshut
Distance	51.6km
Difficulty	Easy
Time	4hr
Height gain/loss	95m/651m
Maps	LGL Freizeitkarte Blatt F509 Waldshut-Tiengen 1:50,000; LGL Landkreiskarte LWT Landkreis Waldshut 1:50,000 (2012)
Refreshments	Numerous possibilities in the villages along the way
Public transport	Public transport to Bonndorf is not possible with bike. Closest public transport access for bikes is train to Neustadt. Return by train from Lauchringen or Waldshut
Access	Take B500 to Schluchsee, or B314 to Stühlingen, then B315 to Bonndorf
Parking	By the disused railway station, Bahnhofstraße in Bonndorf, but this option is not recommended as there is no way to get your bikes back to Bonndorf by public transport.
Webcam	www.waldshut-tiengen.de/freizeit/erleben/webcam
Note	Best done as an overnight trip in conjunction with Stage 1.

An easy and pleasant ride, first across the eastern plateau, then coasting down towards the Rhine, then following the River Wutach through a series of little villages to Waldshut with its picturesque old town centre.

Bonndorf–Stühlingen (21km)
Follow Lindenstraße to the left and turn right at the T-junction. Turn right on Donaueschinger Straße to the next junction and cross the road to turn left on Am Lindenbuck. Continue straight down the tree-lined lane through the fields towards Lausheim. At a small crossing turn left towards Dillendorf, then immediately left again towards Birkle (at *Hunnenfeld*). At *Birkle* continue straight, past *Dillendorfer Buck* towards Langer Haag. Turn left at *Langer*

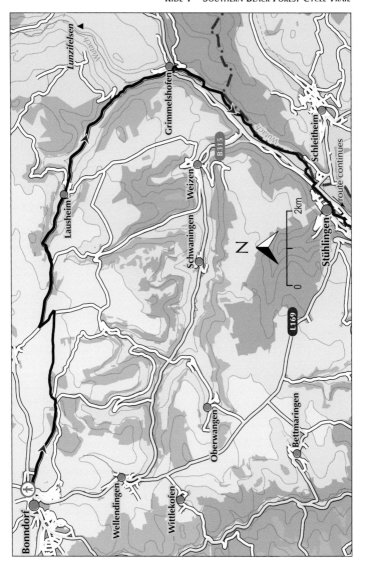

123

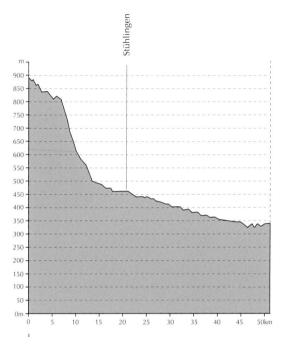

Haag and left again. At the T-junction join the country road to the right and freewheel all the way down the hill for approximately 7km past Lausheim to Grimmelshofen. (Take care – there is no cycle lane.) In Grimmelshofen, at a busy crossroads (B314), turn left across the bridge, cross the road and follow Schleitheimerstraße to the right. At the first corner turn right on Brühlstraße. At a fork take the right-hand trail and cross the river. Follow the river trail along the Wutach towards Stühlingen. After about 5km pass the playing fields and bear right, towards the road. Cross the main road via the subway and follow Bahnhofstraße to Hauptstraße.

Stühlingen–Wutöschingen (12.5km)
Turn right on Hauptstraße. By the catholic church cross the junction to the left and follow Hallauerstraße past a

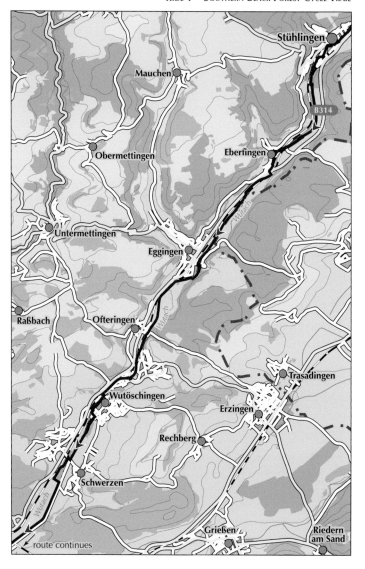

route continues

125

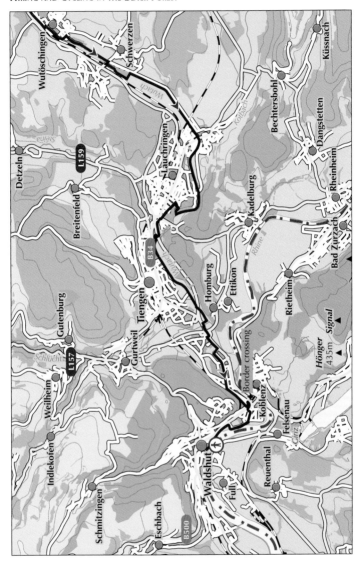

school, then uphill through a residential area. At a fork follow the right-hand trail (in effect straight ahead) on Zinngärten, downhill. Cross the railway tracks. The trail now runs between the tracks and the river. Just before Eberfingen cross the tracks again. Follow Eisenbahnstraße into the village. Turn left across the bridge and continue on Waldshuter Straße to the left. Just after the bend turn left on Köhlerstraße. After 200m turn left across the tracks. Follow the path as it jinks left then right, passing underneath a couple of bridges, then continue straight, between the river and the road. After about 3km turn left across the bridge and immediately right on Forellenweg. ▶ Follow the river for about 3km to Ofterdingen. Pass underneath a bridge and continue straight to cross the road via a subway. Continue along the river to Wutöschingen.

Bonndorf

Note There are no route markings – if you miss this turn you'll end up in Switzerland!

Wutöschingen–Lauchringen (8.5km)
By a bridge at the entrance of Wutöschingen turn left on Hauptstraße and follow it through town (or turn right on Wutachstraße and at the end, by the T-junction re-join Hauptstraße again to the right, to bypass the town centre), and continue along the river. In Horheim, cross the bridge and pass through a subway. Pass the industrial

Wooden covered bridge across the River Wutach

estate and continue along the water. On the outskirts of Lauchringen pass below a railway bridge and continue on the embankment along the river. After crossing a little wooden bridge pass underneath a road and continue along the river to *Riedwiesen*. Turn right towards Unter Lauchringen and circle around the field to the right. Turn left on Wiesenweg and left again on Hauptstraße. Continue straight down to a big junction.

Lauchringen–Waldshut (9.6km)

Take the subway (Radwegunterführung nach Tiengen) to cross the junction and continue straight down, parallel to the road. Just before the bridge fork to the left onto a small path past some allotments. Pass below a big bridge, then cross a wooden bridge. Continue to the left, along the water for about 2.5km. After passing some sports facilities and Tiengen stadium cross another small bridge then pass under a big bridge. Go around the water treatment facility to the right. At the T-junction turn left across the little bridge and continue next to the main road. Pass under a big bridge, then cross the road (B34) via a subway, which emerges at bus stop 'Ettikon Abzw'. The bicycle trail continues next to the busy B34 for about 400m, then turns off to the right, on a quieter route through the industrial estate. Follow Marie-Curie-Straße to Lise-Meitner Ring and turn left through the green. Cross the roundabout and continue straight on. At the end follow the bike path to the left. Cross Kupferschmidstraße, and at the end take a sharp left on Aarbergweg down to the junction and follow the bike path to the right, parallel zur B34.

The border crossing to Switzerland is to the left. Cross the big junction at the traffic lights and continue on Züricher Straße. Take the first left on Klingnauer Straße and turn right on Koblenzer Straße at the next corner. ▶ At the end cross Aarauer Straße and continue on Jahnweg to the Rhine. Pass the outdoor swimming pool and minigolf course to the right. Where Jahnweg forks off to the right continue straight on Rheinweg along the river. By the footbridge across the Rhine a trail forks off to the right (Zollstraße) leading to the centre of Waldshut. To reach the train station, follow Zollstraße to the bridge and turn right on Bismarckstraße, or, to visit the historic town centre, turn left through the city gate. ▶

Note There is no obvious marker here.

The picturesque town centre with its historic city gates, painted facades and outdoor cafés is well-worth a visit.

STAGE 3

Waldshut to Rheinfelden

Start	Zollstraße, Waldshut
Finish	Rheinfelden (hiking signpost Rheinfelden/Adelberg)
Distance	45.5km
Difficulty	Easy
Time	4hr
Height gain/loss	180m/220m
Maps	LGL Freizeitkarte Blatt F509 Waldshut-Tiengen and Blatt F508 Lörrach 1:50,000; LGL Landkreiskarte LWT Landkreis Waldshut 1:50,000 (2012)
Refreshments	Many options in the towns and villages along the way. Laufenburg and Bad Säckingen are particularly good
Public transport	Return by train from Bahnhof, Rheinfelden (Baden).
Access	Both Waldshut-Tiengen and Rheinfelden are situated on the B34 along the Rhine
Parking	At the station
Webcam	www.waldshut-tiengen.de/freizeit/erleben/webcam www.badsaeckingen.de/de/informationen-service/webcam

This is the easiest section of the whole route, following the Rhine all the way. It is also very scenic, as it passes through some very picturesque old towns that offer the opportunity to cross the border into Switzerland via footbridges.

Waldshut-Tiengen–Albbruck (8km)

If starting from the station, cross the busy road and follow Bismarckstraße towards the old town. Just before crossing the bridge turn off on the cycle path (Zollstraße) to the left, to reach the Rhine.

Continue along the Rhine towards Dogern and Albbruck. After passing Waldshut the bike lane runs on the left-hand side, next to the road. By the power plant turn left on Auweg. After crossing a small bridge take the left fork on Rheinstraße.

Pass a sign saying 'Dogern' and keep to the left, along the water. Pass the power plant (on the Swiss side of the Rhine). At a T-junction take a sharp left towards Bad Säckingen and cross the dam. Do not follow the bend to the left, but bear right, around the reservoir and then straight down the 'island'. By a car park where a foot-bridge crosses over into Switzerland take a sharp right and cross the big bridge towards Albbruck. Bear right and cross the road (B34) via the subway. At the first junction

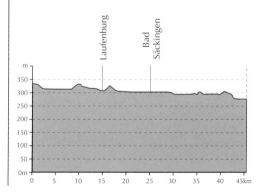

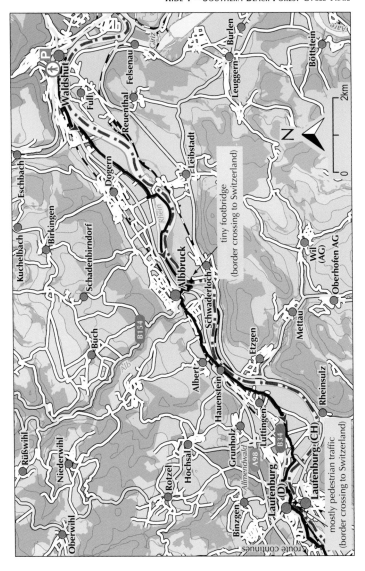

tiny footbridge
(border crossing to Switzerland)

mostly pedestrian traffic
(border crossing to Switzerland)

route continues

2km

cross the big road and continue on Alte Landstraße towards Laufenburg.

View of Laufenburg from the Swiss side

Albbruck–Laufenburg (7km)

Continue straight across the crossroads on Hauensteiner Straße through a residential area and downhill to the B34. Cross the B34 at the traffic lights and follow the cycle lane on the left through Hauenstein. Hauensteiner Straße turns into Luttinger Straße. By the church in Luttingen follow Stadenhauser Straße to the left. By the cemetery fork right on Dr. Rudolph Eberle Straße. Approaching Laufenburg, do not cross the little bridge, but continue straight, along the stream, crossing Stadtweg on Rheinuferweg. After passing below a bridge the path makes a left/right jink and crosses a footbridge. Continue straight along the Rhine to the beautiful town of Laufenburg. Pass the outdoor pool and playground, bearing right. Turn left on Andelsbachstraße and left on Waldshuter Straße. Bearing

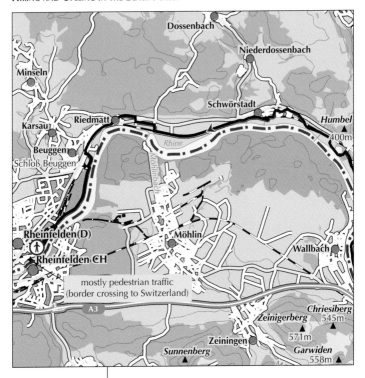

The prettiest part of the old town is on the Swiss side.

left, pass through the archway and follow Hauptstraße down to the bridge. ◀

Laufenburg–Bad Säckingen (10km)

Continue straight ahead, up towards the station and follow the footpath/bike lane to a T-junction. Turn left on Zimmermannstraße and at the end turn left on Säckingerstraße. Just after the factory buildings turn left on Kraftwerkweg. Cross the tracks and follow the bike path to the right along the Rhine. Pass the outdoor pool in Murg and follow the trail around to the left to continue on Rheinuferweg. After passing a water treatment facility continue along the Rhine next to the railway tracks towards Bad Säckingen. After passing the weir follow Rheinallee to Gallusturm, a prominent tower at the entrance of Bad Säckingen. After passing Gallusturm fork off on Fischergasse and walk your bike through the pedestrianised town centre. Turn left on Steinbrückstraße to reach the market square and the Münster (cathedral).

Bad Säckingen–Rheinfelden (20.5km)

Cross the market square (Münsterplatz) diagonally and follow the small street to the right. Turn left on Rheinbrückstraße and immediately right on Wernergasse. ▶

The historic covered wooden bridge, which dates back to at least AD1272, is the longest of its kind in Europe and is still used as a footbridge to Switzerland.

Turn left on Austraße past the park and just after the cemetery follow the cycle path to the left, then continue along the Rhine towards Wehr/Rheinfelden. In Wallbach the trail joins Hauptstraße to the left. At bus stop Wallbach/Bündtenstraße turn left on Bündtenstraße and follow it to the end. Continue to the left on Rötelbachstraße. In the bend turn left past the water treatment facility and cross the little bridge over the River Wehra. Pass a small lagoon and continue along the railway tracks. At a fork go right to pass underneath the tracks. Turn left on the footpath/bike lane next to the main road for approximately 350m before turning left on Baummattstraße. Follow Baummattstraße around to the right. At the crossroads turn left on Rheinstraße. Cross the tracks and continue next to them to the right on Rheinbadstraße. By the hydroelectric power station turn right, pass beneath the railway tracks on Kraftwerkstraße and continue to the left on the access road to the busy main road (B34). Cross and continue straight ahead, then turn left on Brombachstraße through the village.

At the end turn right (*Riedmatt*) towards the road. Follow the bike/pedestrian path next to the B34 for about 1km. Cross the B34 at the traffic lights by the tiny station of Beuggen. Cross the tracks via the subway and follow the path as it jinks left then right and head towards the estate of Schloss Beuggen.

Schloss Beuggen was originally built in AD1268 as the Swabian-Alsace-Burgundy headquarters of the

View from Höllhaken towards the Swiss part of Rheinfelden

Teutonic Knights who occupied the complex for 560 years until the order was dissolved in 1806. Today Schloss Beuggen has been turned into a hotel and seminar centre, see **www.schloss-beuggen.de**.

Cross the yard and continue to the right along the Rhine. Pass the hydropower plant. At the bend continue straight ahead on a track through a wooded area. The trail emerges up on an embankment by some vineyards at hiking signpost *Höllhaken*. Continue straight on along Adelbergstraße to the T-junction where the route splits.

To find the station, turn right and take the footpath up towards the tracks via the ramp. The station is to the left.

STAGE 4A
Rheinfelden to Steinenstadt via Basle and France

Start	Rheinfelden (hiking signpost Rheinfelden/Adelberg)
Finish	Steinenstadt
Distance	54.5km
Difficulty	Easy
Time	4hr30min
Height gain/loss	161m/204m
Maps	LGL Landkreiskarte LLÖ Landkreis Lörrach 1:50,000 (2011)
Refreshments	Many options along the way until Weil-am-Rhein. Nothing between Weil-am-Rhein and Bad Bellingen
Public transport	Train to Bahnhof, Rheinfelden (Baden). Return by train from Bahnhof, Schliengen
Access	Via B34 (runs along the Rhine between Basle and Waldshut-Tiengen)
Parking	At Rheinfelden station
Webcam	www.webcam-basel.ch
Note	Try to avoid Basle during rush hour. You could take a ferry from Rheinfelden to Basle, or bypass this section by taking the train to Weil-am-Rhein.

Although this section of the trail passes through urban and industrial areas, for the most part it is a pleasant and interesting ride, leading past the archaeological site of the ancient Roman city of Augusta Raurica to the old city of Basle. It sneaks into France on quiet back roads before crossing the Rhine back into Germany at Weil-am-Rhein. The part between Basle and the hydropower dam just outside Weil-am-Rhein runs alongside a busy road, but once you are back along the river the ride is easy and relaxing. Unfortunately, the sections through Switzerland and France are not well marked.

Rheinfelden–Kaiseraugst (Augusta Raurica) (8km)
If starting from Rheinfelden station follow the tracks to the left over the road, then take the ramp down to street level. Turn left towards Rheinbrücke to cross into Switzerland.

From hiking signpost *Rheinfelden/Adelberg* turn left on Rheinbrückenstraße and cross the bridge to

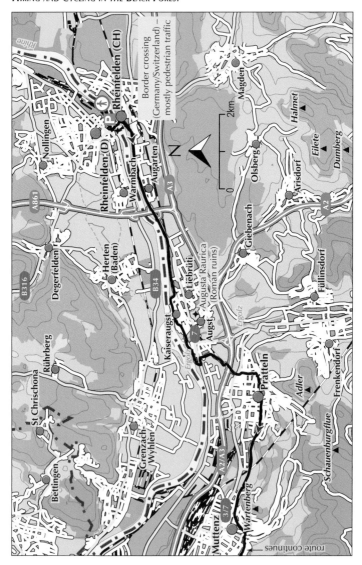

Border crossing
Germany/Switzerland –
mostly pedestrian traffic

route continues

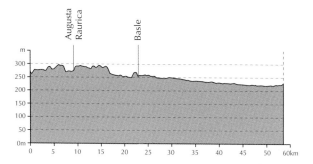

Switzerland. ▸ Turn right towards Kaiseraugst, Pratteln and Basle. At the bend bear right and follow the bike lane, which runs parallel to a big road. Just before the bridge across the train tracks, take the lane to the right that runs parallel to the tracks. The route runs jointly with the EV6/EV15 (European VeloRoute) and forks left on Rohrweg, still running along the tracks. After passing a retirement home turn right on Almendsgasse and follow the bend to the left, which becomes Dorfstrasse.

The old town of Rheinfelden lies to the left.

> There are remains of Roman sites all along the Rhine. **Augusta Raurica** once was the largest Roman settlement north of the Alps, with 18,000 inhabitants. The museum houses an extensive display of artifacts found at the site and provides a fascinating insight into the daily life in this far northern outpost of the Roman Empire. The archeological site can be visited free of charge, entrance to the museum is 8CHF. Various events, including workshops, talks, performances and a Roman Festival, are staged throughout the year, see **www.augustaraurica.ch**.

Kaiseraugst–Salina Raurica–Pratteln (4km)

Continue on Dorfstrasse past the school and around the bend to the left. (On the left-hand side of the road you will see the remains of the old Roman fortifications). Turn right on Friedhofstrasse, follow it around the playing fields and cross the bridge.

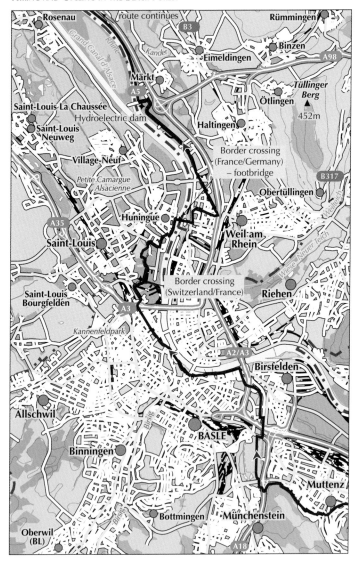

Museum at Augusta Raurica

The road, now called Kraftwerkstrasse, runs along the Rhine, passes the lock and then bends to the left to meet Hauptstrasse 7, a busy road. Turn left on Hauptstrasse for approx. 100m, then take a right on Whylenstrasse and follow it to the end.

Pass the train station of Salina Raurica, then take the left fork along the train tracks. At the end pass underneath the tracks and then cross the motorway via a bridge. Pass the outdoor swimming pool and pass underneath another big road. Follow Griebenacherstrasse until you reach a T-junction at Obermattstrasse. Follow Obermattstrasse to the right, pass underneath a railway bridge and around the corner to the right at the T-junction. Continue straight on this road, which briefly becomes Hauptstrasse and then Muttenzerstrasse.

Pratteln–Muttenz (4km)
Turn left along the tram tracks by tram stop 'Lachmatt', where the cycle path runs half underneath a fly-over and then carries on straight, along the tracks. At the end it joins a residential street (Breitestrasse) and follows it to the end. Bear right on Burggasse and pass the church to the left. Turn left on Geispelgasse, and immediately right on Pfaffenmattweg.

Muttenz–Basle (7.5km)

Follow Pfaffenmattweg, first through a residential area then along the edge of the forest. At the end follow the path around to the right and turn left just before the football pitch. After passing some allotments the trail runs through a bit of forest. Cross the motorway via a bridge, continue to the right and cross the river Birs via a covered wooden bridge. Turn right. After passing below a bridge continue on a paved lane (Grosse Allee) through the playing fields and sports area. Eventually the trail ends by a big road and meets up with the tramline again. Cross the road, turn right and continue on Birsstrasse, next to the river. The road passes underneath a huge train and motorway bridge. Continue straight until the road meets the train trusses and bends to the right. The Velo path runs on the road, in the bus lane. Follow the road down to the Rhine, then turn left along the river on St Alban-Rheinweg.

Basle–Weil-am-Rhein (6km)

Just before the next bridge across the Rhine turn left on Mühlenberg and join St Alban-Vorstadt to the right. Cross the big junction and continue straight on Rittergasse to the cathedral. Cross the square and bearing right, continue on Augustinergasse, which turns into Rheinsprung and ends by a bridge (Mittlere Brücke). Cross the junction and pass the ferry landing at *Schifflände*. Continue straight ahead on Blumenrain. Take the left fork on Spitalstrasse past the hospital. At the junction cross St Johanns-Ring and follow the long street of Lothringerstrasse to the very end by a large roundabout. Take the second exit to the right on Hüningerstrasse towards Huningue, and at the next big junction turn left on Elsässerstrasse. At the end of the tram tracks bear right and turn right on Kohlenstrasse. Take the first turn to the left, across the roundabout, and cross the border into France.

After the border control post use the bike lane on the left. At the junction turn left and circle around the car park. At the junction cross Rue de la Chapelle to the left. At the roundabout take the first exit to the right towards Huningue (D107). Continue straight across the big

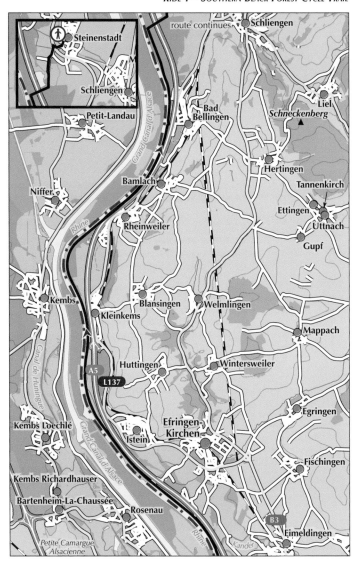

junction (Avenue de Bâle) and continue on Rue des Trois Frontières to the shore of the Rhine. Turn left along the river on Quai du Rhîn. At the bend continue through the little picnic/park area. Cross a small bridge and bear right to continue along the river on Quai de la République to the Passerelle des Trois Pays, a footbridge across the Rhine. Push your bike across the bridge to get back into Germany at Weil-am-Rhein.

Weil-am-Rhein–Steinenstadt (25km)
At the first big junction turn left onto Colmarer Straße. Just after crossing a junction at a bend turn right on Tullastraße. At the end turn left at the T-junction (Riedlinstraße) and then join Alte Straße to the left, in the bend. After about 3km, after passing a water treatment facility, cross the road and continue on the left-hand side of the road. By a factory (Wempfler) turn left towards the hydroelectric dam (*Stauwehr*). Follow the Rhine trail to signpost Schulmeisterkopf, near Steinenstadt.

> At the time of writing a major renaturation project is underway along the Rhine. The aim is to create several artificial **alluvial basins** as water catchment areas in case of flooding. The design is as ecological as possible and integrates cycle tracks and footpaths into the landscaping. At low water levels it may be possible to use the trails next to the river, but in case of high water the fords will be flooded and it is better to take the little detours around the edges of the basins. Although these alternative trails may not be explicitly marked, it is easy to find your way.

At *Schulmeisterkopf* turn right, pass through the subway under the motorway and continue past a private, members only campsite. The track meets a road at a bend and turns right. Shortly after crossing a small stream, cross the big road by hiking signpost *Hohlenbach* (this is where the two routes join again).

Continue on that little lane following the stream to Steinenstadt (if you want to pause there for the night).

STAGE 4B

Rheinfelden to Steinenstadt via Kandern

Start	Rheinfelden (hiking signpost Rheinfelden/Adelberg)
Finish	Steinenstadt
Distance	44.5km
Difficulty	Hard
Time	5hr
Height gain/loss	444m/486m
Maps	LGL Freizeitkarte Blatt F508 Lörrach 1:50,000; LGL Landkreiskarte LLÖ Landkreis Lörrach 1:50,000 (2011)
Refreshments	Gasthaus Waldhorn in Brombach; Bruckmühle; Landgasthof Krone in Kandern
Public transport	Train to Bahnhof, Rheinfelden (Baden). Return by train from Bahnhof, Schliengen
Access	Via B34
Parking	Rheinfelden station
Note	Stamina needed. The 'cycling without luggage' package continues to Müllheim, but you can request accommodation in Steinenstadt.

The rolling hills of Markgräflerland are pretty, but take some legwork. Mercifully, this route is not all uphill, and at the end of the day you can relax at the thermal spa in Badenweiler or Bad Bellingen.

Rheinfelden– Niedereichsel (7.5km)

If starting from the station follow the tracks to the left over the road, then take the ramp down to street level. Turn left towards Rheinbrücke, to find hiking signpost *Rheinfelden/Adelberg*.

At signpost *Rheinfelden/Adelberg* turn right and pass underneath the railway bridge. Continue straight on, on Nollinger Straße to Oberrheinplatz. Turn left on Werderstraße and keep going straight, past the outdoor swimming pool, until the road (now Eichbergstraße) crosses the motorway via a bridge. Immediately

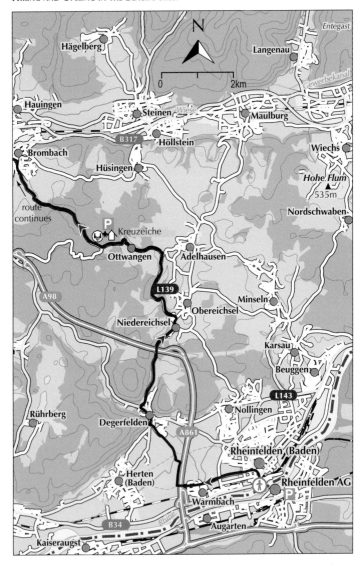

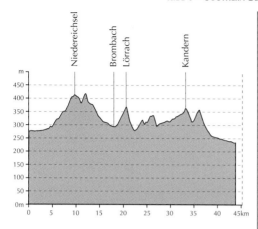

afterwards turn right and follow the bike route next to the motorway (0.5km) before it bends to the left and runs through a plant nursery. At the T-junction the bike route makes a quick right-left wriggle and continues straight on through the fields to Degerfelden. Continue straight on to the T-junction and turn right. Follow Grenzacher Straße through the village, across the little stream and cross the bigger road (Lörracher Straße E54). Just a few metres along on Eichselner Straße the bicycle route branches off to the left but keeps running parallel, (don't head into the woods) above the busy road for about 2.5km, passing below a huge motorway bridge before it reaches Niedereichsel.

Niedereichsel–Brombach (8km)

In Niedereichsel the bike route bends to the left and enters the village on Silbergrabenweg. At the T-junction turn left on Angerstraße and follow it up through the village. By a fork near the end of the village keep to the left. Now a country lane, the route meanders through the woods and fields. By the bench keep to the right and head for the road below. Turn left on this country road to Ottwangen (no bike lane). Pass through the village and climb up the hill. At the trailhead car park at Kreuzeiche

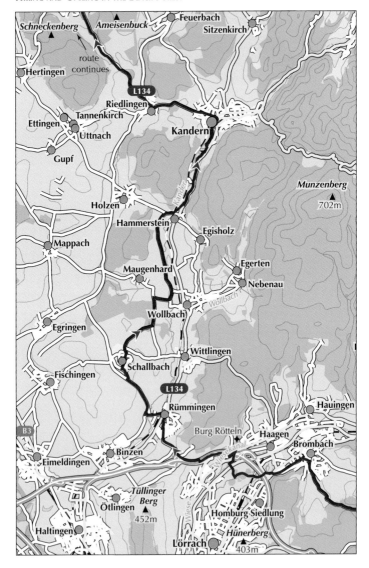

(a 400-year-old oak tree) follow the paved bike lane to the right, downhill through the forest to Brombach. At the T-junction follow Adelhauserstraße to the right, into the town.

Brombach–Lörrach (Rötteln) (4km)

At Gasthaus Waldhorn turn left on Römerstraße. Take the second street to the left (Wilh. Wagner Straße). At the end follow the street right then left and continue on Hellbergstraße through a residential area (traffic from the right has priority). Cross the big road and continue down the dead-end street (Wilhelm Schöpflin Straße) towards Kandern and Rümmingen. After a few metres follow a footpath/cycle path to the right, down into the park. At the bottom turn left. Pass underneath a series of bridges (a motorway access road, a motorway and finally a railway bridge) and continue straight ahead to the football pitches. Turn right just in front of the football pitches and cross a road (B317) and a river (Wiese) via a wooden bridge. Turn right. At the first opportunity (after about 150m) turn left towards Kandern. Pass below a couple

Höllhaken, above Rheinfelden

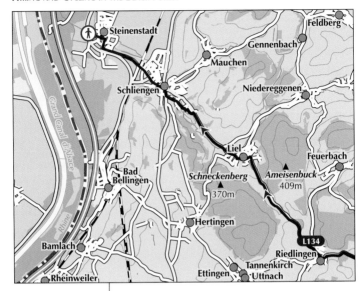

of bridges (a sliproad bridge and a motorway bridge) and cross a small wooden bridge. Continue up to the road. Cross and turn left, passing under the big motorway bridge once more. Immediately afterwards turn right, up the hill on Röttelnweiler, towards Burg Rötteln. At the top, just before another bridge across the motorway (A98), turn left on a small lane that runs parallel to it.

> Straight ahead across the motorway lies **Burg Rötteln**, the third largest castle ruin complex in Baden, which dates back to the 11th century. The castle was largely destroyed in an earthquake that struck Basle in 1356. The ruins are impressive and on a clear day there are great views of Basle and the Bernese Oberland to be had from the top.

Rötteln–Kandern (13.5km)

At the far end turn right through the subway underneath the A98. Turn left, uphill, then down past a car park.

At the end continue to the right towards Rümmingen. The bike lane ends. Continue on the road into the centre of the little town. By Landgasthof Sonne turn left on Binzener Straße and immediately right on Schallbacher Straße. Cross the tracks. At the bend continue straight ahead on Mühlenstraße. Opposite the garden centre follow Alte Kanderner Straße to the right. Cross the road and head down into Schallbach.

Turn right on Rümminger Straße through the village. By the water fountain (*Schallbach/Am Rain*) turn right, on Am Rain, past the fields and into the woods. At the T-junction in the forest (*Schallbach Hölzli*) turn left, along the edge of the forest. At a junction by a farm turn right towards Kandern and Wollbach. At the T-junction turn left. Pass Landgasthof Bruckmühle and a couple of kilometres further on, pass Landgasthof Krone. At the T-junction turn right towards Hammerstein. Before crossing the train tracks turn left along the stream. After crossing the stream and tracks the bike lane briefly runs next to the road, then bears left again. Pass the playing fields and bear left to follow Papierweg into Kandern.

Kandern–Schliengen–Steinenstadt (11.5km)

At the T-junction turn left on Hammersteiner Straße. Cross the bridge and follow the main road (Bahnhofstraße) uphill towards Riedlingen and Liel (no bike lane). At bus stop 'Erlenboden' cross the road and continue on the bike lane on the left-hand side of the road. ▶ Pass through Riedlingen and Liel and continue to Schliengen.

From here to Schliengen the bike lane runs parallel to the road on the left except through the villages.

On the outkirts of Schliengen turn left on Mühleweg. Cross a little wooden bridge to the left and follow Untere Biefang Straße to the village centre. Turn right along the main road to Gasthaus Sonne. Cross the road and follow Eisenbahnstraße towards the station. In the bend turn off on the smaller road to the right and at the fork keep to the left – all still Eisenbahnstraße. Cross the train tracks via the subway under the station, and continue straight on to Steinenstadt. Turn right on Hauptstraße.

STAGE 5
Steinenstadt to Hinterzarten

Start	Steinenstadt
Finish	Kirchzarten station
Distance	57.7km
Difficulty	Medium
Time	5hr
Height gain/loss	315m/153m
Maps	LGL Freizeitkarte Blatt F508 Lörrach and F505 Freiburg, 1:50,000; LGL Landkreiskarte LLÖ Landkreis Lörrach 1:50,000 (2011)
Refreshments	Numerous possibilities along the way. Look out for Straussenwirtschaften to sample local specialities.
Public transport	Train to Bahnhof, Schliengen. Return by train from Bahnhof/ Kirchzarten
Access	A5/B3 to Schliengen/Steinenstadt
Parking	Schliengen station
Note	You will need to do the final part of this stage from Kirchzarten to Hinterzarten by train. Although there is a marked route through the mountains, it is only recommended for mountain bikes or e-bikes, as it involves an altitude difference of about 900m.

This stage is a very pleasant ride through the vineyards and wine villages of Margrave's Land to Freiburg and along the River Dreisam to Kirchzarten.

Steinenstadt–Neuenburg (8.7km)
The two routes meet up again just outside Steinenstadt, where Rheintalstraße meets the L134. By Gasthaus zum Salmen in Steinenstadt, follow Rheinthalstraße out of the village, to the hiking signpost *Hohlenbach* by the L134 country road. Stay on the right-hand side of the big road and continue north, towards Neuenburg.

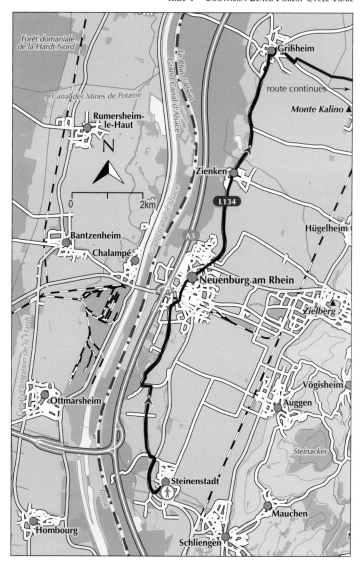

Forêt domaniale
de la Hardt-Nord

Canal des Mines de Potasse

Le Rhin / Rhein
Grand Canal d'Alsace

Grißheim

route continues

Monte Kalino

Rumersheim-
le-Haut

N

Zienken

L134

0   2km

Hügelheim

Bantzenheim

A5

Grand Canal d'Alsace

Chalampé

Neuenburg am Rhein

Zielberg

Vögisheim

La Canal d'Irrigation de la Hardt

Ottmarsheim

Auggen

Steinacker

Rhine

Steinenstadt

Mauchen

Hombourg

Schliengen

153

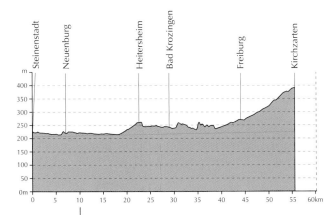

At the next big junction cross the main road again to the left and after about 100m turn right on Steinweg, past fields and farms. At the T-junction turn left and follow the track around to the right past a campsite. Soon after, the bike route passes through an industrial estate of Neuenburg. Cross the junction (Freudenbergstraße) and at the following junction turn right, on Fischerstraße. At the end turn left on Sandroggenstraße, up to Baselerstraße and turn left to the roundabout by Gasthaus Krone.

Alternatively, you can continue along the Rhine to Neuenburg/Hafen and follow the bike route(Mülhauser Straße) to Neuenburg, but there is a lot of traffic at the busy motorway access junction (Am Wurloch) between Neuenburg and the Rhine.

Neuenburg–Heitersheim (13.6km)
From the roundabout follow Breisacher Straße out of town and across the roundabout towards Zienken and Grißheim. In Grißheim turn right on Meierstraße and at the next corner left on Neue Straße, then right again, following Bugginger Straße out of the village. Just after the little cemetery turn left on the access road and right again at the next corner. Continue straight for about 2km then turn left by a small building. Turn right at the next T-junction

on Grißheimer Weg, which passes underneath the railway tracks and straight on through the industrial estate. By the big road (B3) turn left towards the roundabout.

Heitersheim–Bad Krozingen (7.4km)
Cross the roundabout and follow the stream to the right on Im Stühlinger to Heitersheim town centre (Ortsmitte).

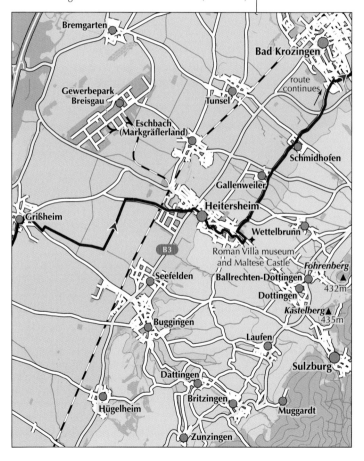

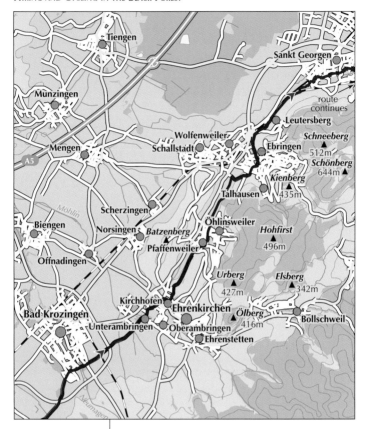

At *Alte Rathaus* cross the little roundabout and continue along the stream on Am Sulzbach. After a couple of kilometres, by Straussenwirschaft Lampp, cross the bridge and continue on the left side of the stream. Turn left towards the road past the playing fields. Cross the main road and follow it to the left, past the Roman Villa museum and the Maltese Castle. Immediately after the Maltese Castle turn right on Staufener Straße. After about 150m, cross the road and turn left through the fields towards Gallenweiler. Oberer Gallenweiler Weg turns into Schmidhofener Straße and after crossing Eschbacher Straße it becomes Felix and Nabor Straße. Cross the country road at Gasthaus Storchen and continue straight on. Cross the bridge over the B3 and follow Schmidhofener Straße to the outskirts of Bad Krozingen.

Bad Krozingen–Freiburg (16.9km)

At the T-junction pass a little chapel to the right, then turn left on Josefstraße. Cross the stream and continue straight to Landgasthaus Adler. Cross the road and continue straight on through the fields towards Ehrenkirchen. Cross the railway tracks and the bridge over the B3. At the T-junction (Krozingerstraße) by a way cross bear right to go through the village following the R6/R7 cycle route markings. Cross the next big junction (Lazarus-Schwendi-Straße), and continue straight on Lairenstraße towards Pfaffenweiler. Turn right on Herrenstraße and follow it

The dreamy wine village of Ebringen

157

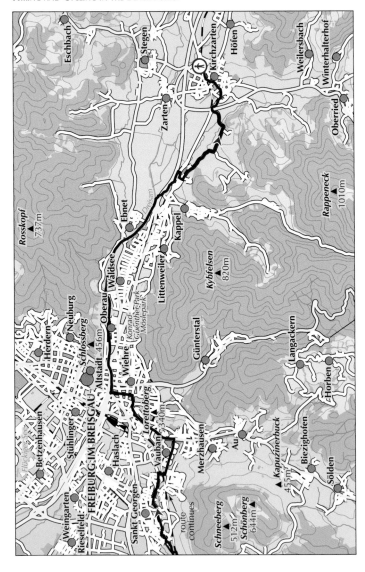

around past the church. Turn left on Batzenbergstraße, then immediately turn off on Bärenstraße to the right, into the vineyards. In Pfaffenweiler pass Columba Church. Cross Weinstraße and continue on Mittlere Straße through the village and into the vineyards.

At a T-junction, where Wiiwegli intersects (signed with a bunch of yellow grapes on red rhombus), turn right, up the hill to *Dürrenberg*; then continue to the left towards Ebringen. Follow Dürrenbergstraße to the centre of the village. Turn left on Talhauserstraße. By the fountain turn left on Schönbergstraße and almost immediately follow Rennweg to the right into the vineyards. Continue along the tracks to the right. Where the lane splits, take the left fork. Immediately the lane splits again; continue straight on (right fork). Cross Schönbergstraße and continue next to the railway line. Follow signs for Markgräfler Radweg and Freiburg-Mulhouse Radweg to the left through a subway underneath the tracks. Before the next set of tracks (railway bridges) continue to the right to the outskirts of Freiburg.

Follow Malteserordenstraße around to the left. Cross the bridge and turn right on Am Dorfbach then left on Obergasse. At the junction turn right on Andreas-Hofer-Straße. By the sports grounds turn right on Innsbrucker Straße and after a railway bridge turn left and continue straight, along the tram tracks through the Vauban district.

Along the Dreisam

By the square (Alfred-Döblin Platz) cross the tram tracks and follow Vaubanallee to the left. By the big road turn left on Merzhauser Straße. At the next big junction follow Lorettostraße to the right. Just after the outdoor swimming pool turn left on Goethestraße. Continue straight across Konradstraße and across Basler Straße to the huge junction by the River Dreisam.

Freiburg–Kirchzarten station (11.1km)

Follow the river trail to the right towards Kirchzarten for about 7km. At the bridge of Fabrikstraße the trail briefly continues on Otto-Wels-Straße, but soon returns to the river. Where the river forks follow the trail to the right, across a little bridge and through a subway. Continue along the railway tracks. By the parking area, bear right across the tracks to the main road, then turn right towards Kappel for about 150m. At the next corner follow Erzweg to the left, to Neuhäuserstraße, and turn left again.

At the end of the village (by a bridge) follow the lane to the right, then turn left on Am Engenberg and follow the left bend, towards the main road. Follow the bicycle trail across the junction towards Kirchzarten, through a subway (here the bike lane ends). Freiburger Straße leads to the centre of Kirchzarten. Turn left on Hauptstraße through the pedestrian precinct. At the far end turn left on Bahnhofstraße to find the train station, from where trains connect with Hinterzarten.

An old-style signpost (Walk 10)

CENTRAL
BLACK FOREST

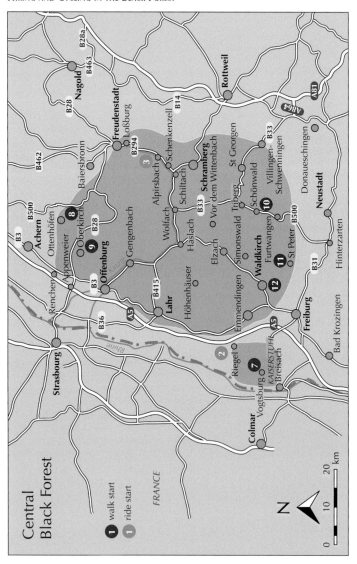

Central
Black Forest

1 walk start
1 ride start

INTRODUCTION

Stretching from Achertal in the north to Elztal in the south the central Black Forest is the true heartland of the region and home to such classic Black Forest icons as the cuckoo clock. Even today Furtwangen, Schonach and Triberg are important centres of cuckoo-clock production. A fascinating clock museum can be seen in Furtwangen (www.deutsches-uhrenmuseum.de).

The central Black Forest's two biggest towns are Offenburg in the west, cultural centre of the Ortenau, and on the eastern edge of the region the twin towns of Villingen-Schwenningen. Villingen is noted for its well-preserved historic town centre. Just 7km to the south lies Bad Dürrheim, home of the only brine spa in the Black Forest. But the cultural centre of this region is Donaueschingen, where the rivers Breg and Briga join to form the Danube. The actual headwaters emerge up in the hills, at the source of the River Breg (Walk 10).

The geography of the central Black Forest is surprisingly diverse: the western edges are draped in vineyards and orchards, while the eastern plateau forms an expanse of rolling hills that makes for easy walking and, thanks to its height, offers fabulous long-distance views.

The main river valleys, with their innumerable side valleys, are open and wide towards the Rhine and increasingly narrow towards their eastern ends. The steep hills give rise to some impressive waterfalls: Triberg Falls at 163m, ranks among the highest in Germany outside the Alps, while Zweribach Falls, near St Peter, are perhaps one of the most romantic of the region.

At the mouth of the idyllic Elz Valley, Kandel (at 1241m the highest mountain of the central Black Forest), towers above Waldkirch. It faces Kaiserstuhl, a miniature mountain range of volcanic origin situated in the Rhine Valley. Although technically not part of the Black Forest it is included here for practical purposes. Kaiserstuhl is almost entirely covered with vineyards and orchards and dotted with lovely little wine villages around the edges of the hills. The most significant town of the region is Breisach, which has been settled since Neolithic times. Due to its strategic position right on the Rhine the town has been overrun and destroyed by wars innumerable times – no doubt the reason why the citizens of this town on 9 July 1950 voted almost unanimously for a unified Europe at the birth hour of the European Union.

Further north lies Kinzig Valley, characterised by a string of picture-perfect timber-frame towns set along the shores of the River Kinzig.

Kaiserstuhl vineyards with view of the Vosges (Walk 7)

Schiltach, Wolfach, Haslach and Gernsbach all derived their wealth from the timber trade boom of the 17th and 18th centuries. Relics of the raftsmen heritage are everywhere to be seen.

Rench Valley is also very pretty but has a more rural character. Its principal town is Oberkirch, with a beautiful old town centre and Schauenburg castle ruins overlooking the town and surrounding vineyards (Walk 9). Neighbouring Acher Valley is equally beautiful. Ottenhöfen at its centre gives access to a number of great walks, including the only real scrambling trail of the Black Forest, known as Karlsruher Grat (Walk 8).

WALK 7
Kaiserstuhl rim route

Start/finish	Oberrotweil station
Distance	21km
Difficulty	Medium
Time	6hr
Height gain/loss	610m
Maps	Schwarzwaldverein Wanderkarte Breisgau Kaiserstuhl 1:35,000; map.solutions Wanderkarte Kaiserstuhl-Tuniberg 1:30,000; Kompass Kaiserstuhl-Tuniberg 1:25,000
Refreshments	Various places in Oberrotweil; Landhotel Rebstock in Bickensohl www.rebstock-bickensohl.com
Public transport	Bus or train to Bahnhof, Oberrotweil
Access	From Breisach on L104 towards Burkheim, turn off on L115 towards Vogtsburg Oberrotweil
Parking	Oberrotweil station
Trail markings	Losshohlwege-Pfad, Neunlindenpfad and Katharinenpfad symbols
Note	This is a long, but mostly easy walk with some short, steep sections. There is not much food or drink to be found along the way, so bring plenty of water and snacks.

Kaiserstuhl appears like the gatekeeper of the Black Forest: a little fortress of mountains that stands guard over the Rhine. A scenic and varied trail through Loess gullies, vineyards, orchards and woods, this walk offers plenty of excellent views towards the Black Forest on one side and the Vosges on the other.

From the station in Oberrotweil turn left towards the main road and follow it to the right through the village, past the church and tourist information to *Sparkasse*. Following the yellow marker turn right on Ellenbuchstraße towards Bickensohl and Lösshohlweg Roggenberg. At *Roggenberg/Ellenbuch* turn left and follow the trail into the vineyards via a *Lösshohlweg*.

Lösshohlwege-Pfad waymark

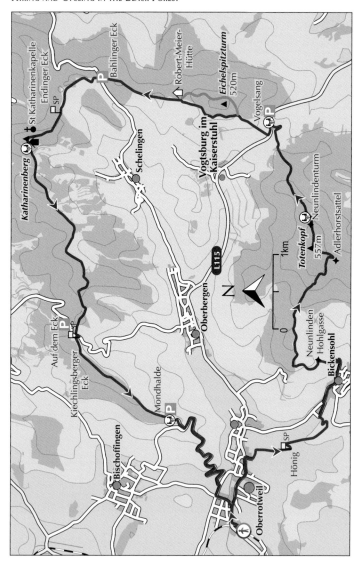

Lösshohlwege, or Loess gullies, are a common landscape feature in the Kaiserstuhl. The thick layer of Loess is the result of thousands of years of wind-blown silt deposits. The silt is very fine, and easy to cut into. It enriches the soil considerably, making the Kaiserstuhl one of the most fertile wine and fruit growing regions in Germany.

In the middle of the gully, at *Hönig*, cross the vineyard to the left, now following Lösshohlwege-Pfad markers (pictured). A small path leads down along the edge of the hill. Turning left, pass the orchards and continue on a residential street (Im Riedgarten) to bus stop 'Riedgarten' and turn right through the village of **Bickensohl**, past *Rebstockgarten* to *Ortsmitte*. Cross Achkarrerstraße and continue straight, on Neunlindenstraße. At the bend, bear left towards **Neunlinden Hohlgasse** (a prominent Loess gully) to reach *Einstieg Eichgasse* at the end of the village.

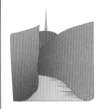

Loess gully

Follow Lösshohlwege-Pfad up through the gullies to a little lane at *Geiser*. Turn left to *Arno's Hütte* and continue on the right fork towards Käfer. In the tight bend continue straight for a few metres on the forest path to *Käfer*, and take the steep trail up the hill to the right, towards Neunlindenturm. At the top (*Strümpfeköpfle*) the trail passes along the edge of the vineyard to *Dachsbuck*. About 50m further along, at another signpost also called Dachsbuck, leave Lösshohlwege-Pfad and follow the yellow marker up through the woods on a small footpath that leads to a road. Bear right on a wider, level forest road to *Adlerhorstsattel*. From here follow Neunlindenpfad up the hill to the left. Pass *Beim Neunlindenturm* and continue to the observation tower (**Neunlindenturm**) and picnic area at the top of **Totenkopf**, which at 557m is the highest peak of Kaiserstuhl.

During the Middle Ages Totenkopf was the site of a **hermitage**, and later a monastery. Climb the tower (Neunlindenturm) for the best 360° views. (Close the hatch at the top when you leave.)

From here the route follows Neunlindenpfad (waymarked with a leaf symbol, pictured) to Katharinenkapelle (about 6.5km further on) around the rim of Kaiserstuhl. At trail junctions follow Neunlindenpfad trail symbols. Between signposts the yellow marker points the way.

Cross the picnic area below Neunlindenturm and continue steeply down the hill towards Vogelsangpass, passing *Herrenweg* and *Gagenhartwald* on the way. At *Schöne Aussicht* take the right fork down to *Vogelsangpass*, cross the road and a picnic area and continue on the other side, up the hill to the left. A gentle climb takes you up onto the ridge to *Blasendobel*.

To climb Eichelspitzturm

If you want to take a side trip up to **Eichelspitzturm**, the second highest point of Kaiserstuhl, follow the path up to the peak and down the other side to **Robert-Meier-Hütte**, then turn left to re-join Neunlindenpfad at *Öhmdsmatten*.

*Kaiserstuhl from
Neunlindenturm –
just above the clouds*

Continue straight past Öhmdsmatten to *Degenmatten*
and cross another road at **Bahlinger Eck** car park. At
Beim Bahlinger Eck Neunlindenpfad goes off to the left
to *Obergrub* and *Endinger Eck*. Querweg Schwarzwald-
Kaiserstuhl-Rhein continues straight to Schönebene. The
two paths meet up again at **Endinger Eck** and jointly
climb up to **St Katharinenkapelle**. ▶

During the summer
months a little kiosk
by the chapel is
usually open for
refreshments at
weekends.

The trail now follows Katharinenpfad (waymarked with
a church symbol, pictured) back to Oberrotweil. Look for
a little footpath by the cross that leads down the hill. The
route is straightforward and mostly runs along the edge of
the forest. Follow the ridge and ignore all trails to the right or
left unless specifically marked, passing *Amolterer Eck* (crucifix), *Schelinger Viehweide*, a shelter hut at *Jungviehweide*,
Lochacker and *Galgenberg* to reach **Kiechlinsberger Eck**
(Auf dem Eck) car park. Cross the road and climb up on the
small footpath on the other side. The trail continues mostly
along the edge of the forest or the vineyards via *Hasenlager*,
Eck and *Geissensee* to **Mondhalde Pavillon**, a picnic area
and car park in the vineyards. Here the trail turns into a
paved vineyard lane that zigzags down the hill. Almost at
the bottom, by a bench (*Panoramaweg*) continue downhill
past the chapel, and left again past the cemetery and memorial. At the corner turn right along the wall and at the next
corner turn left past the supermarket and at the crossroads
follow Bahnhofstraße to the right. After passing the wine
cooperative (Winzergenossenschaft), turn left to reach the
station in **Oberrotweil**.

WALK 8
Edelfrauengrab and Karlsruher Grat

Start/finish	Ottenhöfen station
Distance	11.3km
Difficulty	Medium, except in the scrambling section (1km), which is difficult and can be dangerous
Time	4–5hr
Height gain/loss	530m
Maps	Schwarzwaldverein Wanderkarte Hornisgrinde 1:30,000
Refreshments	Gasthaus Bosensteiner Eck (closed Wed)
Public transport	Train or bus to Bahnhof, Ottenhöfen
Access	Via Achern/Fautenbach on L87
Parking	Tourist information office or at the station at Ottenhöfen
Webcam	www.webcam-ottenhoefen.de
Note	This route is for scramblers and can be dangerous. You must be fairly agile and vertigo-free. Firm footwear with a good grip is essential. Do not attempt it in wet, windy, snowy or icy conditions. However, the dangerous section is short and can be bypassed.

This is an exciting and challenging route – perhaps the most difficult in the whole of the Black Forest. Scramblers will love it. Karlsruher Grat is a ridge broken up by rocky outcrops, so-called *Schrofen*, which run perpendicular to the ridge. There is no delineated path, no steps hewn into the stone, and no safety rope or wire. You have to scramble, sometimes on all fours, to get across the rocks. But even if you choose to bypass the scrambling section, the route is delightful and varied.

From signpost *Bahnhof* by the kiosk at the corner of the little park follow the blue marker across the park. Turn right on Allerheiligen Straße, and by the church turn left on Albert-Köhler Straße. At *Hildahain*, behind the church, follow the yellow marker towards Edelfrauengrab and Karlsruher Grat. After a few metres take the right fork

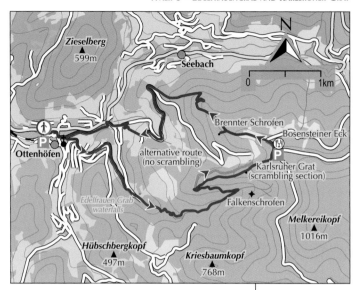

and follow the footpath up to the street. Turn left along the paved road to *Schlosshof* and take the left fork past some houses down to a quarry. Continue straight through the quarry yard, past the office building on the right, to a small car park at the far end. Cross the car park and follow the stream. Soon you reach a waterfall and **Edelfrauengrab**. ▶

The trail leads up through the waterfall and follows the stream through the valley. Shortly after Gottschlägtal the trail splits. Continue straight on (right fork), to a trail junction with some benches and signposts. A steep and narrow path leads up the hill to the left (Klrh. Grat) to Herrenschrofen, a rocky outcrop with excellent views. Continue straight to the trail junction at Standort C.

Scrambling route

▶ Bear right, signed 'Karlsruher Grat, Bosenstein Kletterpartie'. The path across the ridge is not marked. You have to find your own way. Keep to the left where

Edelfrauengrab is a cave hollowed out by the waterfall, which, according to legend, became the grave of the cruel Lady of Bosenstein.

Note For search and rescue phone 07223 19222.

171

Waterfall at Edelfrauengrab

possible. This section can be dangerous – do not take unnecessary risks. The views are wonderful, however, and the passage is exciting. After about 1km of scrambling the trail reaches a trail junction. Continue straight on, along the middle (blue-marked) trail towards Bosenstein.

Alternative/bad weather variation

At *Standort C* continue straight on towards Bosenstein and turn right at *Dreierschrofen*. Ignore Alois Pfad and keep to the right at the next two forks. Follow the narrow trail that climbs up to the ridge at a switchback angle to meet the trail coming from the scrambling section. At the top continue to the left on the blue-marked trail up the hill towards Bosenstein (not the very steep path).

Turn left at the car park at *Bosensteiner Eck* and follow the yellow marker back down to Ottenhöfen. Pass the Bosensteiner Eck **restaurant** and continue straight across the saddle of the hill with sweeping views in all directions. At the far end of the pasture follow the trail along the edge of the forest. A tiny path forks off to **Brennter Schrofen**, another rocky outcrop with fabulous views, only a few metres off the main trail.

Continue on the main trail straight down the hill. Cross a forest road at *Am Grenzweg* and continue down through the forest to a broader forest road where an old wooden signpost points to the right for Ottenhöfen and Seebach. This is a little deceiving as the trail only makes a little right-left wriggle. A few metres further on, it continues to the left on a grassy path down to a lane at *Anfang Grenzweg*. At *Kleineck*, turn right, around the tight bend and continue down the hill following the 'Genießerweg' signs. At the next two forks, keep to the right. At *Hubersloch*, continue straight on, crossing a stream in a tight bend. Continue straight (left fork). After the lane comes out of the woods turn off onto a field track to the right. At the bottom turn right and then follow the lane to the left to Bromberg. Follow Hagenbruck (right fork) into Ottenhöfen. Turn right at the end of the lane towards the main road. Turn left across the street to *Hagenbruck* and cross the car park. Continue over the footbridge and turn right along the stream, past the wooden church to *Hildahain* by the catholic church. Bear right to retrace your steps to the station.

View of Ottenhöfen

WALK 9
Above Renchtal

Start	Oberkirch station
Finish	Oppenau station
Distance	24km
Difficulty	Medium
Time	6hr30min
Height gain/loss	660m/590m
Maps	Schwarzwaldverein Wanderkarte Hornisgrinde 1:30,000
Refreshments	Burgwirtschaft Schauenburg https://burg-oberkirch.de, Klosterhof Allerheiligen www.klosterhof-allerheiligen.de, Gasthaus Blume www.blume-lierbach.de; various restaurants and cafés in Oberkirch and Oppenau.
Public transport	Bus or train to Bahnhof, Oberkirch, Return by bus or train from Bahnhof, Oppenau
Access	Take B3 to Appenweier north of Offenburg, then B28 to Oberkirch
Parking	Oberkirch station
Trail markings	Blue rhombus almost all the way, except for short sections where it may be yellow, or show a Renchtalsteig marker, which shares the same routing much of the way from Oberkirch to Allerheiligen.
Webcam	www.schauenburg.de/schauenburg/ansichten/webcam/
Note	It is difficult to shorten the route as the bus service to Allerheiligen is very poor

A beautiful and varied panoramic route above Renchtal, from the castle ruins of Schauenburg to the remains of Allerheiligen Abbey. From here the trail follows in the footsteps of Mark Twain through the impressive Allerheiligen waterfalls and down the lovely Lierbachtal to Oppenau. Twain, who travelled in Germany in 1878, recorded his walk from Ottenhöfen to Oppenau in *A Tramp Abroad*. From Allerheiligen to Oppenau this walk follows the same route.

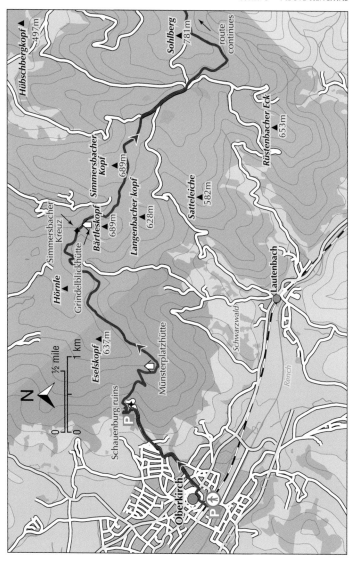

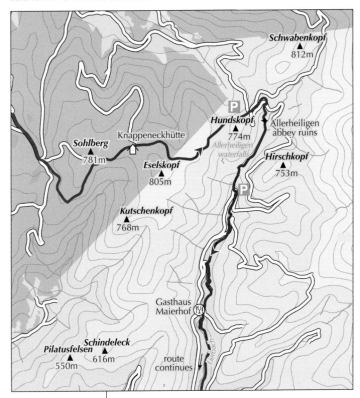

From Oberkirch station walk up Bahnhofstraße to the pedestrian precinct. At the second crossing turn right and follow Apothekergasse around to Hauptstraße. Turn right and just before Romantik Hotel zur Oberen Linde turn left on Stadtgartenstraße towards Schauenburg. At a crossroads continue up the hill on Burgstraße. Pass the first car park. On the top edge of the second car park (for camper vans) at **Schauenburg Parkplatz** a steep little footpath climbs up to a broader track and joins it to the left to reach the castle moat. The gateway to the castle is to the right.

Schauenburg castle dates back to AD1055. From 1650–1661 the author Hans Jakob Christoffel von Grimmelshausen was administrator of the castle while working on his most famous work *Simplicius Simplicissimus*, in which he portrays in literary and often sarcastic style the chaos of the Thirty Years War.

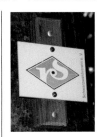

Renchtalsteig waymark

Continue along the moat past the restaurant to *Schauenburg* and take the small footpath to the right signed towards Allerheiligen. At *Schweigmatt* follow the yellow marker to the left on Obere Weg and almost immediately fork left on a winding trail to reach *Oberer Schauenburgweg*. Turn left on the broad forest road past **Münsterplatzhütte** and *Dilgerbrunnen*. At a sharp bend continue straight on to *Mühlebur* from where the blue marker again leads the way. Continue on the broad forest track to *Oberer Spitzenberg* and by the T-junction continue left to **Simmersbacher Kreuz**.

Schauenburg castle ruins

Take the trail that passes **Grindelblickhütte** to the left. At a trail junction by another crucifix continue straight on the gravel track. At **Simmersbacher Kopf** follow the right fork (straight ahead) towards Sohlberg Parkplatz. The gravel track becomes a paved lane and continues straight on to *Sohlebergkamm* and *Sohlberg Parkplatz*. Bear left and by the fork carry on along the field track to the right following the wooden signs towards Allerheiligen and Knappeneck. The trail continues on a gravelly, almost level farm track around the nose of the hill. Eventually it reaches a T-junction and continues to the right. At the picnic area at *Knappeneck* follow the broad gravel path to the left of the **hut** to Eselsbrunnen ('donkey's well').

> According to legend, the Duchess Uta von Schauenburg was determined to found an abbey, but was undecided about its location. In a dream she saw that a **donkey** would reveal the will of God: wherever the animal dropped its heavy load of gold, there the abbey should be built. By the time the donkey reached this spot it was thirsty and started to kick up the dirt, and lo and behold a spring bubbled forth from the ground. A short distance further on he finally dumped his burden and thus the location for the abbey was chosen. Allerheiligen Abbey was founded in 1196 as a Premonstratensian monastery. It burned down soon after secularisation in 1803.

Continue straight on the broad forest road to St Ursula car park and cross the road. Follow Renchtalsteig markings down the hill. Cross another road and continue down through the meadow, past the little chapel down to the ruins of **Allerheiligen Abbey**.

Pass the abbey ruins to the right and continue past the restaurant and souvenir shop down the lane towards the waterfalls. ◀ At the bottom continue straight on through the car park and cross the road. Follow the thin trail to the left. Just around the bend the path starts dropping below

At **Allerheiligen waterfalls** Lierbach plunges down the gorge over several steps, losing 100m of altitude over a distance of about 1km.

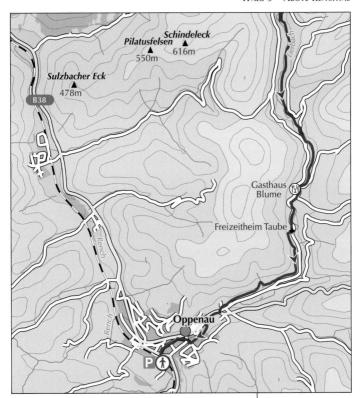

the level of the road and continues down the valley as *Lierbachtalweg*.

At *Windschlägwald* the trail emerges from the woods and continues along a little lane to the crossing of Wahlholzstraße and Hohlengrundstraße. Bear left along the edge of the meadow.

At *Lierbach Haus Wasserfall* the trail joins the lane again and continues down the valley. At *Maierhof* bear right across the bridge and pass **Gasthaus Maierhof** before crossing back over another bridge to continue along the stream.

Allerheiligen waterfalls

Cross a bridge again at *Einkehr*, pass *Bürgerhaus* and continue straight on. At **Gasthaus Blume** head towards the road but turn left in front of the guesthouse to *Mühleloch*. Follow the footpath to the right, closer to the stream. After the Kneipp pool the trail comes up by a bridge by Freizeitheim Taube. Bear right and pass in front of **Freizeitheim Taube**. For about 150m the trail continues on the road itself before it crosses over and starts climbing steeply up the hill to follow a very narrow ledge path above the road to the outskirts of **Oppenau**.

Eventually the trail reaches a lane. Continue to the right to *Rußdobel*. Follow the steps down the hill, cross the road and continue along the footpath next to the stream through the park. At the end bear right on Farnweg. Continue on Inselweg and turn left on Karl-Friedrichstraße to reach the station.

WALK 10

To the source of the Danube

Start/finish	Schönwald town centre (Ortsmitte)
Distance	21.5km
Difficulty	Easy
Time	5hr
Height gain/loss	440m
Maps	Elztal & Simonswäldertal Tourismus Wandererlebnis ZweiTälerLand 1:30,000
Refreshments	Naturfreundehaus Küferhäusle www.kueferhaeusle.de (open on weekends and public holidays), Kolmenhof www.kolmenhof.de (closed Wed, but they provide a snack dispenser for when they are closed), Berggasthaus Brend www.berggasthofbrend.de (closed Tues), Naturfreunde Haus Brend www.naturfreundehaus-brend.de (closed Mon & Tues)
Public transport	Bus to Ortsmitte, Schönwald (Schwarzw)
Access	B500 (between Triberg and Furtwangen)
Parking	In the centre of the village (Landschaftspark)
Webcam	www.berggasthofbrend.de
Trail markings	Yellow, red, blue
Note	The West Way has recently been re-routed. At the time of writing changes were not yet reflected on most available maps.

Despite its length, this is an easy, interesting and delightful walk around a high plateau of the eastern Black Forest. The area is full of springs and moors, which make for interesting botanical discoveries. At an altitude of 1110m the headwaters of the Danube bubble forth as a little brook called Breg. Many passages through open pastureland offer fabulous views in all directions.

Starting from the tourist information board at *Landschaftspark* in the centre of Schönwald, cross the street and head up the hill on Bourg-Achard Straße (yellow marker). Turn right by the war memorial and pass the cemetery. Just before the football ground

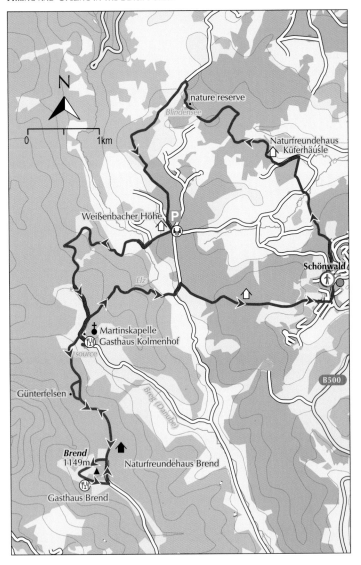

turn left into the forest. At *Rüttwald* bear right towards Weißenbachertalblick. The trail follows the edge of the forest. After crossing a stream continue straight up the hill, across the little lane and up through the field. At *Weißenbachertalblick* turn right and follow the blue marker to the little crossing at *Küferhäusle*. Turn left towards Blindensee. Leave the lane and bear right, passing through the car park of the **Naturfreundehaus Küferhäusle** and heading into the forest on the broad forest road towards Blindensee. After crossing a stream continue straight on, up the hill on a smaller track (no markers). The trail passes a shrine and a derelict hut before reaching a junction at *Blindenhäusle*. Follow the broad forest road to the left, and at *Blindenhof Süd* turn left again to *Brand*. Here follow West Way (red marker) on the small footpath to the right through the **nature reserve** to **Blindensee**.

Blindensee nature reserve

183

Blindensee is entirely rain fed and embedded in a rare peat moor habitat. The water in the lake is very acidic and does not support much life. However, some specialised species have adapted to this extreme environment. Please stay on the boardwalk to protect the fragile habitat.

On the other side of the reserve turn left down the lane (yellow marker) and pass the wind turbines to the left. At the bend continue on the field track straight on, past *Weißenbacher Wald*. The trail joins another track to the left that leads to a lane at *Farnberg*. Turn left to reach the forest car park at **Weißenbacher Höhe**. Follow West Way down through the valley to the right along the edge of the field. On the other side, at *Vogte*, cross the lane and, following the yellow marker, head gently uphill towards Martinskapelle (signed 'Farnberg 11–10'). After passing Rimprechtshof the lane starts to level out. The trail leaves the lane and continues uphill to the left on an old forest track. At *Steinbühl*, turn left past *Käsmatte*

View from Brend towards the Rhine Valley and Vosges

(blue marker), pass a barrier and continue to ski hut Martinskapelle. Turn left to *Forsthaus Martinskapelle*. Join West Way to the right, to the corner of **Reiterstation Martinskapelle**, and bear left to head towards **Gasthaus Kolmenhof**, opposite the little **chapel**. ▸

Retrace your steps to the turn off just before Gasthaus Martinskapelle and follow West Way down Brendweg to the left. Continue straight past *Kolmenkreuz* to *Naturfreundehaus Brend* (red marker). Leave West Way and turn right towards Brendturm (yellow marker). At *Brendhäusle* a grassy track leads up the hill to the top of **Brend**.

After taking in the views pass the **restaurant** and look for a trail to the left of the car park that leads through the trees back to the lane. Return along the lane past **Naturfreundehaus Brend** towards *Kolmenkreuz* to reach Forsthaus Martinskapelle following the red marker.

West Way makes a little detour to a bizarre rock formation, a mass of piled up boulders, called **Günterfelsen**, which lies just off the forest road. Look out for a red marker pointing to the left about 1km after Naturfreundehaus Brend. Follow the 'sticks and stones' trail to the rocks. Follow the small trail to the right to re-join the forest road.

At *Forsthaus Martinskapelle* continue on Brücklerainweg past the source of the River Elz to *NSG Briglirain* (red marker). From here follow the blue marker towards Zinswald. At the T-junction turn left down the lane and at the next corner turn right along the edge of the field and into the forest. At an unnamed signpost in the forest follow the left fork towards Schönwald (yellow marker). At *Zinswald* continue straight on past a hut. After crossing a field, the trail turns into a paved lane. Continue straight down the hill, past the church to the main street of **Schönwald**. *Landschaftspark* is to the left.

A path marked 'zur Donauquelle' runs through Kolmenhof property and leads to the **source** of the River Breg, the most distant headwaters of the Danube.

WALK 11
Zweribachfalls and Vosges chapel

Start/finish	St Peter bus station (Zähringer Eck)
Distance	18km
Difficulty	Medium/hard
Time	5hr
Height gain/loss	560m
Maps	Schwarzwaldverein Wanderkarte Hochschwarzwald 1:35,000; Kompass Titisee-Neustadt 1:25,000
Refreshments	Plattenhof www.plattenhof-ferienwohnung.de (closed Mon and Tues)
Public transport	Bus to Zähringer Eck, St. Peter (Schwarzw)
Access	From Kirchzarten via Stegen on L127, or from Waldkirch via Kandel (mountain) on L186, or from Denzlingen via Glottertal on L112, or B500 to Thurner, then L128 via St Märgen
Parking	By the bus station or at trailhead car park Hirschmattenweg or Potsdamer Platz
Webcam	www.meteoblue.com/en/weather/webcams/kandel_germany_2893245
Trail markings	Yellow; white K on red rhombus; Zweitälersteig symbol (green rhombus with red heart); blue
Note	If arriving by car the walk can be shortened to 11km by starting and finishing either at trailhead car park 'Wanderparkplatz Hirschmattenweg' or 'Potsdamer Platz'. Firm footwear is essential.
	Walkers must be surefooted and vertigo-free. Most of the route is perfectly safe and easy, but the section through the waterfalls can be dangerous in inclement weather. Do not attempt in snow/icy conditions. In case of emergency call Bergwachtrettungsdienst 19222.

This is a fabulous walk for those who like a bit of an adventure: a visit to the magnificent Zweribach waterfalls is followed by a scramble up Hirschbachfalls through a Bannwald (strict forest reserve). The way back leads along the ridge, accompanied by sweeping views across Dreisam valley towards Feldberg and the southern mountains.

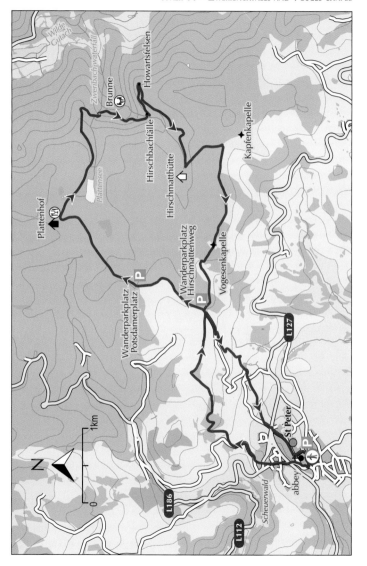

Starting at the bus station follow Zähringer Straße up the hill, towards the **abbey** (Klosterkirche/Ortsmitte). Cross the abbey courtyard and exit through the gate on the left. Turn right, down the hill (*Schierbrückle*) and cross the road. Walk straight up on Scheuergasse past *Baumeisters Kreuz* towards Scheuerwald. By the last building follow the small footpath to the right. Cross another road and a lay-by and continue on the footpath through the woods to **Scheuerwald**. From here follow Kandelhöhenweg (white K on red rhombus) towards Auf der Eck and Plattenhof. The trail reaches a lane by a caravan park. Turn right and follow the lane around the bend to the left, up the hill.

Shortly after passing Steingrubenhof the trail forks off to the right on Steingrubenhofweg. Just inside the forest bear to the right up the hill following the yellow markers. Before reaching the top turn left on the crossing forest road, still heading uphill. The path comes to the edge of the forest and continues to the left, then emerges in a

Picnic area at Brunne

field. Follow the line of trees along the edge of the field to a trail T-junction at *Auf der Eck*. Turn right towards Vorderwillmen.

At *Vorderwillmen* turn left on the paved lane, past two car parks (**Wanderparkplatz Hirschmattenweg** and **Potsdamerplatz**) to *Schönhöfe* and on to **Plattenhof**. From here follow Zweitälersteig markers down the lane to *Platte/Langeckerhof*. Turn right, into the forest. Soon you start hearing the waterfalls. Pass the little bridge at *Brückle*, and continue down through the falls to a wonderful picnic spot at **Brunne**.

At *Brunne* leave Zweitälersteig and follow the yellow marker towards Hirschbachfälle. This trail is a little bit tricky to pick out. It is marked, but the markers are sometimes in odd places. In a couple of spots it looks as though the trail continues straight when it actually turns to the right. However, you can't go far wrong, as the other paths are dead ends that will only take you to look out spots from where you can view the falls. The trail zigzags up the hill to a little bridge at **Hirschbachfälle**. Cross the bridge and continue to the left, up the side of the hill, to emerge on a regular forest road at *Bannwald Zweribach*. ▶

At the top turn right along the forest road towards Kapfenkapelle. Just before reaching a picnic area at **Hirschmatte**, follow the blue marker to the left towards Vogesenkapelle. After crossing a forest road the trail reaches *Rotes Kreuz* at the edge of the forest. On clear days the views from here across the whole valley and the high mountains beyond are fabulous.

Follow the yellow marker to the right, first along the edge of the field (not on the forest road), then along a paved lane. At *Bei der Vogesenkapelle* continue on the stony path to the left to reach **Vogesenkapelle** chapel by a little clearing. Continue straight on through the woods and around the edge of a field. Pass the farm and continue through the forest to return to *Vorderwillmen* (the Hirschmattenweg car park is just a few metres to the right).

Turn left down the lane towards St Peter. After about 300m walk down the driveway on the left and turn right,

To find **Hohwartsfelsen**, a rock outcrop with great views across the valley, follow an unmarked, narrow trail that continues straight on where the main path makes a sharp bend. Be very careful here.

189

The trail towards St Peter

past the house and follow the field track down the hill. Just before reaching the next farm continue on a farm track straight on, which leads to a way cross on a country lane. Turn right and continue down the hill. Just after the bend bear left, past a couple of houses. The trail makes a tiny left/right wriggle and follows a farm track down towards St Peter. By the T-junction turn left and cross the big road via a subway. Continue straight past the school on Mühlegraben, and left on Schulweg to return to the bus station at Zähringer Eck.

WALK 12
Zweitälersteig

Zweitälersteig

Start/finish	Waldkirch
Distance	108km
Time	5 days
Terrain	The first two and a half sections are often steep and rugged, using small trails to traverse rocky slopes. After that the route becomes a panoramic ridge trail mostly on field tracks and broad paths. The first 2km of Stage 2 run almost level through the forest, but parallel to a road which on weekends is popular with bikers and motorists.
Refreshments	Take plenty of food and water, especially for Stages 1 and 2, where there are practically no restaurants along the way.
Warning	Stage 2 requires sure-footedness and sturdy footwear with good grip. The section through the waterfall can be dangerous in adverse weather conditions.
Website	www.zweitaelersteig.de – check 'Aktuell' for current information about trail conditions
Trail markings	Green rhombus with red heart (pictured)
Note	The best season to walk this trail is from May to the end of October, as long as the ridges are free of snow and ice.

Zweitälersteig (two valley trail) is a fabulous and highly diverse circular route of 108km that traverses the ridges above Elzach Valley: wild and adventurous on one side, peaceful and idyllic on the other, with wonderful, sweeping vistas all around. With a total of about 4000m in height gain Zweitälersteig presents a challenging but rewarding excursion into the heart of the central Black Forest.

In 2011 Zweitälersteig was certified as a 'Quality Trail'. It is conceptualised as a 5-day tour made up of individual stages of up to 26km. Extra days could be added to make it a little easier. Those who want to walk the full length of the route can take advantage of the 'walking without luggage' packages, which are available either with a luggage-forwarding service, or with a fixed base. The luggage-forwarding option is easier logistically, as it is independent of bus schedules.

Buses serve all the official beginning and end points, but don't necessarily connect the two points directly. For day tours it's best to park at the nearest train station and take the bus to the trail head. It will be easier to get back to the train station than to the trail head at the end of the day.

At the end of Stage 1 an alternative descent to St Peter is given. To continue on Zweitälersteig from there, take either the bus back up to Kandel, or use the slightly harder route described in Walk 16 to reach Plattenhof (climbing an extra 250m). It is worth the extra effort for the sweeping views down to St Peter, St Märgen and Dreisamtal below, with Feldberg in the distance across the valley.

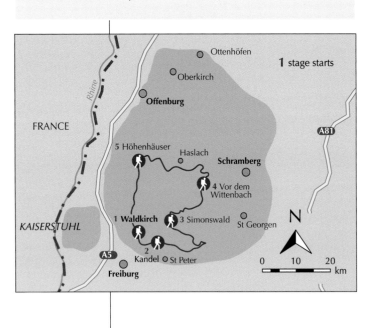

Waldkirch to Kandel (or St Peter)

Start	Waldkirch station
Finish	Kandelhof (or St Peter)
Distance	10km (19km to St Peter)
Difficulty	Hard
Time	4hr30min (6hr30min to St Peter)
Height gain/loss	970m/30m (1090m/610m to St Peter)
Maps	Elztal & Simonswäldertal Tourismus Wandererlebnis ZweiTälerLand 1:30,000; Schwarzwaldverein Wanderkarte Elztal Gutachtal 1:35,000
Refreshments	Bergwelt Kandel www.bergwelt-kandel.de (closed Mon)
Public transport	Bus or train to Bahnhof, Waldkirch (Breisgau), return via Zähringer Eck, St. Peter (Schwarzw) (there is no direct bus back to Waldkirch)
Access	Take B3 to Denzlingen, then B294 to Waldkirch
Parking	By the station
Webcam	www.meteoblue.com/en/weather/webcams/ kandel_germany_2893245
Note	Take plenty of food and water, as there are no restaurants along the way until you reach the top of Kandel, and nothing much on the way down to St Peter either.

If there is a tour for peak-baggers in this book it has got to be this one. Although Kandel is not the highest mountain in the Black Forest, none other requires overcoming 1000m of altitude to get to the top. Kandel rises almost straight from the Rhine Valley to 1241m above sea level. Most of the route runs through cool, shady forest, but the top is entirely open, offering fabulous views across the Rhine Valley towards Kaiserstuhl and the Vosges on one side and Elz Valley and the central Black Forest peaks on the other.

A big signpost and orientation board opposite the train station welcomes walkers to Zweitälersteig, which starts to the left, following Bahnhofstraße across the River Elz and to the pedestrianised town centre. At the far end of Marktplatz, at *Mohreneck* turn right on Kirchstraße and follow signs for Schwarzwaldzoo. At the bend

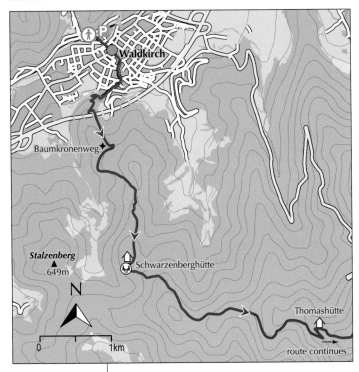

continue to the left on Propsteistraße to the corner of Schwarzenbergstraße and turn right through a residential area. Cross the big junction and continue half-right on Am Buchenbühl to reach Schwarzwaldzoo.

Cross the car park and follow the zigzagging trail up the hill to join the 'Path of the Senses', an exploratory trail for children, past a couple of wooden benches at *Kanapee* to **Baumkronenweg**, a tree-top adventure trail (entrance fee).

Pass the picnic area by the entrance of the canopy trail and follow the bend around to the left to *Am Fohrenbühl*. Take the left fork, which turns into a narrow path that climbs steeply up the hill and emerges on another forest road by a timber landing at *Kienzleebel*. Zweitälersteig continues to the right on Schwarzenbergweg to reach a picnic area and hut at **Schwarzenberghütte**. ▸

Zweitälersteig continues on the small trail to the right of the hut. Crossing a couple of forest roads it steadily climbs up the hill and eventually reaches a more open area with good views across the valley. The trail now continues along the ridge. Cross another forest road and continue on Moosbühlweg to *Am Kranzenkopf*, where Zweitälersteig is joined by a blue-marked trail. Together they continue past *Gullerkopf* to *Moosbühl* where the trail splits. Take the steep 'sticks and stones' trail up towards Thomashütte. After crossing a couple of forest roads it reaches a junction. The marker is not very obvious here. Continue across the junction and up the hill on the left-hand track. The path gradually becomes narrower as it ambles past rocks and boulders on its way to **Thomashütte**, perched on a rocky precipice, with great views across Glottertal and Freiburg in the distance.

If you have extra energy you can make a short detour to take a look at the ruins of Schwarzenburg castle via a small trail to the right.

The path up to Kandel

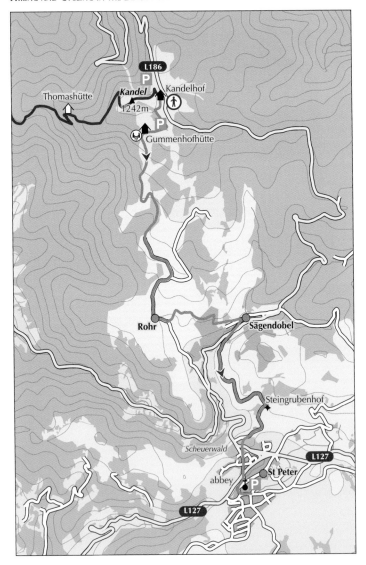

Continue on President Thoma Weg, above the hut to the right. At *Bei der Thomashütte* follow the stony trail straight up to *Hoschgetkreuz* and continue to the left. Join Damenpfad to the right for the final ascent. An elevated shelter hut marks the summit. The bus stops by the **Kandelhof** guesthouse/restaurant below the summit.

> **Kandel** is steeped in mythology and is known locally as a 'witches mountain', a place where witches were believed to gather on Beltain's Eve to dance with the devil. According to legend, a huge reservoir of water is sealed inside the mountain, held back only by Kandelfelsen, a massive rock below the summit. Superstition holds that if the rock was displaced the valley below would become flooded (which, according to another story, the devil has already attempted, in days gone by...)

Alternative descent to St Peter
At *Kandel/Pyramide* take the right-hand trail (blue marker) towards St Peter. Pass *Kreuzacker* and continue straight on to *Kaibeloch Parkplatz*. From here follow

The path down towards St Peter

the yellow marker to the right, across a pasture towards **Gummenhofhütte**. Behind the hut (*Gummenhütte*) the yellow marker leads down through the valley towards the hamlet of Rohr. At the bottom of the field continue on the dirt road to the right to Gummenhof and follow the lane to the left past *Oberhalb Dilgerhäusle*, *Neubauern Ebel* and *Neubauernhof* towards Rohr. At the crossroads in the centre of the tiny hamlet of **Rohr** turn left towards Felsenhof and left again at the next corner up towards Nazihof.

> This farm, Nazihof, derives its **unfortunate name** from its original owner, Ignaz Hummel, who died in 1737. Apparently Ignaz, then a common name, used to be abbreviated to 'Nazi' before that term acquired its sinister associations.

By the chapel of Nazihof, look for a small footpath that leads across the field to the right. Pass through a line of trees and continue straight on. Cross the forest road to the left and just a few steps further on continue on the small trail down to a paved lane. Follow the paved lane around the dog-leg bend towards Sägendobel. At *Felsenhof* walk straight past the farmhouse and follow the footpath down the side of the hill to the village of **Sägendobel**.

At the sawmill (*Sägendobel Säge*) continue to the right, and cross the road at bus stop 'Sägendobel', now following Kandelhöhenweg markings (white K on red rhombus) up the paved lane opposite, to St Peter via *Haldenhof*, *Heitzmannhof* and **Steingrubenhof**. Cross the yard of Steingrubenhof and just after the campsite look for a footpath through the forest on the left, still following Kandelhöhenweg. At **Scheuerwald** follow the yellow marker to St Peter. Cross Glottertalstraße and continue straight on the narrow path to a lane. Turn left, pass *Baumeisterkreuz* and cross the main road at the bottom. Head up the hill towards the **abbey** and the centre of the **St Peter** To find the main bus station, follow the road around to the left through the village to *Zähringer Eck*, the bus stop in the centre.

Kandel to Simonswald

Start	Kandel Rasthaus
Finish	Alt-Simonswald (hiking signpost Rathaus)
Distance	26km
Difficulty	Hard
Time	7–8hr
Height gain/loss	530m/1380m
Maps	Elztal & Simonswäldertal Tourismus Wandererlebnis ZweiTälerLand 1:30,000; Schwarzwaldverein Wanderkarte Elztal Gutachtal 1:35,000
Refreshments	Bergwelt Kandel www.bergwelt-kandel.de (closed Mon), Plattenhof www.plattenhof-ferienwohnung.de, Bergvesperstube Hintereck www.hintereck.de (weekends Apr–Oct and public holidays), Gasthof-Hotel Engel www.hotel-engel.de, Gasthaus-Pension Rebstock www.rebstock-simonswald.de, Café-Restaurant Huber. Carry food and water, as there are not many restaurants along the way until you reach Simonstal. Fresh water fountains can be found at Brunne and at Hintereck hut.
Public transport	Kandel Rasthaus, Waldkirch (Breisgau) (via St. Peter). Return by bus from Rathaus, Simonswald
Access	B294 to Waldkirch. Take the bus from Waldkirch, St Peter or Denzlingen up to Kandel as retrieving your car from the towns will be much easier than fetching it from the top of Kandel.
Parking	At Waldkirch station, Denzlingen station or St Peter bus station
Note	The route can be shortened to Gasthaus–Hotel Engel (Simonswald Engel). There is a bus stop right in front of the hotel. Endurance and sure-footedness are essential. In wet or icy conditions the steep sections are dangerous and should not be attempted. Walking poles may be useful. For an alternative route from St Peter to Plattenhof see Walk 16.

This section of Zweitälersteig reveals the wilder side of the Black Forest. Waterfalls, gorges and rock-strewn slopes as well as sweeping vistas make this walk wonderfully varied and exciting, but it requires excellent stamina.

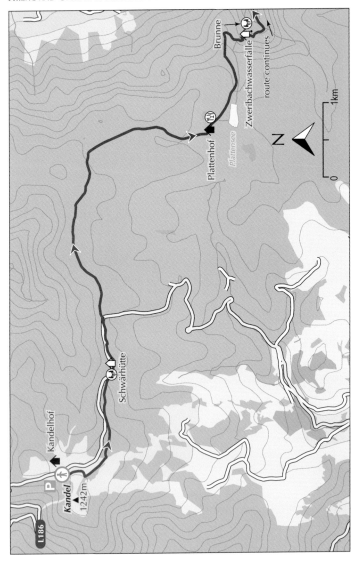

View of Simonstal

From the bus stop at Kandel Rasthaus head up the track towards the peak, but before reaching the top turn left at *Tischle Bank*. At *Kreuzacker* turn left towards *Kaibeloch* car park and continue straight down to the bottom of the meadow. Cross the dirt road at *Rohrallmend* and continue on the forest trail to the left, parallel to the road towards Plattenhof, for 2.5km.

Shortly after passing **Schwärhütte**, cross the road at *Auf der Linie* and continue straight on the broad forest road, past *Dreispitz* to *Kaltenbrunnen*. Here take the right fork towards *Militärschlag* and continue straight past *Bei der Bockhornhütte*. Soon the trail emerges from the forest on the plateau known as Platte, with sweeping views and exposed mountain pastures. Turn left at the T-junction, past **Plattenhof** and down towards Zweribachwasserfälle. At *Langeckerhof* turn right and follow the trail into the forest, which soon turns into a steep 'sticks and stones' path that meanders through rocks and boulders down to the **waterfall**. ▸ Cross the bridge and continue down along the falls to **Brunne**, a beautifully situated picnic

The falls are especially impressive when water levels are high – but that is also the time when the trail can be dangerous. Do be careful – fatal accidents have occurred here.

area on the site of an old farmstead, which was abandoned after it burned down.

The trail continues down the track past Bruggerhof towards Teichschlucht. At the T-junction turn left across the stream and right across the next bridge. Follow the street around the hill to *Luxenhof*. Here take the left fork down towards Pfaffmühle. After the last building the trail continues as a footpath through the field. Just after crossing a brook turn left down the field and across the footbridge to *Vitenhof*. Walk up to the right, cross the road

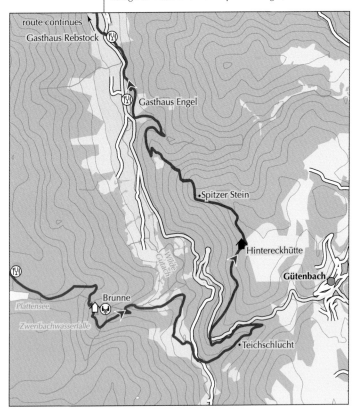

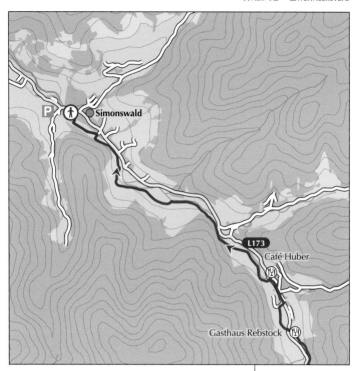

and head for bus stop 'Pfaffmühle' by the Wild Gutach village sign.

Turn left at *Pfaffmühle* and follow the stream on a forest path that soon turns into another adventure trail as it steadily climbs up through the rocky gorge. By a huge boulder at **Teichschlucht**, continue up to the left towards Hoheneck. The small trail becomes almost alpine as it crosses a small scree slope. At *Vitenbühl* take the steep little path up to the road. Cross carefully and continue up the hill on the broad forest road on the other side (Probstwaldweg). After about 1km it turns into a grassy track and terminates at a timber landing. At the far end a small footpath leads across a tiny bridge and immediately starts climbing steeply up the hill to the right, to **Hintereckhütte** hut, a good place to rest and fill up the water bottle.

Continue on the track behind the hut to the left. At a T-junction continue to the left, towards Schöne Aussicht. At *Am Spitzen Stein* bear left to *Unterer Spitzer Stein* on an adventurous and difficult path down a steep, boulder-strewn slope. At the bottom briefly join a forestry road to the right and just after the bend continue on a narrow trail steeply downhill to the right. Cross another forestry road at *Saulache* and again continue on a small trail down the hill. At the bottom turn right and after the bend, by a big wooden signpost, turn right on Breitackerweg towards Simonswald Engel. At *Unterer Kilpen* follow the stream to the left to reach **Gasthaus Engel**.

Look for the continuation of the path behind Gasthaus Engel, leading to the right past the deer enclosure. At *Wildgehege* follow the narrow trail down through the trees to the left and pass the playing field to the left. After crossing a parking area continue next to the **Wilde Gutach** river.

Pass Stegenhof to the left, cross the busy road and follow the path past the little gardens to continue along the river. At the next bridge turn right towards **Gasthaus Rebstock**, cross the road and continue past **Café Huber**. Cross the road and the wooden footbridge to continue along the river, past *Kaspersbrücke* and *Grün*. At *Ibendörfle* turn left and continue on the lane for about 1km. Just before a tight bend take the trail down to the river. At *Brennerbrücke* continue to the left along the river to *Eiskeller* and turn right to cross to *Ochsenbrücke*. Follow Staubfreier Weg to the left and turn right by the tennis court. Cross the big car park by the watermills to reach the centre of **Simonswald** (*Simonswald/Rathaus*).

Start	Alt-Simonswald (hiking signpost Rathaus)
Finish	Gasthaus Rössle, Oberprechtal-Vor dem Wittenbach
Distance	26km
Difficulty	Hard
Time	9hr
Height gain/loss	1090m/950m
Maps	Elztal & Simonswäldertal Tourismus Wandererlebnis ZweiTälerLand 1:30,000
Refreshments	Hörnleberg chapel hut (only when chapel is open); Schwedenschanze (weekends and public holidays) and Kapfhütte (May-Oct, Sun and public holidays)
Public transport	Bus to Rathaus/Simonswald. Return by bus from Rössle/Oberprechtal
Access	Take the B294 between Waldkirch and Elzach and turn off on L173 to Simonswald
Parking	In the centre of the village, by the mini-golf and watermills
Note	The route can be shortened to Rohrhardsberg (bus service on weekends only). This stage is not technically difficult, but requires good stamina. Bring plenty of food and water, as there are not many places to buy food along the way.

This stage is a wonderful ridge walk high above Yach (pronounced 'Ee-ach') and Elz Valley. The trail climbs steeply up to Hörnleberg, an ancient sacred site that was 'converted' into a Christian pilgrimage site in about AD700. From there the route continues as a typical ridge walk – much of it through the forest on small trails, but with many excellent vantage points to enjoy the beautiful views.

From the centre of Alt-Simonswald, at *Rathaus,* walk up Kirchstraße and bear right, towards the church. At the far end of the cemetery the trail continues as a footpath, following a stream to the next village. At **Gasthaus Ratsstüble** turn left up the lane and continue on

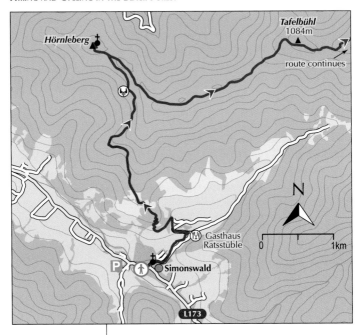

Hesshackenweg into the forest. Ignore Sackgasse, which is a cul-de-sac, and follow the main track around the next tight bend where it emerges on a panoramic field track. At *Simonswald/Hesshackenweg* a narrow path leads up the slope and joins a broader forestry track to the left. Pay close attention to the markers. The trail climbs up the hill in steep zigzags and at some point takes a sharp, somewhat unexpected left through the trees. After a fairly level section on a grassy track it reaches a forest road at *Elme*.

Turn left towards the trail junction in the bend and walk down Mattengrosshofweg for a few metres to find the continuation of Zweitälersteig up a steep track to the right. From here the trail follows a 'Stations of the Cross' pilgrims' path to Hörnleberg chapel. After the fifth station it briefly joins a broader forest road to the left, to the junction at Impfel, before climbing up the hill on

Hörnleberg-Dobelweg. After the ninth station the trail reaches a timber landing and continues to the left on Hörnlebergpfad, past a **picnic bench** and a way cross. *Am Hörnlepfad* marks the saddle. Climb up to the **chapel** to the left to enjoy the great views overlooking Elz Valley, Kaiserstuhl and the Vosges in the distance.

> Ancient records attest that **Hörnleberg** has been used as a sacred site since pre-Christian times. After it was Christianised in AD727 a chapel was built to honour Our Lady of Hörnleberg, and the site became hugely popular, attracting up to 3000 pilgrims a day. Despite being struck by lightning twice and almost being abandoned during secularisation in the 18th century, Hörnleberg retains its pilgrim appeal. The chapel is only open on weekends and Wednesday afternoons from 1–5pm during the summer months. The most important pilgrimage day is Maria Ascension Day, on 15 August.

Return to the saddle and continue half right, on Hörnlepfad towards Tafelbühl and Braunhörnle. At

Ancient pilgrimage site of Hörnleberg

Paragliders take to the skies up here from two different spots: one just below the summit, overlooking Elz Valley, and the other on the top of Tafelbühl, with beautiful views over Simonstal and across to Kandel.

Oberer Weg bear right and follow the markings through the forest, mostly on small paths or on broader, disued forestry tracks, either straight on or just slightly bearing right or left along the ridge or just below it. At a junction of many unmarked trails continue straight on to **Tafelbühl** (4km). Just below Tafelbühl Zweitälersteig is joined by Yacher Höhenweg (marked by a Capercaillie symbol). ◄

Follow the trail across the clearing at the top and down past *Dorerbühl-Hütte* to the junction. Continue to the left on the forest road. At *Bei der Dorerbühl-Hütte* the trail turns sharply to the left to climb up to **Braunhörnle**, another great spot for a picnic, with picnic tables and beautiful views.

A small path continues towards Rohrhardsberg. At *Breitbühl* turn left and follow a ridge trail across a clearing. As soon as the trail goes back into the woods turn left on a rocky track to climb up the hill to **Yacher Höhe**. Here Zweitälersteig continues to the left on an almost level trail. Just before the end briefly bear to the left towards the edge of the forest to reach *Heiliggeistloch*. Turn right along the edge of the forest to *Schwedenschanze* and follow the lane down the hill. (The **hut**, which is open during the season on weekends, lies just off the lane, a bit obscured by the trees.) Just before the bend take the shortcut across the field to the right.

After passing the farm (Schänzlehof) you will see a small trail to the left, which leads to the remains of an **old trench** that dates back to 1688. Although this remote mountain pass seems like the epitome of rural idyll, it has not always been so peaceful up here. During the Thirty Year War this area was frequently overrun, despite this line of defence, which originally extended over many miles.

Follow the gravel road to *Am Schlagbaum* and turn left. Almost immediately Zweitälersteig forks off to the right along the edge of the hill, past *Ober den Siebenfelsen* and a striking rock formation (Gfels), to the trail junction of Hagschachenweg and Ochsentannenbühlweg.

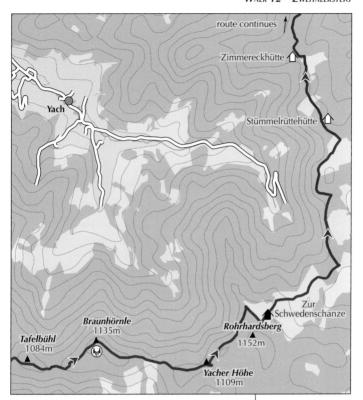

Continue to the left on Hagschachenweg. Just after passing another rock formation by an information board at Am Watzeck, Zweitälersteig forks off to the right on a smaller trail, which leads to a forest road. Turn left to the trail junction of Stümmelrütteweg and Ochsentannenbühlweg and continue to the left on Stümmelrütteweg, past a pyramid-shaped shelter hut (Stümmelrüttehütte). At a bend bear left to continue on an old forest track to another T-junction. Turn left to reach a trail junction at *Zimmereck* where Yacher Höhenweg and Zweitälersteig part company. Pass the hut (**Zimmereckhütte**) to the right to reach

Lache, where the trail joins the right-hand fork of a forest road and continues more or less straight on. A few metres further on, take the left fork to reach *Wolfsgrube* and continue straight to **Wolfsgrubenhütte**.

Follow the small footpath to the left of the hut. It splits almost immediately and continues on the left fork up the hill. At the next fork continue on the right-hand trail to reach **Fentzlingsbank**, a fantastic vantage point high above Elz Valley.

The small path continues through the woods to a forest road and joins it to the left to reach the junction of Langmattenweg and Gschasikopfweg. Turn left past **Langmattenhütte** and at the fork continue to the right, to a wooden sign that marks the 'summit' of Langmatten. At a bend a few metres further along the trail forks off to the left on a track that leads steeply downhill. At the bottom turn briefly to the left before continuing downhill to the right on a smaller path, past *Schwiegrube*, to the fabulously situated **Kapfhütte**.

At *Kapf* a narrow footpath leads down the side of the hill towards Rössle. At the bottom turn right on the grassy track to reach a T-junction and follow the bigger

View from Kapfhütte towards the central Black Forest

210

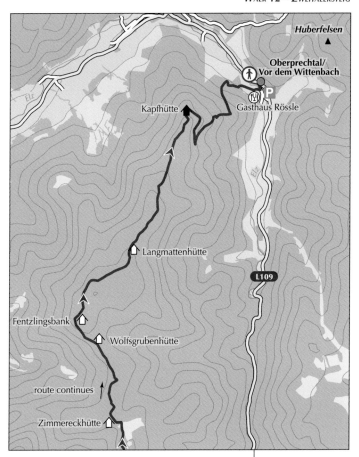

forestry road to the left. At the bend, at *Hänslisbühl*, continue down on the steep path to the left. By the nature reserve sign the trail makes a 90-degree turn to the left, crosses the logging road and continues down the hill. At *Am Schatzweg* turn left to reach the **village**. Pass the first houses to the right and turn left along the lane to the main road. **Gasthaus Rössle** and the bus stop are to the right.

STAGE 4
Oberprechtal and Höhenhäuser

Start	Gasthaus Rössle, Oberprechtal-Vor dem Wittenbach
Finish	Gasthaus Zum Kreuz, Höhenhäuser
Distance	25km
Difficulty	Medium
Time	7hr30min–8hr
Height gain/loss	740m/520m
Maps	Elztal & Simonstal Tourismus Wandererlebnis ZweiTälerLand 1:30,000
Refreshments	Landwassereck www.gasthaus-landwassereck.de/ (closed Wed), Funis Vesperstube www.funihof.de, Gasthof Rössle-Biereck, Höhengasthaus Zum Kreuz www.hoehengasthaus.de (closed Mon and Tues)
Public transport	Bus to Rößle, Oberprechtal. Return to Bahnhof/Elzach from Höhehäuser, Geisberg (Schutter) (SBG-Bus 7206). Limited seats available.
Access	Take B294 from Waldkirch or Haslach to Elzach. For easiest access take the bus from/to Elzach station.
Parking	Elzach station
Note	This stage covers easy terrain without challenging ascents, except at the beginning to reach Huberfelsen and a short but steep section near the end.

A picture-perfect rural idyll on a beautiful ridge walk around the top end of Elz Valley. The trail ambles easily through the forest and across high pastures with many open vistas across the rolling hills and valleys below.

From *Vor dem Wittenbach/Rössle* follow the main road for about 100m up the valley to the right and turn left on Im Hederle. At the fork follow the left-hand track up the valley. By a bench turn right, up a side valley and follow the left fork into the forest. A few metres into the forest Zweitälersteig starts climbing up a serpentine trail to reach a broad forest road at *Hirtzdobel*. Turn left to

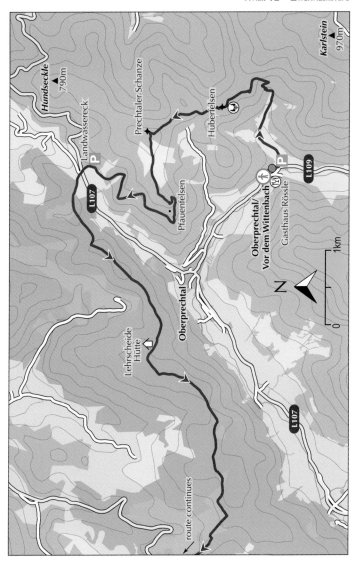

Huberfelsen, a strange rock formation that juts out from the forest floor like a rhino horn (there is a picnic table here).

A tiny footpath leads around the back of the rock and it is possible to climb up to the top. Continuing around the rock, the trail forks. The right-hand path leads back to the picnic table, while the one to the left (red marker) re-joins the forest road a little bit further along. Continue down the forest road, straight past the trail junction at *Huberfelsen*. Just before a clearing bear left up the hill towards Westweg/Schanze. ◄

Pass the trenches to **Prechtaler Schanze** and turn left, towards Pfauenfelsen, across highland pastures and open woodland. After the second stile the path bears left through the firs, then ambles down to Pfauen Kreuz, a crucifix by **Pfauenfelsen**, another wonderful vantage point overlooking Prechtal. Continue to the left down to a broad forest road at *Pfauen* and turn right to *Landwassereck*.

Cross the road (**Landwassereck Parkplatz**) and continue on Landwassereck Höhenweg/Holzerkopfweg behind Gasthaus Landwassereck. The route passes *Burggraben*, *Kirchberg* and *Lehrscheide* on the way to Heidburg Pass. At a bend, by Lehrscheide **shelter hut**, Zweitälersteig forks off to the right on a smaller track. At the T-junction continue to the left on a fairly level stretch to a small clearing where the trail splits. Continue on the right fork, across a trail junction and straight along the gravel path, which joins another forest road to the left to *Bösmatte*. Follow Finsterkapfweg for about 50m. Zweitälersteig turns off to the right on a small path leading to another track and joins it to the left. Cross the fields and follow the tiny trail to the right along the edge of the forest. Halfway down the trail bears to the left and soon reaches a lane at *Griessbaum's Wegkreuz*. Pass the way cross and the telephone mast and continue down to the road and car park at **Heidburg Pass**.

Cross the road and follow Schlosshofweg. Just after passing **Funihof** fork to the right and continue on a gravel track. The trail emerges from the forest above a hamlet. At

The well-preserved trenches (Schanze), built during the 19th century as a defence against the French, serve as an eerie reminder that peace can be transient in even the most remote and seemingly serene places.

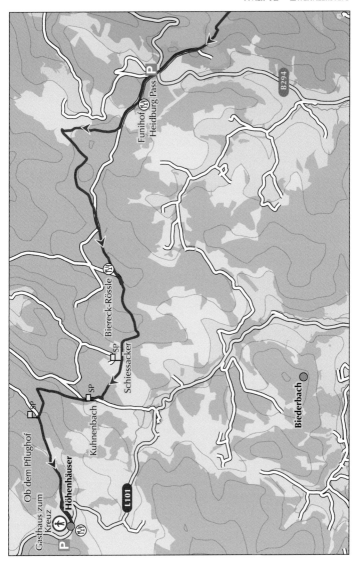

Flachenberg, turn sharply to the left, towards the woods.
By the edge of a clearing bear right to join a broader
track, which leads to a large clearing at *Bei der Heidburg.*

> The **castle** that once stood was completely disman-
> tled during the 19th century as local farmers quar-
> ried the ruins for building materials. Now only the
> name 'Heidburg' remains.

Cross the clearing and continue through the forest
on the right-hand trail. Join the paved lane to the right to
Schlosshof. Continue on the 'sticks and stones' trail up
the hill (not many markers here). At the fork follow the
right-hand trail down to *Biereck* and turn left along the
lane to **Biereck-Rössle** (*Ob dem Biereck*), a historic inn
with great views to the north.

After passing the inn continue to the right past the
field, then bear left on a forest road to **Schiessacker.** Cross
the field and continue through the woods to **Kuhnenbach.**
Take the 'sticks and stones' path on the right to a paved
lane and join it to the right. Just before reaching the farm
(*Lachen*) climb up the hill on the steep little trail along
the edge of the forest to **Ob dem Pflughof** (also signed
Auf der Breitebene) and turn left to the timber landing.
Look for the trail on the left to continue through open
woodland past *Ob dem Lebersteinhof* to the hamlet of
Höhenhäuser. The lane leads down to **Gasthaus zum
Kreuz** by the main road. The bus to Elzach stops right
next to the restaurant.

STAGE 5
Höhenhäuser to Waldkirch

Start	Höhengasthaus zum Kreuz, Höhenhäuser
Finish	Waldkirch station
Distance	24.5km
Difficulty	Medium
Time	6–7hr
Height gain/loss	390m/790m
Maps	Elztal & Simonswäldertal Tourismus Wandererlebnis ZweiTälerLand 1:30,000
Refreshments	Höhengasthaus Zum Kreuz www.hoehengasthaus.de, Luegemol www.luegemol-freiamt.de (weekends and public holidays), Bergkiosk Wandertreff am Hünersedelturm (weekends only), Wanderheim Kreuzmoos (Fri-Sun and public holidays), Gasthaus Zum Gscheid (closed Mon and Tues), Berggasthof Linde www.berggasthof-linde.de (closed Tues); various cafés and restaurants in Waldkirch
Public transport	Bus to Höhenhäuser, Geisberg (Schutter). Return by bus or train from Bahnhof/Waldkirch
Access	From Elzach take the bus up to Höhehäuser, Geisberg (Schutter), return to Elzach from Waldkirch station
Parking	Elzach station
Note	On weekends the bus to Höhenhäuser is a call-bus (bus service 7206.5). Call 07682–9209976 1hr in advance to register. For most of this stage, Zweitälersteig runs jointly with Kandelhöhenweg (white K on red rhombus).

The last section of Zweitälersteig gets top marks for sweeping views. Running jointly with Kandelhöhenweg for most of the way, this is a very scenic ridge trail with beautiful views towards Elz Valley and Kandel to the south, the Vosges and Kaiserstuhl to the west and Kinzig Valley and the northern Black Forest peaks. The route described includes a detour to Hünersedel, which adds a couple of kilometres, but it is well worth it.

At Gasthaus zum Kreuz the trail starts behind the inn on a panoramic field track along the edge of the forest.

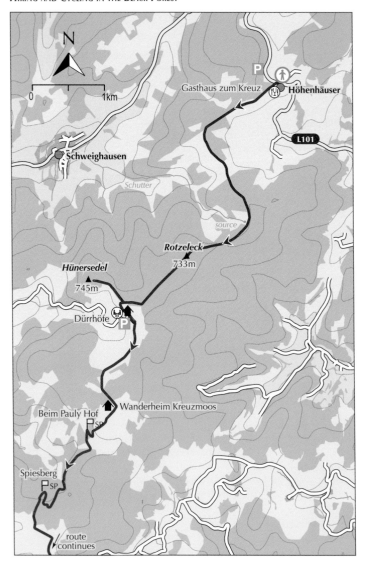

Source of the Schutter River

After passing *Schwabenkreuz* and Schwedenkreuz it soon reaches **Schutterquelle**, the source of the River Schutter (*scutro* is Celtic/German for 'fast flowing'), at the far end of a large open field. Just after the trail junction (*Schlegelsberg*) the track splits (at another signpost, also called Schlegelsberg) and Zweitälersteig continues on the right fork towards Hünersedel. To climb to the top of **Hünersedel** follow the blue-marked trail to the right at *Bei den Dürrhöfen* and turn right on the gravel path at the T-junction. ▸

On a clear day this short side trip is well worth the effort. The views from the top of the observation tower are fabulous, encompassing almost the entire Black Forest range.

To re-join Zweitälersteig retrace your steps down to the junction, but continue to the right on the broad farm track past a field to the picnic area at **Dürrhöfe** and straight on to **Dürrhöfe Parkplatz**.

Turn right towards Wanderheim Kreuzmoos, a walkers' hostel, and after 100m take the right fork across the field. At *Kreuzmoosmatte* follow the track to the left past the hostel to **Wanderheim Kreuzmoos** and turn right, across a field towards Pauly Hof and Schillinger Berg. At the bottom the trail makes an s-curve through some trees to reach the junction at **Beim Pauly Hof**. Continue downhill to the left to another junction. Cross the lane and follow the lower trail to the left. Pass the two-farm hamlet of Pauly Hof and continue on the paved lane to the right to the junction of Am Paulyhof and Bildsteinstraße. Turn

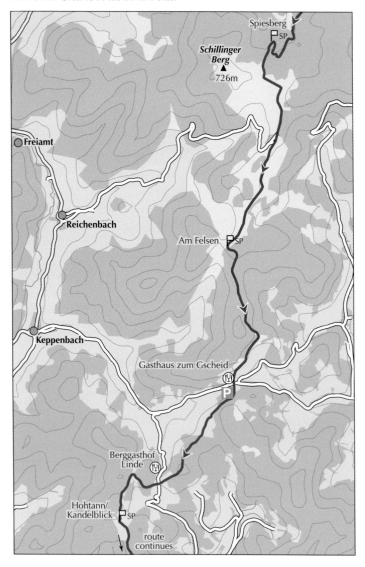

right and at a tight bend follow the left fork to **Spiesberg**. Continue to the left towards Scheerberg and after about 50m bear left on an old track along the edge of the hill. At *Scheerberg* turn left to *Schillinger Berg*, where Kandelhöhenweg rejoins Zweitälersteig and both continue to the right along the edge of a field. Follow Schwarzenbergstraße straight on. After a bend the trail splits and Zweitälersteig continues on the right fork to **Am Felsen** and straight on to *Eckleberg* and *Tannlebühl*. Take the left fork past a farm, heading towards the mountain pass at Gscheid and **Gasthaus zum Gscheid**.

Kastellburg ruins

Cross the road and the **car park** to reach *Vor Gscheid* and continue on the field track up the hill. At the crossroads at *Kuriseck Spick* follow the right fork and cross the road at *Lindenbühl/Sexau* to continue to *Plätzer Ebene*. Follow the bend around to the left towards **Hohtann/ Kandelblick** and enjoy the lovely view of Kandel across the valley to the south. The trail turns sharply to the left down a steep and narrow path that leads to a forest road junction. Continue to the left on Steingrabenweg towards Naturfreundehaus and Kohlenbachereck. After about 350m leave the forest road and continue on a smaller track to the left (wooden signpost to Kohlenbachereck/ Naturfreundehaus). The trail emerges from the woods and continues along the edge of the forest to *Sexauer Haseneckle* and straight on along the edge of the field to the next junction. Turn left through the forest on Langenmoosweg towards Kastellburg.

At *Tannenwiese* bear left and then left again at the next fork. Cross the timber landing and follow the trail until it emerges from the forest by a field. Bear right, slightly uphill towards *Waldkircher Haseneckle*, near a crucifix. Continue straight on for about 100m. Just

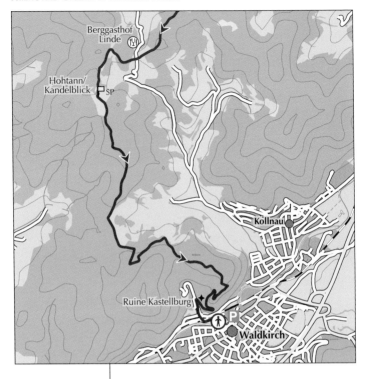

before joining another forest road fork off to the left on a small footpath. After about 1km the path reaches *Beim TV Umsetzer* and briefly joins the forest road to the left before turning off sharply to the right on a steep and rough track down to the **castle ruins** of Kastellburg. Enjoy a last panoramic view across Elz Valley before heading down the hill to Waldkirch.

Follow Ritterweg, a children's trail lined with cut-out knights, for about 100m to *Vor der Burg*. Continue to the left down the hill on the serpentine trail. At the bottom pass the building and car park and turn left down the road. After crossing the train tracks turn left to reach **Waldkirch** railway station.

RIDE 2
Kaiserstuhl Radweg

Start/finish	Riegel-Malterdingen station
Distance	64.5km
Difficulty	Easy
Time	6hr
Height gain/loss	182m
Maps	Schwarzwaldverein Wanderkarte Breisgau Kaiserstuhl 1:35,000; Kompass Kaiserstuhl-Tuniberg 1:25,000
Refreshments	Many options in the villages along the way
Public transport	Train to Riegel-Malterdingen (DB), Riegel (Kaiserstuhl)
Access	From A5 take exit 59
Parking	At the station
Website	www.kaiserstuhl.eu/aktiver-urlaub-am-kaiserstuhl/radfahren/kaiserstuhlradweg/
Trail markings	Black 'Ka' on red background
Note	A tiny train runs around Kaiserstuhl and is never far from the bike route, making it easy to shorten the route. However, at peak times and weekends the trains are often packed, leaving little or no room for bicycles

A lovely and mostly easy ride through the vineyards, orchards and wine villages of Kaiserstuhl, this route has some interesting highlights along the way. The historic town of Breisach with its grand cathedral and the medieval villages of Burkheim and Endingen are worth taking a look around.

Riegel–Bahlingen (6km)

If you arrive by train from Freiburg cross the tracks via the subway to the station building. Follow Bahnhofstraße towards Riegel. Pass underneath a motorway bridge and another big road via a subway. Cross the bridge over the river Elz and follow Hauptstraße to the centre of the village. At the Y-junction by the town hall take the left fork on Kehnerstraße. (There is a dead-end sign, but bikes can get through). At the T-junction turn left on Hauptstraße

223

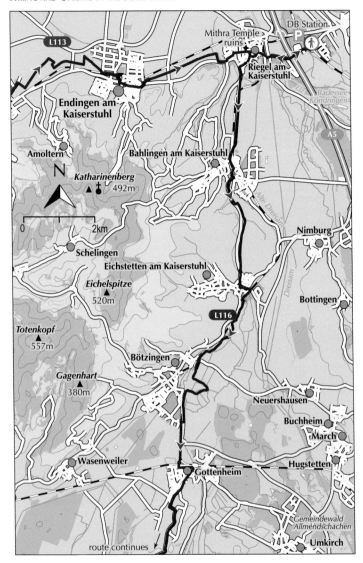

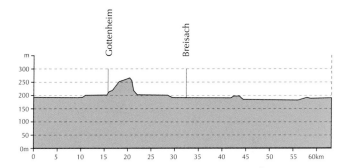

to the big road (L116) and continue alongside this road for about 300m on the left-hand side. Where the bicycle path ends, the route turns off to the left on a small access lane through the fields. At the end the trail runs next to the train tracks and reaches Bahlingen by the little station. Conitnue on the small lane that runs alongside the tracks (Hirschmatten) until it meets Teninger Straße at a bend.

Bahlingen–Eichstetten (3km)

Turn right to the next junction (bend) and turn left on Eichstetter Straße (take care – it's a horrible crossing and there is no bike lane for about 150m). At the end of the village, switch to the bike path on the left side of the road. After 500m the bike path bears to the left across a tiny bridge and follows the stream. Cross back to the right-hand side of the stream. Continue to the outskirts of Eichstetten at Brunnenhof Hiss.

Kaiserstuhl Radweg waymark (red sign on the right)

Eichstetten is known as a **bio village** – it has the greatest number of organic producers in all of Baden-Württemberg and prides itself on its organic, regional specialities and heritage breeds. It is worth checking out some of the farm shops for some unusual products and seeds or visit the 'Kaiserstühler Samengarten' **www.kaiserstuehler-garten.de**, an in-situ seed conservation project.

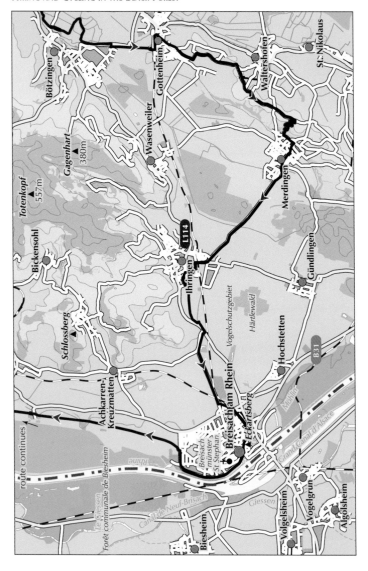

Eichstetten–Bötzingen (5km)

Continue straight ahead to Hauptstraße and turn left. By the tower cross the tracks, but not the bridge and turn right along the train tracks. By the level crossing turn left across a small bridge and then immediately right, along the stream. After a couple of kilometres, cross Neuershauser Straße to the left and continue on Im Grün, around the outskirts of Bötzingen. At the T-junction turn right, back towards Bötzingen.

Bötzingen–Gottenheim (2km)

Turn left along the stream before crossing the bridge into Bötzingen. After about 2km the bike lane reaches a bridge by a roundabout. Turn right, across the road and go around the roundabout. Take the second exit. After crossing the railway tracks immediately turn left to follow the bike path next to the railway tracks to Gottenheim. The trail reaches the carpark of a supermarket before leading down to the main road. Cross the level crossing and turn left towards the station on Bahnhofstraße.

On Tuniberg, with view of Kaiserstuhl

Gottenheim–Tuniberg–Merdingen (5.5km)

Follow Bahnhofstraße past the station, around the bend to the right to Hauptstraße and turn right, through the village. Just after Gasthaus Krone turn left on Tunibergstraße through a residential area and pass the playground to the right. Continue into the vineyards on Tuniberg Höhenweg, a paved access lane that runs across the top of Tuniberg. At the T-junction turn left. At the end turn right and steadily climb up the hill on Tuniberg Höhenweg.

At the T-junction at the top continue to the right towards Breisach and Merdingen. Pass the big wooden raised relief map of Tuniberg. At the corner by the crucifix bear left. At the next T-junction turn right. Pass a large metal cross. At the next corner turn off Tuniberg Höhenweg and follow a steep lane to the right that zigzags down to Merdingen.

Merdingen–Ihringen (4.5km)

In Merdingen turn left on Hochstraße to the main road (Langgasse). Turn right through the village (no bike lane).

Cross the roundabout and switch to the left side of the road. Continue on the bike lane next to the road to Ihringen.

Ihringen–Breisach (6.5km)

Just before Ihringen switch to the other side of the road. Turn right on Gündlingerstraße. Cross the railway tracks and turn left on Breulstraße. Take the third street to the right (Vogesenstraße). Cross Poststraße and follow Josental to the left. At the end briefly bear right and immediately continue to the left through the orchards. At the T-junction turn left and at the next corner turn right towards Weingut Trottenhof. Pass through the orchards to a T-junction. Turn left across a little bridge. Continue to

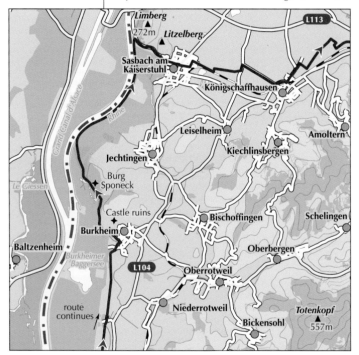

The medieval village of Burkheim

the right towards the main road. Cross via the subway. Bear left along the stream. Pass a little pond and picnic area. Cross the road and turn left towards *Breisach*. After crossing the railway tracks switch to the right-hand side of the road. Turn left on Im Gelbstein, by the big bottle factory. Continue straight ahead to the train station.

Breisach–Burkheim (9.5km)

Pass the train station to the roundabout. Take the second exit and follow Neutorplatz to the centre of Breisach. Pass the market square and continue to the waterfront. Turn right along the ramparts on Josef-Bueb Straße. Pass the industrial harbour. Cross Krummholzstraße. At the next, somewhat awkward junction (Burkheimer Landstraße) cross the road to the left and follow the right fork towards Burkheim. Continue straight, past Jägerhof, through fields and orchards to *Burkheim*. ▶

Burkheim is a lovely little medieval village and well worth taking a look around.

Burkheim–Sasbach (6.5km)

Enter Burkheim on Plonweg. Cross the bridge. Turn left on Laz. v. Schwendi Straße, cross another, old bridge. Skirt around the ramparts to the left. The trail turns into an unpaved path through riverside forest. After about 2km, pass the car park below Burg Sponeck. ▶

The historic 'castell' was originally built by the Romans as a strategic watchtower.

Continue to the left towards Sasbach (marked as scenic route). At the fork bear left to reach the Rhine. Follow the river path along the embankment to the end, where you

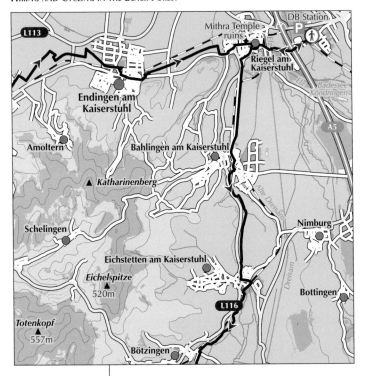

have to cross a bridge to the right by a beer garden. Turn right towards Sasbach. By the junction on the outskirts of Sasbach turn left on Limburgerstraße. Cross Wyhler Straße and continue straight, now on Kaiserstuhlstraße. Turn left on Ankerstraße and at the T-junction turn right on Endinger Weg to head out of the village.

Sasbach–Endingen (9km)

Just after the quarry the bike route turns left. At the T-junction turn left and at the next turn right. Continue to just before Königschaffhausen, but turn left before crossing the train tracks. Turn left on Gehrmatten. By the T-junction turn left on Bahnhofstraße and in the bend

continue straight on, on Königsweg. Turn right by the football field and just before reaching the road turn left and
continue through the orchards. At the crossing turn right
and follow the paved lane in an S-bend through the fields
to the main road. Cross the road and continue straight
on. Turn left at the T-junction. At the next T-junction turn
right and right again at the next corner. At the end bear
right alongside the train tracks then cross the tracks and
follow Forchheimer Straße up to the main street. Turn left
through the town gate of Endingen. Endingen is a very
picturesque little town, full of wineries and artsy shops.

Endingen–Riegel (7km)

Follow Hauptstraße through Endingen and at the other
end continue on Riegler Straße to the roundabout. Turn
left at the roundabout and immediately turn off to the
right on Lichteneckstraße. Follow it through the fields for
about 2km. At the T-junction turn right, to the main road
and turn left. Shortly after turn left on Kaiserstuhlstraße
through the outskirts of Riegel. At the left bend turn right
on Üsenbergstraße to Hauptstraße.

> Look out for the archaeological site on the right side
> of the road just before Hauptstraße. These are the
> remains of an ancient **Mithra temple**. The Persian
> mystery cult of Mithra spread through central
> Europe with the Romans. It flourished during the
> second and third centuries, but quickly diminished
> in importance once the Roman Empire adopted
> Christianity during the fourth century.

Turn right on Hauptstraße and at the next corner turn
left, on Kehnerstraße, which takes you back to the town
hall (Rathaus). Turn right on Hauptstraße to Messmer
Kunsthalle. Switch to the other side of the road to cross
the busy main road via the subway and continue straight
down Bahnhofstraße to Riegel station.

RIDE 3

Kinzigtal Radweg – Alpirsbach to Offenburg

Start	Alpirsbach station
Finish	Offenburg station
Distance	65km
Difficulty	Easy
Time	4hr30min–5hr
Height gain/loss	210m/490m
Maps	LGL Freizeitkarte Blatt F504 Freudenstadt 1:50,000; LGL Freizeitkarte Blatt F503 Offenburg 1:50,000
Refreshments	Many places along the way
Public transport	Train to Bahnhof, Alpirsbach. Return by train from Bahnhof, Offenburg
Access	Alpirsbach lies on the B294 between Freudenstadt and Haslach
Parking	At Alpirsbach station
Trail markings	Stylised K
Note	The route can be shortened at many points as it runs close to the Kinzig Valley railway line. Kinzig Valley Cycle Trail actually starts in Freudenstadt, but the first section has quite a lot of very steep up and downhill sections. If you don't have a mountain bike or e-bike it is better to start from Alpirsbach.

Kinzig Valley has been a thoroughfare between the Neckar and Rhine rivers since Roman times. Later it became an important artery for the wood trade, from which the pretty timber-frame, medieval towns derived their wealth. Traces of the age-old rafting tradition abound.

Alpirsbach–Schenkenzell (6km)

Starting by the fountain in front of the old abbey follow the road down to the corner of Marktplatz and Krähenbadstraße (Restaurant Löwen-Post) and turn right towards B294. Cross the car park and continue straight. Where Krähenbadstraße bends to the right keep going

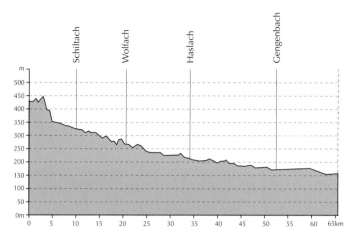

straight, along the tracks. Pass below the tracks and immediately turn right on a residential street (Fried-Preuning-Straße). Cross the tracks again and follow Elmeweg to the left. Pass underneath the tracks and turn right, along the main road for about 220m. Bear right on Hinterer Weg towards Schiltach (no-through road) and follow it around to the right. Cross the tracks and continue up the hill. In a tiny hamlet pass the old border demarcation between the Kingdom of Württemberg and the Grand Duchy of Baden. Follow the left fork down the hill. Turn left at the T-junction to the outskirts of *Schenkenzell*.

Schenkenzell–Schiltach (4km)

By Restaurant Schlössle, bear half-left down a no-through road. Cross the main road and follow Hansjakobstraße through a residential area. At the T-junction turn left on Kinzigstraße and follow it along the river to the main road. Cross and continue to the left. Just after passing the station, cross to the left side of the road. Follow the cycle lane towards Schiltach. After the bend by the ruins of Schenkenburg castle cross the bridge and turn right along the river for a bit before the trail re-joins the cycle lane and continues to the left along the main road.

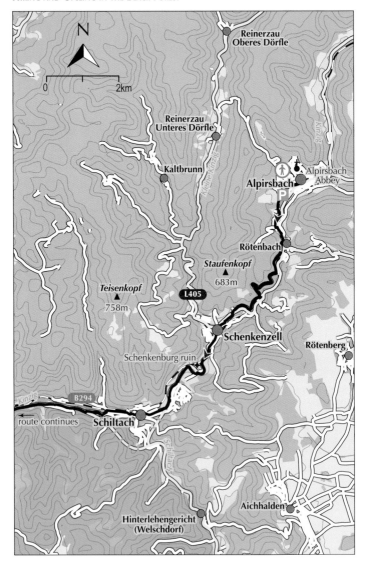

Schiltach–Wolfach (11km)

At the entrance of Schiltach cross the road via a subway and continue along the road. Take the right fork through the village of Hauptstraße. ▸

Just after the church cross the river to the right on Bahnhofstraße. Pass the station and the car park. At the end cross the bridge and the road to follow the cycle lane down the valley. By bus stop 'Hohenstein' cross the B294 via a subway and continue on the left side of the road. After passing a couple of hamlets, cross the tracks just before entering Halbmeil. Bear left at Gasthaus Löwen, cross the tracks again and continue on Schulstraße. Turn left by Gasthaus Engel and right at the next corner, on Baumgartenstraße. Turn right to follow Dörflestraße out of the village and continue to the outskirts of Wolfach. Cross the bridge and briefly continue along the road before crossing it via a subway. Turn left, and left again at the end of the football field, crossing first a canal, then the river. Continue on the left-hand side of the river. The trail ends in St Jakobsweg, which leads to Hauptstraße, by the 'peace oak' monument.

Schiltach is one of the most picturesque medieval timber-frame towns in the whole of Kinzig Valley.

Kinzigtal Radweg waymark (bottom sign on post)

Wolfach–Haslach (13km)

Turn left on Hauptstraße. Opposite the town hall turn right on Kirchstraße. ▸ Cross the bridge and follow the bike path to the left on Am Mühlegrün passing the rafting museum and café. Cross a tiny bridge and continue on the left fork along the river on Herlinsbachweg. At the T-junction turn right on Hausacher Straße (bike lane marked on road). At the end, just before the big junction (B294), briefly turn off to the right on Untere Zinne, and cross via the subway. The bicycle lane continues along the river.

Note If you miss this turn you can continue to the end of the village, and cross the bridge after the station to meet up with the signposted route again.

Just before Hausach the bike path comes up to the main road and crosses the river. Immediately after the bridge the bike lane drops below the level of the road and comes to a little T-junction. Turn left to loop underneath the road and continue along the river. Pass underneath another bridge and keep following the river. After crossing a small road and passing underneath another

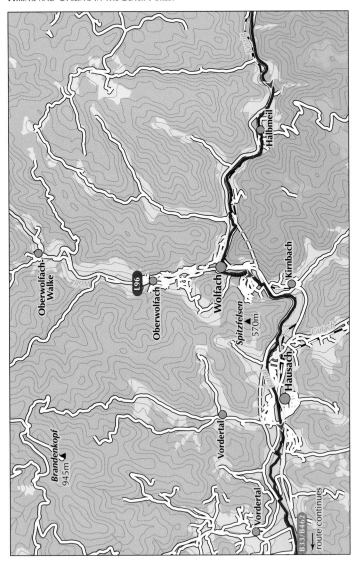

bridge the bike path crosses a footbridge and continues on the other side of the river to Eschau/Fischbach (orientation board). Bear left and continue on the dam.

After bypassing the village cross the river again and continue to the right. At a bend continue straight, on a paved lane parallel to the train tracks. Pass some industrial buildings and follow the trail as it jinks right then left. At the crossroads turn left to pass below the bridge. Cross the big road via the pedestrian crossing and circle around the back of the large supermarket to the left to enter Hausach via the back streets. Follow Im Spießacker to the next junction. Turn left to Mühlenstraße and then turn right. Cross the B294 and bear right, across the square to continue on Engelstraße.

Haslach–Steinach (5km)

Follow Engelstraße to Hauptstraße and turn left through the centre of town. At Marktplatz turn right to the junction. Cross to the left and continue on Klosterstraße. Take the second street on the right (Kampfackerstraße)

Alpirsbach Abbey

towards Steinach and Biberach. By the cemetery turn left on Strickenweg and bear right towards the sports facilities. Go round the top end of the first football field and turn right along the train tracks, down to the big road. Pass underneath the railway bridge and cross the road at the traffic lights. Continue on the bike lane, which soon bears right to continue parallel to the road across the fields. Cross the river and continue next to the B33. Cross Schnellinger Straße and turn left on Allmendweg. Turn left on Kinzigstraße and continue through the fields on Neumatt. At the little T-junction turn right and by the crucifix turn left (signed 'zum Vesperstüble'). Cross the road via the subway and continue to the right. Cross the river and follow the paved lane half-right into *Steinach*. Cross a road (Kinzigstraße) and continue straight through the archway.

Steinach–Biberach (5km)

Cross Hauptstraße and continue half-right. Pass the cemetery and fork off to the right on Kapellenstraße. At the second crossroads briefly turn left on Kolpingstraße and then immediately right on Biberacher Straße. Pass the chapel to the left, cross underneath the railway tracks and continue straight on, first through another hamlet and eventually to Landgasthaus Kinzigstrand. Continue straight to the T-junction. Pass the quarry to the right. Turn right across the bridge and circle around the top end of the field. Turn left through the subway and continue straight to the river. Follow the bicycle lane across the footbridge into Bieberach and continue straight on Strandbadweg to Hauptstraße.

Biberach–Gengenbach (9km)

There are two turn-offs to Bruch, but if you take the first one you may shoot right past the village. If you take the second you can't miss the route.

Turn left on Hauptstraße. At the bend continue straight on Mitteldorfstraße to a T-junction. Join the big road to the right and immediately turn right again on Brucherstraße. Cross Friedenstraße and follow Brucherstraße past a leisure centre and out of the village. Pass underneath the train tracks and take the **second** turn to the left, towards Bruch. ◄ Pass the village to the left and continue through

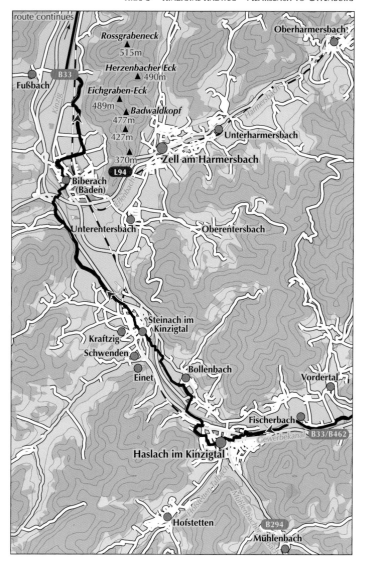

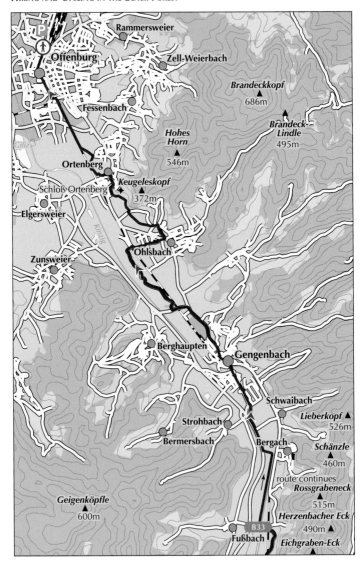

the fields. In Fröschbach turn left, cross the tracks and immediately turn right, crossing the tracks again. At the next T-junction turn left across the tracks and the river. (From here to the other side of Gengenbach the trail is badly marked. Follow signs to Offenburg.) After the bridge turn right and continue below the dam on the paved lane, until it bends to the left to join the cycle lane along the main road to the right, towards *Gengenbach*. Cross the bridge and pass through the city gate. ▶

One of Gengenbach's city gates

Gengenbach has one of the best preserved historic town centres and is well-worth exploring on foot.

Gengenbach–Ortenburg (8km)

The markings through Gengenbach are terrible! Follow Hauptstraße around to the left past the market square and out of town. By a large shopping centre cross the road at the traffic lights and continue on the bike lane on the left-hand side. At the roundabout turn left. After the train tracks, cross to the other side of the busy road with care and bear right past the water treatment facility on Alte Landstraße. (If there is too much traffic, continue to just before the river and cross underneath the bridge. Turn right on the track, past the water treatment facility.)

Turn left before the tracks and follow the lane through the fields for about 2km. By the T-junction turn right, cross the tracks and continue to the right, following a little stream, first through an industrial estate then through a residential area to a bus stop by the main street. Continue to the traffic lights and cross the road to the left. Follow Hubergasse to the end. Turn left and at the bend continue straight on along a farm road through the fields. At the T-junction, below the castle of Schloß Ortenburg, turn right and immediately left by the crucifix. Pass the archery range and circle around the vineyards and outskirts of Ortenburg on Hinterer Burgweg to reach Hauptstraße.

Ortenburg–Offenburg (4km)

Turn right on Hauptstraße. At the roundabout turn left and immediately cross the road to continue on Kochgässle to the left through the orchards. At the T-junction turn left (Bruchstraße) and just before the level crossing turn right to follow the tracks into Offenburg. After about 1.5km cross the bridge to the left on Philosophenweg. Turn right at the next corner to a big junction at Grabenallee. Cross and continue straight on Lange Straße. At the end turn left on Gustav-Ree-Anlage and right on Hauptstraße to find the train station.

NORTHERN
BLACK FOREST

Kaltenbronn nature reserve (Walk 16)

INTRODUCTION

The northern Black Forest is dominated by narrow valleys and dark, tall firs. Yet even here there is surprising variation and many wonderful walks. This part of the Black Forest is more densely populated than the south and peppered with beautiful old villages and small towns. Geographically it comprises the area between Pforzheim, Achertal and Freudenstadt.

Freudenstadt, a pretty market town founded by Duke Frederic I of Württemberg in 1599, is the cultural centre of the northeastern Black Forest. It boasts the largest market square in Germany, thanks to the fact that the Duke's castle, which was planned to take 'centre stage', was never actually built. Despite its location, very much on the eastern edge, it is surprisingly well connected via the Black Forest high road, the B500.

Close by lies the little town of Baiersbronn, which consists of several villages. It holds the distinction of being a gastronomic hot spot, as there are more Michelin starred chefs per square kilometre found here than anywhere else in the country (Walk 18).

Along the eastern periphery a string of beautiful historic towns line the River Nagold on its way to Pforzheim: Nagold has a pretty, old town centre, although on the outskirts it has sprawled to fill the whole valley. Its castle, overlooking the river,

Mummelsee (Walk 15)

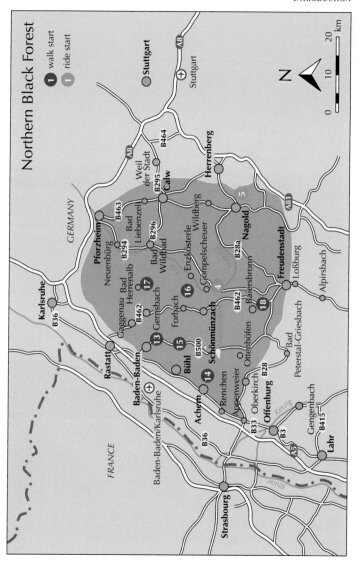

Northern Black Forest

1 walk start
1 ride start

was once a Celtic settlement. Further downstream lies Calw, birthplace of author Hermann Hesse, with pretty timber-frame buildings, and neighbouring Hirsau, once the site of a highly influential monastery of which only the ruins remain. Bad Liebenzell, the next town along, has a long tradition as a spa town and boasts not one but seven thermal springs, which Swiss physician Paracelsus (c 1493–1541) praised for their healing benefits.

In Pforzheim the River Nagold joins the River Enz (Rides 4 and 5). In the days of the raftsmen this was an important port for the timber trade. Pforzheim is not a pretty town as it was almost completely destroyed during World War II and reconstruction took place in a hurry. Interestingly, it has a tradition of goldworking, which is still alive today, and the town has a fascinating jewellery museum www. schmuckmuseum.de.

The laid-back and somewhat secluded ambience of Enz Valley belies the fact that Neuenbürg an der Enz is one of the oldest settled regions of the Black Forest. In Celtic times it was an important centre for iron production. Over the centuries both mining and the wood trade turned the valley into an incredibly industrious zone. Later, Bad Wildbad, in the centre of the valley, boomed during the 18th and 19th century, when spa tourism became popular. Today its old-fashioned charm is a little worn, and, considering the royalty that used

to assemble here, it has a remarkably humble atmosphere.

Further up in the hills lies the largest upland moor in Germany, Kaltenbronner Hochmoor (Walk 16). It may not be very big, compared to, say, Dartmoor in the UK, but the nature reserve protects many rare species. On the other side of the hills is Murg Valley, another important rafting area. The river meanders through handsome towns and villages, such as Schönmünzach, Forbach and the pretty town of Gernsbach, which all made their fortunes from the 'green gold' of the Black Forest. Nearby Bad Herrenalb is another spa town with a relaxing, old-world ambience (Walk 17).

The famous royal town of Baden-Baden is considered by many to be the crown jewel of spa towns. In its glory days it was the summer playground of the rich and famous from all over Europe and Russia. Even now it oozes with aristocratic ambience, and the seasonal meets at the nearby horse race track of Iffezheim regularly attract a well-heeled crowd. The town is also blessed with an enchanting setting (Walk 13).

Just to the south the lovely Bühl Valley stretches into the hills towards Hornisgrinde, the highest mountain in the northern Black Forest. At its base lies Lake Mummelsee, one of the most popular tourist destinations in the whole region (Walks 15 and 18). On its flanks the village of Sasbachwalden (Walk 14) nestles amid vineyards and orchards that fringe the western side of the Black Forest.

WALK 13

Romantic circuit above Baden-Baden

Start/finish	Parkplatz Wolfsschlucht
Distance	11km
Difficulty	Easy
Time	3hr30min
Height gain/loss	360m
Maps	Schwarzwaldverein Wanderkarte Albtal 1:35,000
Refreshments	Café Wolfsschlucht www.hotel-cafe-wolfsschlucht.de (closed Thur), many places in Baden-Baden, Hotel Restaurant Merkurwald www.merkurwald.de
Public transport	Bus to Wolfsschlucht, Ebersteinburg
Access	From Baden-Baden take Schlossbergtunnel on L79a (Rotenbachtalstraße) towards Gaggenau and Eberssteinburg.
Parking	Car park by bus stop 'Wolfsschlucht'
Trail markings	Ebersteinburg Rundweg (blue ring)
Note	Some of the signs in this area are 'old-style' – they show the position name and altitude at the top.

This is a beautiful scenic walk in the immediate vicinity of the historic royal spa town of Baden-Baden. It has many highlights: great panoramic views, a small gorge, rugged red sandstone formations and romantic castle ruins.

Starting from the bus shelter at 'Wolfsschlucht' cross the car park and follow the footpath to the right, up the hill towards **Engelskanzel**. Keep to the right at the fork.

> **Engelskanzel** (Angel's Pulpit) is a rocky precipice overlooking the valley. On the opposite side of the road is a similar precipice called Teufelskanzel (Devil's Pulpit). According to legend, in the days when Christianity was a new religion the angel of God and the devil held shouting matches from

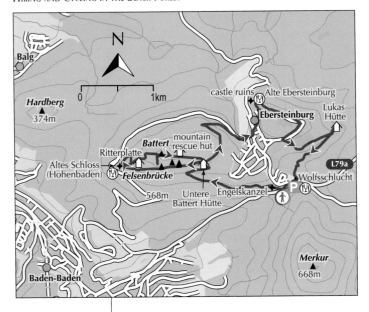

Ebersteinburg
Rundweg waymark

these promontories, in an attempt to dissuade each other's followers.

Cross Engelskanzel and follow the trail down the hill to *Kapffelsen*. Take the right fork towards Battert. The almost level trail (Furtwängler Weg) joins another path to the left. At the big trail junction cross Badenerweg and continue up the hill to the right at *Daubenhauerweg* on a trail that zigzags to the junction at **Untere Battert Hütte**. Turn left on Unt. Felsenweg, which passes below the huge rock formations and partially eroded sandstone columns on its way to the ruins of **Altes Schloss** (Hohenbaden Castle).

The trails around **Battert Felsen** are some of the oldest established walking paths in Germany. Inaugurated in 1839, they are a perfect example of the ideal landscape propagated by the Romantic

Movement, which was popular at the time as a reaction against the growing trend towards industrialisation. Today Battert Felsen is protected as a nature reserve, though in some parts rock climbing is permitted.

In front of the castle is a picnic area and there is a restaurant inside. Continue either on the little trail that leads up the hill around the back of the castle, towards Ritterplatte, or walk through the ruins, past the restaurant. Both trails meet up and jointly head up the hill.

Built between the 12th and 15th centuries, the formidable **Hohenbaden Castle** was the home of the Margraves of Baden. At the end of the 16th century it was destroyed by a fire. The castle is said to be haunted by the 'Grey Lady', a Margravine who was infamous for her cruelty towards her servants and subjects. One day she took her young son to the

Battert Felsen, the rugged red sandstone cliff overlooking Baden-Baden

249

Ebersteinburg Castle ruins

top of the tower to show him the land that would one day be his. But the child slid from her hands and fell to his death among the rocks below. Ever since then, the Grey Lady has been searching for him around the castle, but in vain. The castle ruins can be explored free of charge.

Follow the trail up to the trail junction at **Ritterplatte**, a platform of rocks that offers excellent views over the castle and Baden-Baden below. Take the left fork up the hill on a stony path, which becomes wilder upon entering the Bannwald forest reserve. Climb up the steps to the right to Obere Battert Hütte.

Felsenbrücke is a little bridge that connects a couple of stone columns that stand slightly apart from the main rock massif. It can be accessed from July to November by following the trail to the right, signed 'zur Felsenbrücke'. At all other times it is closed in order to protect it as a nesting site for ravens and peregrine falcons.

Continue straight on to the **mountain rescue hut** (*Bergwacht*) on Oberer Felsenweg, an area that is popular with rock climbers. From here the path gradually meanders down to the lower trail (Unt. Felsenweg). At the bottom turn left and continue past the **hut** (*Untere Battert Hütte*) on Bienenwaldweg towards Ruine Eberstein. At the bend continue straight on, following Bienenwaldweg to Franzosenweg. Follow Franzosenweg down the hill to *Gemeindezentrum Ebersteinburg.* Walk up to the main road and turn left. Follow Brunnenlinde up the hill, bearing left towards Ebersteinburg **castle ruins**.

The trail continues towards Wolfsschlucht on a small footpath to the left behind the wall by the car park below the castle and leads down to a little trail junction. Cross and continue uphill on the other side. The path meets a little road, crosses it slightly to the left and continues on the other side.

A little bit further along cross the lane again and take the steep little shortcut down to another track. Turn left and take the right-hand path down the hill, which leads to a trail junction. Follow the trail up the hill to the left and straight across another trail junction towards **Lukas Hütte**, a little hut perched on a rock precipice. Just before reaching the hut a narrow trail leads down the hill towards Wolfsschlucht. At the bottom it merges with an old forestry track to the right and then forks off down the hill to the left. At the bottom, cross the forest road to the right and follow the narrow footpath down into the 'mini-gorge' (**Wolfsschlucht**) and up again on the other side. Continue to the left, past the car park to the main road. The bus stop and car park are to the right.

WALK 14
Sasbachwalden idyll

Start/finish	Kurhaus, Sasbachwalden
Distance	10.5km
Difficulty	Easy
Time	3hr30min
Height gain/loss	530m
Maps	Schwarzwaldverein Wanderkarte Hornisgrinde 1:35,000
Refreshments	Numerous options in Sasbachwalden
Public transport	Bus to Gaishölle, Sasbachwalden. Return by bus from Sparkasse, Sasbachwalden
Access	Take B3 to Achern then L86 towards Hornisgrinde/ Mummelsee
Parking	By the Kurhaus
Webcam	www.blumen-weindorf-wetter.de/webcam2.htm
Trail markings	Mostly yellow and Ortenau Weinpfad: blue grapes on red rhombus

A charming circular walk high above the pretty village of Sasbachwalden, with idyllic views across the Rhine Valley and the Vosges. The trail leads through vineyards and orchards up to a scenic viewpoint by the castle ruins of Brigittenschloss, and returns to Sasbachwalden via the romantic Gaishölle Gorge with its cascading waterfalls.

The walk starts at *Sasbachwalden/Kurhaus*, just a short way up the road from bus stop 'Gaishölle'. Look for the trail towards 'Dorfmitte' (village centre), which starts by the little traffic island and follows a stream into the park. At *Altenrain*, climb up the hill on Ortenauer Weinpfad. Cross the lane and continue on the other side towards Grieseneck. At the top turn left along the lane and then take the right-hand fork further up the hill, skirting the vineyards. By the lane turn left to the T-junction and continue to the right on Auf der Eck, past *Kappelberg*.

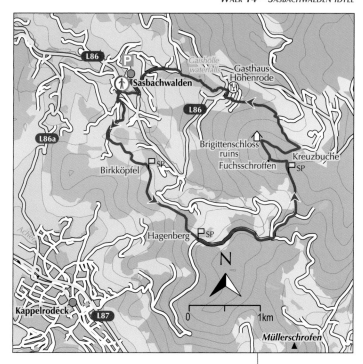

At *Grieseneck* leave Ortenauer Weinpfad and follow the left fork (yellow markers) towards Birkköpfel. Just after the farm leave the lane and continue straight on along a grassy track through the orchards. Bear left by the statue of the Virgin Mary and head straight up the hill. At the top bear left along the edge of the forest to **Birkköpfel**. Continue to the right towards Hagenberg. From here the trail turns into a kind of ridge path that runs along the rim of the valley. Pass *Wolfersberg*, cross the junction and continue straight up the hill. By the bench follow the left fork up the rough track. Cross another track and join a forest road to the right. The trail emerges from the forest, crosses the ridge and climbs up the grassy path to the left of the houses to **Hagenberg**.

Turn left along the lane, past *Brünnele* to a junction near Schönbüch. Cross the road and continue straight on, up the lane towards Brigittenschloss. Just after the bend, follow the stony trail to the right, parallel to the road. Before the trail meets the road again head on, turn sharply to the left across the junction at *Hinterer Wasen*. Continue straight on this little lane to *Hilsenberg*, where the trail continues on the right-hand fork up the forest track towards Kreuzbuche.

At the forest road junction of **Kreuzbuche** turn left on the broad track. The trail soon forks off to the right and after about 200m along that trail, it again turns right, up the hill. Keep to the left at the forks. Soon the trail becomes a little more adventurous as it passes through a jumble of boulders and meanders around an outcrop of rocks called Fuchsschroffen before reaching a shelter hut below the rather sparse remains of **Brigittenschloss**.

Also known as Schloss Hohenrode, the original castle of **Brigittenschloss** dates back to the middle of the 11th century. Although only a small part of the outer wall has survived the ravages of time, it nevertheless makes for a lovely picnic spot with beautiful views across the Rhine Valley and the Vosges.

After exploring the ruins retrace your steps to the little hut and continue to the left down to *Buchwald*. Take the left fork to *Bure Berg* and left again towards Gaishölle. At *Weidberg* (where the signpost is somewhat obscured by trees) the path comes out of the forest and continues sharply down the hill to the left on the gravelly forest road. After about 350m bear right on a smaller path. At the bend turn left across the orchard (no marker). Pass to the left of the farm down to the driveway at *Honsmathise* and turn left for about 100m. At *Schlossberg* follow the forest road to the right down the hill and eventually out of the forest.

After passing a couple of houses cross the residential street to the left and take the stairs down the hill to another street. Cross to the right and again continue further down the hill to Am Schloßberg. Turn right to the corner and then turn left, past the **restaurant**, and cross the road.

At *Gaishölle oben* a footpath leads into the gorge and weaves back and forth across the **waterfalls**. About halfway through the gorge choose the left-hand fork down to *Gaishölle unten* and turn right to *Gaishölle Einstieg*. Follow the lane to the left down the hill, past the triangle junction, and then turn left, down to the main road at **Sasbachwalden**. The bus stop and the Kurhaus are to the left.

Fuchsschroffen outcrop of rocks

WALK 15
Upland moors (Hornisgrinde)

Start	Chapel and bus stop at Sand
Finish	Mummelsee
Distance	14km
Difficulty	Medium
Time	4hr
Height gain/loss	540m/340m
Maps	Schwarzwaldverein Wanderkarte Hornisgrinde1:35,000
Refreshments	Hochkopf Stub www.Hochkopf.de, Zur Großen Tanne www.zurgrossentanne.de, Wanderheim Ochsestall www.wanderheim-ochsenstall.de (open at weekends and public holidays)
Public transport	Bus to Kapelle, Sand (Schwarzwald). Return by bus from Mummelsee, Seebach (Baden)
Access	At the crossroads of B500 and L83
Parking	Car park at Sand
Webcam	www.mummelsee.de/en_US/informations/webcam-2/
Trail markings	Red and yellow rhombus
Note	It is best not to do this route at weekends as it's not far from the B500, which is very popular with bikers and other motorists and can be noisy.

This pleasant, panoramic route takes you across some of the high moors of the northern Black Forest, with beautiful vistas and interesting plantlife along the way.

The trail starts by the junction of the B500 and the L83 at *Sand/Kapelle* and follows red West Way markers on a broad forest road towards Mehliskopf. After about 400m, at *Schwarzbergle*, turn left, now following the yellow marker to *Skihang*. Continue straight across the slope to where the lift passes overhead and zigzag up to the right, towards the forest. The trail now continues on a smaller forest path up to **Mehliskopf tower**. Cross Mehliskopf and continue straight, on the broad forest road. Turn right at

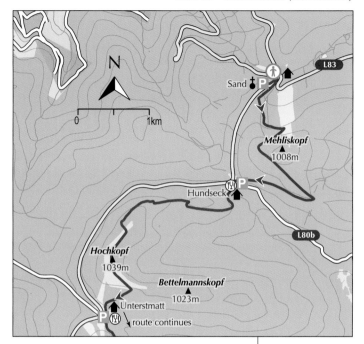

Westliche Drei Kohlplatten and head straight down to
Hundseck.

Pass the restaurant and car park and cross the road.
From here the trail follows the red marker again towards
Hornisgrinde. Cross the road and continue on the dirt
road to the left. After passing underneath a ski-lift at
Hundseck Sprungschanze follow the right-hand fork up
the hill, which soon reaches a timber landing. Look for a
narrow footpath in the top right-hand corner and follow
it through the forest. It joins a broader, old forestry track
to the left. After passing through an area of new growth
the trail bears to the left on a narrower path up the hill to
a forest road junction at *Hinterm Riesenköpfle*. Continue
straight up the hill. By a big wooden board at *Schonwald
'Hochkopf Pfriemackerkopf'* continue on the trail up the

hill to the left to the top of **Hochkopf**, a typical *Grinde* or upland moor.

Cross the top and continue down the hill on the other side towards **Unterstmatt**. After crossing a forest road continue straight, through the bushes to the top car park and then across the lower car park at *Unterstmatt/Tanne*. Head towards the ski-lift on the other side and pass the barrier. Look for the red marker at the back of the cashier's booth and follow the trail into the forest. Cross a forestry road and continue up the hill on the other side (Hans-Reymann Weg). After crossing a little waterfall the path joins a

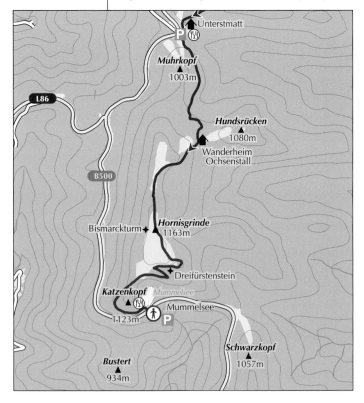

forestry road to the left. At the fork follow the right-hand path up the hill towards **Wanderheim Ochsenstall**, a walkers' hostel. The trail emerges on another forest road and turns left. Just before the hostel turn right on the forestry road and immediately before the barrier follow the trail up the hill. At the top pass the power mast to the left and continue along the edge of the hill, past the wind turbines (*Hornisgrinde/Windpark*) towards **Bismarckturm**, the observation tower on top of **Hornisgrinde**.

> During World War II **Hornisgrinde** was occupied by the French. In parts it still has the ambience of a derelict military compound as it was only opened to the public again in 1998. Efforts are underway to restore the natural features and to protect the rare bog plants, such as the insect-eating sundew, cotton grasses, and a myriad of mosses.

At *Hornisgrinde/Bismarckturm* continue along the edge of the hill on the narrow paved track, which soon turns into a boardwalk across the moor to **Dreifürstenstein**. ▶

Hochkopf is a typical Grinde or upland moor

Just a little bit further along a huge flat stone dating from 1722 marks the former border between the territories of the Margraviate Baden, the Duchy of Württemberg and the Bishopric of Strasbourg.

259

Hornisgrinde

Continue towards Hornisgrinde Turm and Mummelseeblick past another tower. The trail turns into a paved lane and leads to the main access road at *Hornisgrinde/Segelflughalle*. Turn left down the hill and after passing some buildings at *Hornisgrinde/ Wachgebäude* follow the yellow marker to the right around the flanks of **Katzenkopf** to **Mummelsee Berghotel**, a beautiful spot, but also a tourist trap best avoided at weekends and on public holidays.

WALK 16
Kaltenbronn Moor

Start	Schwarzmiss (car park C)
Finish	Bad Wildbad
Distance	15km
Difficulty	Easy
Time	3hr30min–4hr
Height gain/loss	96m/590m
Maps	Schwarzwaldverein Wanderkarte Oberes Enztal 1:35,000
Refreshments	Hotel Sarbacher www.hotel-sarbacher.de in Kaltenbronn (closed Mon and Tues), Grünhütte www.gruenhuette.de (closed Mon), Hotel Sommerberg www.sommerberg-hotel.de in Sommerberg, Hotel Auerhahn www.auerhahn-badwildbad. de (closed Wed and Thurs); many in Bad Wildbad
Public transport	Bus to Schwarzmißhütte/Kaltenbronn. Return by bus or train from Bahnhof, Bad Wildbad
Access	Take B462 to Hilpertsau, then L76b via Reichental to Schwarzmiss, or, from Bad Wildbad or Enzklösterle, turn off at Sprollenmühle towards Kaltenbronn on L76b
Parking	Schwarzmiss is a big car park on a mountain pass. There is no village. There are several more car parks between Kaltenbronn and Schwarzmiss.
Trail markings	Yellow, red, red rhombus with white line in the middle.
Note	For a shorter route, park at car park F and follow Rundweg 1, which takes the same route as described below to Weißensteinhütte, but then turns left to circle back around to Wildgehege (300m from car park), via Middle Way markings (red rhombus with white line in the middle). To avoid the very steep descent to Bad Wildbad take the funicular railway from Sommerberg.

From the Hohlohturm observation tower the trail passes through an extensive upland moor with many rare plants and animal species. This is an easy walk almost without any climbs, but a few steep downhill sections.

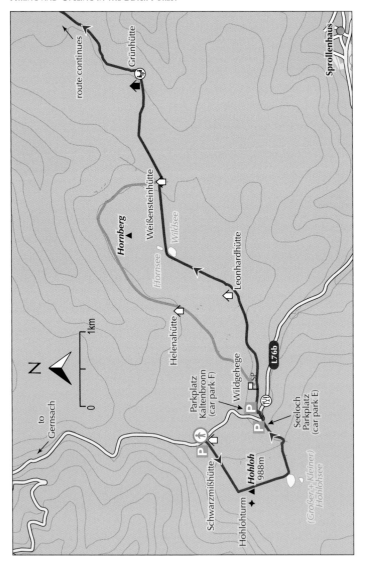

Wildsee

At Schwarzmiss follow the yellow marker on the right fork of the car park towards Hohlohturm. Leave the paved lane at the bend and continue on the sandy path straight to the observation tower. After climbing Kaiser-Wilhelm Turm (**Hohlohturm**) and taking in the views follow the red markers to the left. A boardwalk leads across the bog to **Hohlohsee**.

> **Kaltenbronner Hochmoor** represents the most extensive upland moor in Germany. Its origins date back to the end of the last ice age, 10,000 years ago. Favoured by low temperatures and high precipitation, peat mosses and grasses populated the underlying Bunter, a type of water-resistant sandstone. As the layers of peat grew, the plants on the surface lost access to the underlying mineral-rich bedrock and depended solely on rainwater for their nutrients. Very few species can survive in such an extreme habitat. Thus the resulting ecosystem

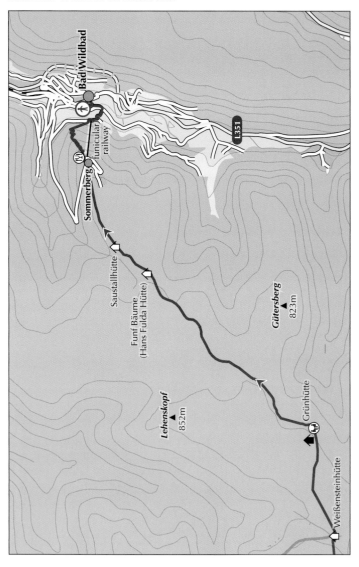

forms a community of highly adapted, rare plants and animal species. Kaltenbronner Hochmoor was declared a nature reserve some 60 years ago and the areas around the 'lakes' are designated as a strict forest reserve (Bannwald).

Follow the trail to a forestry road, cross and continue on the other side, following Middle Way markers on a gravelly path down the hill to *Seeloch Parkplatz* (**car park E**). Cross the road to the right and head across **car park F** (*Parkplatz Kaltenbronn*) to continue on the broad gravel path past *Schlittenhang* and the deer enclosure. At **Wildgehege** continue straight on, now following yellow markers past **Leonhardhütte** to *Wildseemoor*.

Just after Leonhardhütte there is a large tree trunk with a time scale marked on it, which shows the growth of the peat layer over the centuries. Right next to it a little path to the right leads through the strict forest reserve on the boardwalk across the bog. On the other side, at **Weißensteinhütte**, turn right and follow Middle Way markers on the broad forest road. Just after *Blockhauswald* the trail bears to the right to **Grünhütte**, a large picnic area and hut. Still following Middle Way markers bear left, past *Langenwald*. Follow the right fork to *Langenwaldebene*. Cross the forest road and continue straight on to *Laternenbuckel* and on to **Fünf (5) Bäume**.

Now following yellow markers bear right, then take the left fork past *Bächlesweg* and shortly after, again follow the left fork to **Saustallhütte**. Continue half-right past the hut towards **Sommerberg**. ▸

There is now a canopy walkway/ tower, a mountain bike area, and the latest addition: Germany's longest pedestrian suspension bridge. It is a thrill, but not a cheap one.

Soon the ski hut and the mountain bike park come into view. Continue straight on, to the hill station of the **funicular railway**. The Sommerbergsteige footpath (Zickzackweg) starts to the left of the mountain station and follows the yellow-marked trail in steep, tight zig-zags down the hill, crossing a couple of forest roads on the way. At the bottom turn right on Panoramastraße and continue down the hill on Straubenbergstraße to reach the centre of **Bad Wildbad**.

WALK 17
Großes Loch and Teufelsmühle

Start/finish	Rathausplatz, Bad Herrenalb
Distance	17km
Difficulty	Medium
Time	4hr30min
Height gain/loss	570m
Maps	Schwarzwaldverein Wanderkarte Oberes Enztal 1:35,000
Refreshments	Plötzsägmühle www.plotzsaegmuehl.de, Höhengasthaus Teufelsmühle (open weekends), Hahnenfalzhütte (open Sun and public holidays, closed Sep 15-Oct 15)
Public transport	Bus to Rathausplatz, Bad Herrenalb
Access	Take B462 to Gernsbach, then L564 to Bad Herrenalb via Löffenau
Parking	By the station or at Rathausplatz
Trail markings	Blue and yellow
Note	The section around Großes Loch can be dangerous in very wet or icy conditions. Firm footwear with good grip is advised.

A wonderfully varied walk and a bit of an adventure trail through the ravine at Großes Loch ('the big hole'), an alcove carved into a sandstone cliff. From there, the path climbs up to Teufelsmühle (908m), offering great views towards the Vosges. The route returns to Bad Herrenalb via an old border path, and passes the fabulously located Hahnenpfalzhütte on the way down into the valley.

At *Rathausplatz*, walk through the archway and across the old monastery grounds past the church and down the little alleyway next to Klosterscheuer. Climb up the stairs and turn right on Albtalweg, past the cemetery and along the edge of the valley. Pass *Albtalweg/Jagdhaus* and a picnic spot at **Härtwig Hütte** to continue to **Plotzsägmühle**.

Follow the yellow marker down to the restaurant and turn right to cross the ford behind the main building.

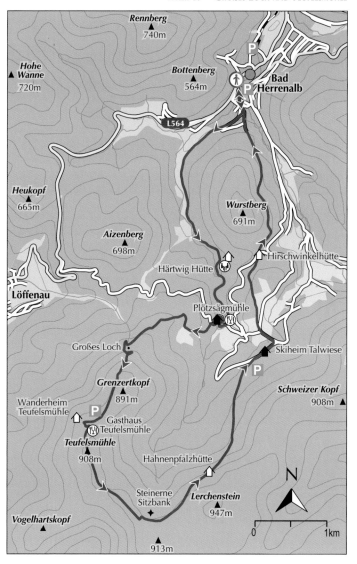

Continue up the paved lane to *Sandgrube*, where a footpath to the left heads up the hill through an old dry gully. At *Vogelwiesen* cross the forest road and continue straight on, towards Michelsrank. At the junction turn left up the hill on the broad gravel track, leading to a paved lane. Turn left to reach *Michelsrank*, and follow the grassy trail to the right towards Großes Loch.

The path soon narrows to a thin ledge along the edge of a ravine with a steep drop on one side and big sandstone boulders towering above. On the rock face opposite, the alcove high up on the cliff face comes into view. At **Großes Loch**, climb up the hill on the steep and narrow path to reach a forest road. (Halfway up, by a kind of landing, a narrow trail to the left leads to the alcove.) At the top, turn left for a few metres and look for the continuation of the path to the right, up the hill. The small trail crosses a forestry road and continues further up the hill on a track opposite. At the next forestry road turn right to **Grenzertparkplatz**. Just to the left of the signpost a little footpath leads through the trees up towards **Teufelsmühle**, crossing the road a couple of times on its way to the top. Continue straight past the restaurant towards the tower on the edge of the mountain. ◄

After taking in the views walk back on the broad track to **Gasthaus Teufelsmühle** and turn right, through the restaurant's car park. In the top right-hand corner a

The tower houses a self-service walkers' hostel owned by the Schwarzwaldverein.

Großes Loch

Teufelsmühle

trail (marked with a red dot) leads into the forest. About 100m down that path at a signpost called *Teufelsmühle* bear left on an old border trail through the forest.

At *Langmartskopf* turn left, now following the yellow marker down to **Steinerne Sitzbank**, where the trail emerges on a forestry road with sweeping views towards Bad Herrenalb and the northern edges of the Black Forest. Continue to the right until the track meets another forestry road at a bend. Follow the left fork down to **Hahnenpfalzhütte**. Look for a rocky, blue-marked trail (Brudesweg) to the left, which leads down towards Bad Herrenalb.

On its way down into the valley the trail crosses three forestry roads before it eventually meets a paved lane. Turn right past the **car park** and follow the left fork by the triangle junction (**Skiheim Talwiese**). Follow the lane to the left across the field. By the bus stop continue on the left fork down the dirt road straight through the forest down to a junction by a **shelter hut**.

The trail continues on Schanzenweg, immediately to the left of the hut (no markers) and leads around the hill to the outskirts of **Bad Herrenalb**. Head straight down the hill on the residential street, which leads back down to *Albtalweg*. Retrace your steps down the stairs and through the old monastery grounds to return to *Rathausplatz*.

WALK 18
Seensteig

Start	Baiersbronn
Finish	Schönmünzach
Distance	71km
Time	4 days
Terrain	The first 1½ stages lead mostly through the forest with quite a lot of up and down and a few small trails. After that the route runs along the main ridge of the Black Forest to Mummelsee, often quite close to the B500. At weekends it can be busy and noisy. Stage 4 is quieter and less dramatic. Many sections on small trails go through windfall areas.
Refreshments	Take plenty of food and water, especially for Stages 1 and 4, which do not pass any restaurants or serviced huts.
Warning	In general, this is a pretty safe and easy route. In bad weather or icy conditions the narrow path leading up along Sankenbach falls may be unsafe. Likewise, Abenteuerpfad, which leads down into the valley from Ellbachsee (Stage 1), can also be dangerous. Be prepared for wet feet as this path passes right through a little stream. Stages 2, 3 and 4 did not have any dangerous sections (except for the detour down to Wildsee via the narrow trail mentioned in Stage 3). The final leg of Seensteig was not walked for this guide so no information is available for that section.
Website	www.baiersbronn.de, www.nationalpark-schwarzwald.de/de/erleben/unterwegs-im-park/wegesperrungen (for temporary and seasonal closures)
Webcam	www.baiersbronn.de/de-de/service/webcams
Trail markings	Stylised landscape with a blue S in a green-rimmed diamond
Note	The best season for this route is from May to the end of October, as long as the trails are free of ice and snow. It is easiest to spend the night locally at the end of each section as the public transport connections are not straight forward and may require changing buses.

Seensteig is a wonderfully varied route that takes in some of the best spots of the northern Black Forest over a total distance of 84km spread over five day stages. Although the focus is on the little tarns that are so emblematic of the northern Black Forest, there is a lot more to this walk than bogs. Although the hills here are not particularly high there is still plenty of up and down, as well as some wonderful ridgeway sections with excellent, far-reaching views. The route also passes through upland moors and some areas damaged by storms, where new growth is emerging among the uprooted trees, slowly rejuvenating the forest.

At the time of writing, the last section of Seensteig (from Schönmünzach to Baiersbronn) was closed due to storm damage, so unfortunately could not be included in this guide. The walk presented here covers the first four stages of the route.

Stages 2 and 3 run quite close to the B500 and include some of the busiest hotspots of the northern Black Forest, such as Lotharpfad, Schliffkopf, Ruhestein and Mummelsee. Seensteig can be done as individual day walks from a fixed base (such as Baiersbronn), however, if you are planning to do the full circuit it would be better to do it as a point-to-point package with a luggage-forwarding service. That way you are not tied to bus schedules and can do those busy sections during the week, when there is less traffic. 'Walking without luggage' packages can be booked through Baiersbronn Touristik (www.baiersbronn.de).

Seensteig has recently been certified as a Quality hiking trail and now has its own rhombus shaped marker. In Stage 3 there are two options marked for the section from Schliffkopf to Ruhestein. You can either follow the route here described, or continue straight on, with Westweg.

Some parts of this walk run through the new Black Forest National Park, which has its headquarters at Ruhestein.

Visit Baiersbronn Touristik (www.baiersbronn.de) to make sure all sections of the trail are open and walkable. Baiersbronn Touristik has an excellent and very helpful Wanderzentrum ('walkers information point') at Baiersbronn station.

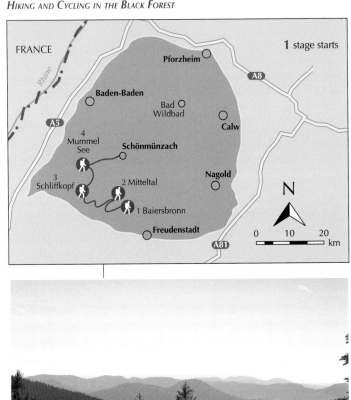

View from Steinmäuerle viewing platform (Stage 2)

Start	Baiersbronn station
Finish	Gasthaus Lamm, Mitteltal
Distance	15.5km
Difficulty	Medium
Time	4hr
Height gain/loss	450m/430m
Maps	Baiersbronn Touristik Wanderkarte Wanderhimmel Baiersbronn 1:25,000
Refreshments	None along the way, but there are cafés in Kniebis (small detour)
Public transport	Bus or train to Bahnhof, Baiersbronn. Return by bus from Lamm, Mitteltal
Access	From Freudenstadt take B462 to Baiersbronn
Parking	By the station
Webcam	www.bergfex.de/kniebis-freudenstadt/webcams
Note	The trail up along Sankenbach waterfall can be dangerous in bad weather.

A lovely varied route that climbs up to Kniebis plateau via the impressive Sankenbach waterfalls, and back down again to Mitteltal. Much of the way is on small paths through different types of terrain.

The trail starts near the bottle bank in the car park opposite the station. Look for Uferweg and follow it along the stream towards Sankenbachsee. Cross the bridge at *Mühlkanal* and continue to *Stöckerwiesen*. Bear right and after crossing another little bridge turn left on Sankenbachstraße. After the last houses, just before the bridge, follow the blue marker to the right, along the stream. Pass the playground at *Sankenbach Spielplatz* and cross the bridge at *Sankenbachbrückle*. Turn right to *Sankenbach-Furt* and cross the little bridge to follow the path next to the stream up to the **Sankenbachsee**. Circle halfway around the lake to the left and just before the picnic area look for the trail that climbs up the hill to Sankenbach **waterfall**. ▶

The sign warns that this trail may be dangerous and that you use it at your own risk.

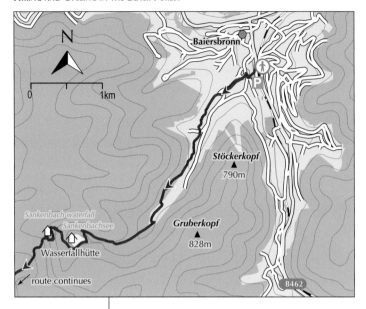

A pine tree with tapping incisions demonstrates the once widespread practice of bleeding pines for resin as a raw material for tar and pitch. This practice was abandoned due to its damaging impact on trees.

The trail crosses the waterfall and clambers up the hill to a forest road at **Wasserfallhütte**. Turn right and a few metres further along, just after the bend, look for a small path that leads further up the hill and crosses another forest road slightly to the right along the way. At the top join the gravel track to the left to reach *Bucheck*. Walk up to the big junction and turn left towards Kniebis Ochsen. At *Ochsenhardt* turn right. Keep to the left at the fork and left again at a triangle junction before finally following Grabenweg to the right. ◄

Seensteig joins Heimatpfad to the right next to a pine tree exhibit and meanders through the forest to a clearing above the village of **Kniebis**.

The *apartment building* that mars the view is a monument to the ill-conceived town planning strategies of the 1960s and 1970s. Originally there were plans to develop the whole Kniebis plateau as a spa town. This apartment building was the first to go up – and promptly galvanised resistance from the locals, which eventually culminated in a court injunction against any further development, on environmental grounds.

Continue along the edge of the forest to the left, past Hexenhütte and bear right on Heimatpfad through the bushes.

By the stone weather station continue to the right along the lane past *Buchschollen* to the car park at the end. Seensteig joins Heimatpfad again to head into the forest towards *Ellbachseeblick*. Soon it meets a forestry road and continues to the left. There is a new viewing platform at Ellbachseeblick, which offers great panoramic views of Ellbachsee below and the hills beyond stretching into the distance. Return to the forest road and continue along the forest road to **Ellbachseeblickhütte**, where a trail leads down the hill to a hut and picnic area at **Ellbachsee.**

Cross the junction to the right and continue down the forest road (blue and yellow marker). At a bend the

Ford across Sankenbach

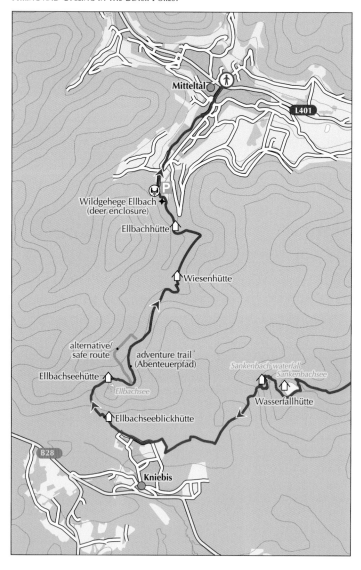

Mitteltal

L401

Wildgehege Ellbach
(deer enclosure)

P

Ellbachhütte

Wiesenhütte

alternative/
safe route

adventure trail
(Abenteuerpfad)

Sankenbach waterfall

Sankenbachsee

Ellbachseehütte

Ellbachsee

Wasserfallhütte

Ellbachseeblickhütte

B28

Kniebis

Ellbachsee

blue marker points to the left. This is the safer and easier alternative path, which should be used in bad weather conditions. The other path, marked with the Seensteig symbol, turns left a short distance further along and descends steeply down the side of the hill through the bushes. This is the Abenteuerpfad ('adventure trail'), which can be dangerous in wet or icy conditions.

The adventure trail passes through the bushes and leads right through a little stream before reaching a level section. Turn right for approximately 800m and look out for the Seensteig marker pointing to another narrow trail on the left to continue down the hill. At the bottom the trail joins the blue-marked trail on the forest road.

Turn right, past the magnificent 260-year-old silver fir to a forestry commission compound called **Wiesenhütte**. Follow the track that forks off to the left, opposite the last building. Bear left at the fork. The trail soon turns into a rocky path, goes down some steps, crosses an old forestry road and continues down some more steps before joining a path to the right. Pass the **Ellbachhütte** picnic area at *Gutellbachwegle* and follow the blue marker on the trail to the left. Cross the bridge and follow the stream down the valley to reach the deer enclosure at **Wildgehege Ellbach**. Continue to the right, towards Mitteltal. At *Forsthaus Mitteltal* turn right to *Gutellbachbrücke*, cross the bridge and follow the stream into the **village**.

STAGE 2
Mitteltal to Schliffkopf

Start	Gasthaus Lamm, Mitteltal
Finish	Schliffkopf
Distance	19km
Difficulty	Medium
Time	5hr
Height gain/loss	790m/330m
Maps	Baiersbronn Touristik Wanderkarte Wanderhimmel Baiersbronn 1:25,000; Schwarzwaldverein Wanderkarte Hornisgrinde 1:30,000
Refreshments	Hotel Schliffkopf www.schliffkopf.de, Hotel Zuflucht www. hotel-zuflucht.de
Public transport	Bus to Lamm, Mitteltal. Return by bus from Schliffkopf, Schliffkopf
Access	Take B462 from Freudenstadt to Baiersbronn, then L401 to Mitteltal
Parking	There is a trailhead car park by the wildlife enclosure (*Wildgehege*) and playground. At Restaurant-Gasthaus Lamm turn off on Ellbachstraße. Turn left at Forsthaus Mitteltal and continue to the car park by the playground and picnic area.
Note	Much of the route runs relatively close to the B500 (Schwarzwald Panorama Road), which unfortunately means that at weekends there will be a lot of traffic as well as other walkers and cyclists on the trails.

A wonderful section of Seensteig, which includes one of the most beautiful and panoramic stretches on the famous West Way, from Lotharpfad to Schliffkopf. After the initial climb most of the walk is on fairly level ground, except for the loop down to Buhlbachsee.

From the centre of Mitteltal, at the corner of Gasthaus Lamm, follow Ellbachstraße up the valley. At *Ahornweg* turn right along the river. Cross the little bridge at *Gutellbachbrückle* and turn right, to *Forsthaus Mitteltal* and left towards the forest, past the car park

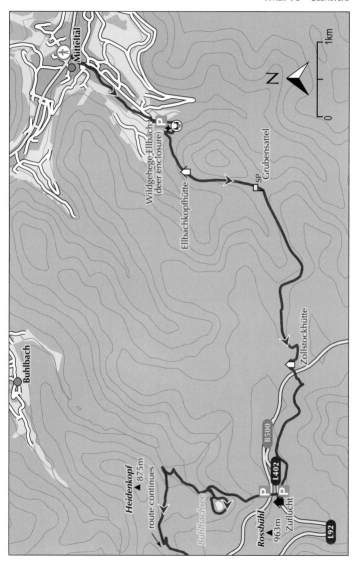

279

and playground. At the far end of the deer enclosure (**Wildgehege Ellbach**) follow the yellow markers towards Ellbachkopfhütte. The trail starts climbing up the hill to the right, skirting around the enclosure before turning sharply to the left on a footpath, which reaches **Ellbachkopfhütte** soon after crossing a forest road.

Pass to the left of the hut up the hill to reach the saddle (**Grubensattel**). Bear to the right of the benches past *Sauerbrunnenwegle* and straight past a hut by a bridge that lies just to the left. At *Ellbachschläger* continue straight on towards Zuflucht. Just after the bend look for a rough track that climbs up the hill, to *Täfele*. At the top join the forestry road to the left, past **Zollstockhütte**.

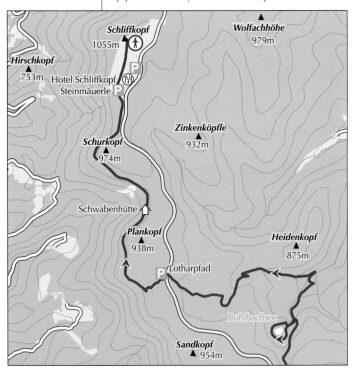

Lotharpfad

Cross the car park and the road and continue straight on to *Abzweig Zollstockhütte*, where Seensteig joins West Way to the right (red marker). At *Härtle* follow the red marker half right to **Zuflucht**.

Just before reaching a road Seensteig joins the blue-marked trail to the right. Cross the road and walk next to it for a few metres to the right. Ignore the mountain bike trail, but follow the track next to it, to the left (marked towards Obertal). Cross the B500 with care and the **car park** (*Parkplatz Bärenteich*) to continue down the hill on an uneven track. After a while the trail evens out as it follows the edge of the hill through the forest. Look for a sharp left turn that leads further down the hill, to a forest road junction at **Buhlbachsee**.

The lake lies about 200m to the left (yellow marker). You can circle around it, but on the far side the path starts to meander through the bushes close to the shore and is a little difficult to follow. Retrace your steps to signpost Buhlbachsee and continue on the broad forest road down the hill (blue marker). Ignore the first junction, but follow the second forest road to the left to *Spaltbächle*. Turn left up the hill on the old forestry track, towards Lotharpfad. At the top join a forestry road to the left and turn right at the T-junction. At the next T-junction turn right, then left at the following T-junction. Continue straight past *Hahnenmisse* to *Buhlbacherläger*. Turn right to reach the B500, by the Lotharpfad **car park**. ▶

Lotharpfad is closed during the winter if snow and ice make it unsafe to walk there.

West Way panorama

Lotharpfad takes its name from **Hurricane Lothar**, which devastated thousands of acres of woodland throughout the Black Forest in December 1999. The path leads through a windfall area that has largely been left undisturbed in order to gain insights into the self-regenerative processes of nature.

Cross the road and follow Lotharpfad through the jumble of trees past a viewing platform and down the hill to another forestry road at *Lotharpfad*, where Seensteig meets West Way again. Jointly they continue to the right towards Schliffkopf on a wonderful track with sweeping panoramic views across the Black Forest and the Vosges. Continue on the right forks at *Haferrütterank* and at *Schwabenrank* to reach the information board at **Steinmäuerle**. Climb straight to the top of **Schliffkopf** from Steinmäuerle, following the narrow trail up the hill. Alternatively, Tausendmeterweg continues straight past the viewing platform and *Jakobshütte* to *Am Tausendmeterweg*, where it turns uphill to the right.

To find the bus stop, return to *Steinmäuerle*, cross the car park and pass directly in front of the hotel. The bus stop is in the car park on the other side.

STAGE 3
Schliffkopf to Mummelsee

Start	Schliffkopf
Finish	Mummelsee
Distance	15.5km
Difficulty	Easy
Time	4hr
Height gain/loss	400m/400m
Maps	Baiersbronn Touristik Wanderkarte Wanderhimmel Baiersbronn 1:25,000; Schwarzwaldverein Wanderkarte Hornisgrinde 1:30,000
Refreshments	Hotel Schliffkopf www.schliffkopf.de, Ruhestein Schänke, Seibelseck www.seibelseckle.de, Darmstädter Hütte www.darmstaedter-huette.de, Berghotel Mummelsee www.mummelsee.de
Public transport	Bus to Schliffkopf, Schliffkopf. Return by bus from Mummelsee, Seebach (Baden) (limited services during the week)
Access	Schliffkopf lies on the B500 (Schwarzwaldhochstraße) between Mummelsee and Kniebis
Parking	At Schliffkopf Hotel off the B500 or Steinmäuerle car park on the other side of the hotel
Note	Schliffkopf, Ruhestein and Mummelsee are among the most popular spots in the northern Black Forest. At weekends it can get very busy. It is best to do this section during the week, when there is less traffic.

This is a very nice and easy section of Seensteig that runs mostly through the forest on small trails and through varying terrain. The walk can be extended to include a little detour down to Wildsee.

From the bus stop at Schliffkopf walk up past the hotel and across the car park to **Steinmäuerle**. Follow the trail to the right up to the top. Turn right by the summit cross and pass the war memorial, towards Roter Schliff (red markers). At *Hübscher Platz* you have a choice of either

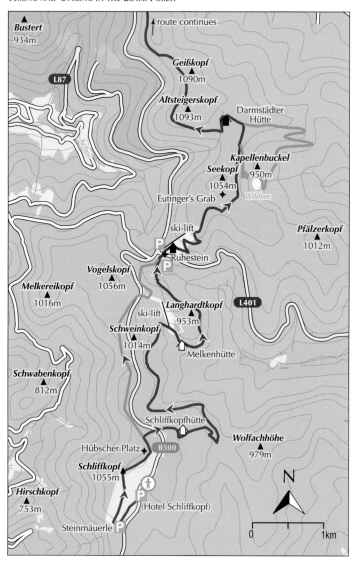

Schliffkopf

following Seensteig as described below, or to continue with West Way down to Ruhestein, the national park HQ.

Follow Seensteig towards the road to the right (yellow marker), cross carefully and continue down the hill on the other side. Pass a hut (**Schliffkopfhütte**) and by the little trail junction turn left down the hill.

At *Roter Schliff* follow the broad forest road to the left, towards Ruhestein. Soon after passing the ski-lift the trail reaches **Melkenhütte**, by a pond. Follow the 'sticks and stones' trail to the left, ambling first through blueberries and heather then through open woodland and finally through the forest to reach a ski jumping ramp. Head for the hut and turn right to cross the road at **Ruhestein**. ▸

Follow the red marker up to the top (or take the ski-lift) and continue straight on, past the information hut at **Seekopf** to **Eutinger's Grab**.

The memorial marks the grave of **Dr Euting**, a German orientalist, who also had a love for the Black Forest and the Vosges. He was a founding member of the Vosges Club and among the first to

If this section is closed, it is possible to continue to Ruhestein via the Westweg (red markers).

realise the touristic potential of the Black Forest and the Vosges as a holiday region for walkers.

Just after the memorial the trail splits. Continue on the small path straight past Wildseewegle and at the end join the broad gravel track to the right.

The trail to Wildsee is subject to seasonal closures to protect wildlife. The section from Eutinger's Grab to Seibelseckle is also affected, but there is an alternative route on a forest road.

Detour to Wildsee

Wildseewegle leads down the side of the hill through a strict forest reserve (Bannwald) to Wildsee. This trail is very steep and can be dangerous. Those attempting to go down this way must be surefooted and free of vertigo. Firm shoes with a good grip are essential. There is an easier way to get down to Wildsee a little further along, at *Bannwald*. ◄

At *Bannwald* turn left to reach **Darmstädter Hütte**. By the restaurant turn left down the broad forest road to *Ski-lift Darmstädter Hütte*. Turn right and cross the bottom of the ski slope, pass underneath the ski-lift and head towards the edge of the forest, where the trail continues as a little

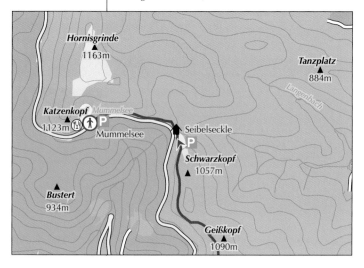

footpath through the woods. It soon emerges in a wind-fall area and meanders through heather, blueberries and many fallen trees. By a junction of unmarked paths bear left down the hill on the broader track. After about 150m follow the small path to the right through the bushes, down to a ski-lift at **Seibelseckle**.

Darmstädter Hütte

Cross the car park and continue to the right of the little eatery, following West Way markers up the hill on the broad track. At the fork continue to the left. Just before reaching the road and car park at the top bear to the right on a smaller path that leads to the West Way portal by the chapel. The **Mummelsee** is to the left. The buses leave in front of the hotel, by the big car park.

STAGE 4
Mummelsee to Schönmünzach

Start	Mummelsee
Finish	Schönmünzach
Distance	21km
Difficulty	Easy
Time	5hr30min
Height gain/loss	410m/990m
Maps	Baiersbronn Touristik Wanderkarte Wanderhimmel
	Baiersbronn 1:25,000
Refreshments	At Mummelsee and Schönmünzach, none along the way
Public transport	Bus to Mummelsee, Seebach (Baden). Return by bus or train from Schönmünzach (better service at weekends, check schedule in advance)
Access	Mummelsee is on the B500, access from Baden-Baden, or from Achern via Sasbachwalden on L86
Parking	At Mummelsee Berghotel
Note	Public transport back to Mummelsee is only feasible at weekends. Make sure to check bus and train schedules in advance. Some sections of the route are closed between November and May to protect wildlife. The National Forest service posts alternative routes in case of trail closures.

This section of Seensteig explores Hornisgrinde, the highest mountain of the northern Black Forest. From there it takes an easy amble around its slopes and along a ridge trail with open views to Schönmünzach.

Walk up on the access road behind the hotel. At *Berghotel Mummelsee* follow the red marker up towards Hornisgrinde. Take the right fork at *Markwaldweg* and at the next fork follow the stony trail up the hill to **Katzenkopf**. West Way goes off to the left, while Seensteig continues a little bit further up the hill and then turns left by the bench to re-join West Way. By the mountain

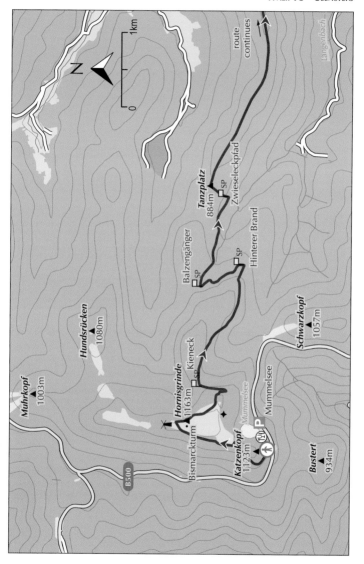

Dreifürstenstein

During the winter this section is open as a snowshoe trail and may not be safe to walk in regular hiking boots.

rescue hut Seensteig leaves West Way and continues straight on, skirting around the edge of **Hornisgrinde** on a narrow trail. ◄ Once it comes out onto the plateau continue straight on towards the wind turbines. On the other side of the plateau turn right to visit Bismarckturm.

Return to the slab stone-paved rim trail and continue along the edge of the mountaintop. Cross the moor on the boardwalk to reach the signpost for the **Dreifürstenstein**. Take the yellow-marked trail to the left, down through the strict forest reserve (Bannwald) to *Dreifürstensteinwegle* and turn left to **Kieneck**. Cross the trail junction and follow the grassy path straight down to a forest road. Continue to the left until the forest road ends at a timber landing. Look for Seensteig in the right-hand corner, leading steeply down the hill. At **Hinterer Brand** turn left to **Balzengänger** and continue on the little trail to the right. At the bottom join the forest road for about 1km to the left.

At **Zwieseleckpfad** Seensteig turns left and immediately forks off to the right on a rough track that leads steeply up the hill. It crosses a forest road and continues almost to the top before turning right to climb up to the ridge, first through the forest and then across a windfall area with views of the mountains in both directions. After about 4km the trail emerges on a forest road, turns right to the T-junction and continues to the left to reach a hut (**Bombenhütte**). ◄

Just to the right, hidden by the trees, lies another tarn, **Blindsee**, which has become almost completely overgrown.

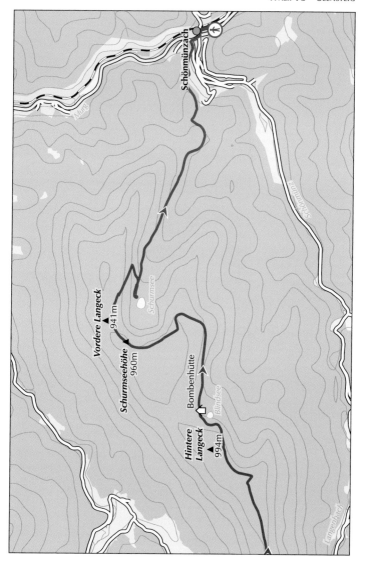

291

Ridge trail to Schönmünzach

Continue straight on to the crossroads at *Blindsee Abzweig* and take the left fork up the hill. At a trail junction Seensteig continues to the right and reaches **Schurmseehöhe**, where a wooden sign reads 'Aussicht mit Sitzbank', and points to a thin trail that leads to a nice bench with a lovely view down to **Schurmsee** and across the valley.

Only 200m to the right lies Schurmsee, almost completely round and surrounded by wooded hills.

Continue down the forest road for about 1km before following the blue marker down the hill, first to the right and then left on a rough track, past *Schurm* and straight down to *Schurmsee Abzweig*. ◄

Turn left towards Schönmünzach. At a T-junction where Murgleiter joins the blue-marked trail for the rest of the way, cross the forest roads and continue on a small path to another forest road junction. Briefly turn right and at the T-junction look for the footpath to the right of the raised hide, leading out of the forest to a panorama path. Continue along the edge of the field. Pass behind the second bench to join a gravel track to the left, which merges with another track.

Soon the trail forks off to the right and leads steeply down the hill, passing behind a house on a narrow trail to the left. Briefly follow the lane to the left before continuing on the little footpath to the right. At the bottom turn left to reach the main road. The station in **Schönmünzach** is across the bridge to the right.

RIDE 4

Enztal Radweg – Gompelscheuer to Pforzheim

Start	Gompelscheuer
Finish	Pforzheim
Distance	45km
Difficulty	Easy
Time	3hr30min–4hr
Height gain/loss	180m/600m
Maps	LGL Freizeitkarte F502 Pforzheim 1:50,000
Refreshments	Many options along the way
Public transport	A bus runs up to Gompelscheuer, but the capacity for carrying bicycles is limited. The next nearest best public transport access is from Bad Wildbad train station.
Access	Take B264 from Pforzheim to Calmbach, turn off on L351 to Bad Wildbad
Parking	It is best to park in Bad Wildbad (parking garage near the station) and take the velobus to Gompelscheuer
Trail markings	Picture of a raftsman
Note	Enztal Radweg continues beyond Pforzheim to Walheim, where the Enz joins the Neckar, but as this part goes beyond the geographical confines of the Black Forest it is not described here. It would be possible to combine Enztalradweg and Nagoldradweg as a multistage tour using Tälerrunde Radweg as a bridge between the two sources (not described in this guide).

High up in the hills above Enzklösterle the River Enz emerges as a bubbling brook. The cycle route follows the course of the river via Bad Wildbad, Höfen an der Enz and Neuenbürg to Pforzheim, where it meets the River Nagold.

Although a quiet backwater today, this area was extremely industrious throughout the 19th century, when the Enz was still a **major traffic artery** for transporting trees down to Pforzheim for further distribution. The 19th century also saw the birth of spa

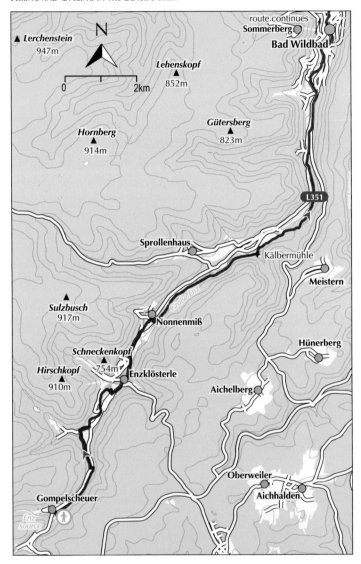

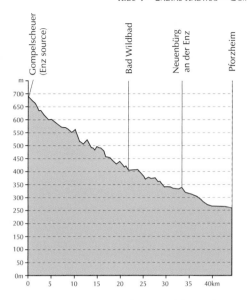

tourism in the region as the rich and famous from all over Europe started to flock to Black Forest spa towns such as Bad Wildbad.

Gompelscheuer–Enzklösterle (5km)
The source of the River Enz lies just to the left of bus stop 'Gompelscheuer'. The cycle route crosses the road and follows Sägmühleweg to the edge of the forest. Turn left on the forest track for about 2km. Cross the road to the left across a bridge and immediately turn right. Pass a trout farm and some playing fields. At the T-junction by a bus stop turn right, cross the bridge and continue along the river. Cross a small lane and continue straight. By the campsite bear right, past the Kindergarten to the main road. Turn left through Enzklösterle.

Enzklösterle–Bad Wildbad (13km)
After the village (by the sign for 'Sporthalle'), switch to the bike lane on the left. At bus stop 'Fabrik' follow

Source of the Enz

Enzauenweg through riverside meadows to bus stop 'Grüner Baum'. Cross the road and turn right for 50m. Cross the bridge and continue to the left along the edge of the forest to a trail junction at *Kälbermühle*. Briefly bear left, then continue to the right (before reaching the bridge). Pass the log sprinkling facility. After about 2km follow the left fork to a parking area and picnic spot by the road. Briefly continue next to the road. Turn right, uphill on Wasserleitungsweg. After about 1km cross a lane and continue on the other side on Alt-Aichelbergstr to the outskirts of Bad Wildbad. Cross the road and follow the bike path to the left, down to another lane. Turn left, across the bridge and along the river to the right. Just before the end of the last playing field bear right on the cycle path through the 'Kurpark'. By the little pagoda turn right, towards the road. Bypass the tunnel to the left and continue on the left-hand side of the street, past bus stop 'Kurpark' to the centre of Bad Wildbad.

Enztal Radweg
waymark (on the left)

Bad Wildbad–Höfen an der Enz (7km)
Cross the river and pass straight through the town to a roundabout (watch out for the trams, which run through the middle of the narrow street!). By a second roundabout bear half-left towards Calmbach and Höfen. Fork

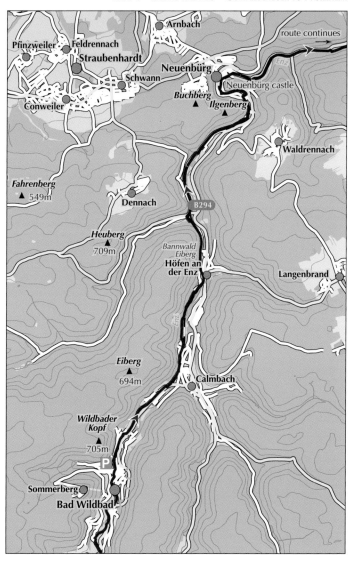

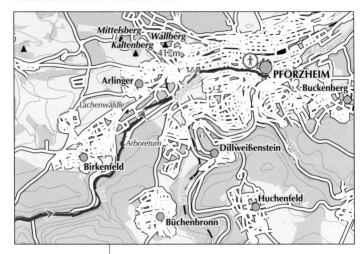

to the right on Paulinenstraße. At a junction continue to the right on Alte Calmbacherstraße. In Calmbach cross the train tracks. Follow the small path to the left. Bear left on Bahnhofstraße, past the station and continue straight, next to the tracks. At the end of the bike path cross the tracks and follow them to the right. At the first fork continue on Alte Höfener Straße. Pass the barrier at *Franzosen Brunnen* and bear right.

Höfen an der Enz–Neuenbürg (7km)
In Höfen cross the tracks and continue on the left side of the river. Cross the tracks again and follow them towards Neuenbürg. Pass the barrier and continue straight towards the road, turn right and cross carefully. Continue on the bike lane to the left of the tracks. Cross the tracks at Rotenbach station. Continue on the bike path next to the tracks past the train stop of 'Neuenbürg/ Freibad'. Cross the tracks to the left and continue straight through an industrial area of Neuenbürg. At the corner of Schlößlestraße turn right (there is a an unnamed walkers' signpost pointing towards Südbahnhof and other destinations). Cross the bridge and turn left on

Wildbader Straße. Turn left along the main road towards the town. ▸

Neuenbürg–Pforzheim (13km)

At the bend bear right towards Pforzheim. Follow Bahnhofstraße out of town. Pass underneath the train tracks and a bridge (B294) and turn left on Untere Reute (marked 'no-through road'). Continue to the end, past the water treatment facility. Bear left, slightly uphill and follow the bike lane next to the road. It soon drops below the level of the road. At a tight bend turn right (not back up towards the road) and cross a little footbridge. Follow the river to the left (West Way markers) all the way to the suburbs of Pforzheim, crossing the river a couple of times along the way. Turn left on Waldmeisterweg. At a bend continue straight on Herrenstrietweg. By Fingerhutweg bear left across a footbridge and follow the river to the right. The bike path joins Fritz-Ungerer-Straße. Just before a big junction bear right and pass below a bridge. After about 3.5km pass a huge car park to another bridge at Benckiserstraße. Cross the road via the underpass below the bridge and continue on Simmlerstraße. Follow the Enz to the confluence with the River Nagold, by the Convention Centre. To find the train station, retrace your steps to the last big road (Dillsteinerstraße/Leopoldstraße). Follow Leopoldstraße up the hill and bear right on Bahnhofstraße.

To get off the main road, continue on Uferweg just before the bend. Follow the lane to the right on Mühlstraße. At the T-junction turn right to the next corner and turn left on Bahnhofstraße.

Neuenbürg an der Enz

RIDE 5
Nagold Radweg – Nagold to Pforzheim

Start	Nagold
Finish	Pforzheim
Distance	56.5km
Difficulty	Easy
Time	4hr
Height gain/loss	250m/400m
Maps	LGL Freizeitkarte F502 Pforzheim 1:50,000
Refreshments	Many options in the little towns along the way
Public transport	Train to Bahnhof/Nagold. Return by train from Bahnhof/ Pforzheim
Access	Take M81 to Herrenberg, then B28 to Nagold, or B463 from Pforzheim
Parking	At Nagold station (follow Bahnhofstraße to Marktstraße)
Trail markings	Stylised landscape on green background
Note	The source of the River Nagold is up in the hills, near the hamlet of Urnagold, some 40km upriver. However, that first section is badly marked, and from Nagold Reservoir to Nagold much of the way runs on, or along a major road. The best part of this cycle route runs from Nagold to Pforzheim, almost entirely on quiet back roads and cycle paths.

This ride offers a very beautiful and culturally interesting tour that follows the River Nagold through a string of picturesque, small towns, famous for their historic timber-frame buildings. Some of these towns are also known for their healing waters.

Nagold–Wildberg (13km)
From the centre of Nagold follow Marktstraße to Oberamteistraße. Turn left, past the police station to the river and follow it to the right. Pass through the car park and bear left. Continue on Neuwiesenweg. After crossing

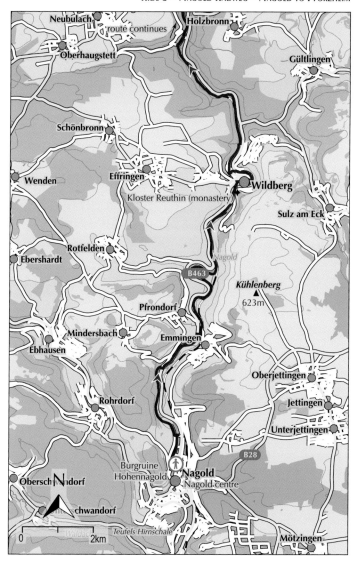

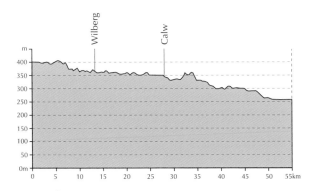

*Nagold Radweg
waymark*

the bridge the trail runs through river meadows. Take the sharp right turn towards Calw, pass underneath a bridge and continue on the right-hand side of the road for about 2km. Cross a wooden bridge and continue on the right-hand side of the river. Briefly join a little road to the left; then bear right, and stay on the right-hand side of the river, all the way to Wildberg. On the outskirts of Wildberg pass the old monastery of Reuthin and go through the park. Cross a covered wooden bridge and continue to the left. By the stone bridge turn left and follow the road to the right. At the junction turn left on Talstraße towards the town hall and the station.

Wildberg–Calw (15km)

By the station, cross the tracks and turn right, through the car parks. Follow the tracks and after 1km pass underneath them to continue on the other side. Follow the path to the hamlet of Seitzental and turn right at the T-junction. Continue straight past the restaurant to the next hamlet, Kohlerstal. Turn right towards the bridge, but follow the bike path along the river on a slightly hilly path before crossing the bridge. ◄ The trail ends by a road at Hotel Teinachtal. Turn right to the T-junction and right on the bigger road. By the fly-over, switch onto the bike lane on the left-hand side of the road and follow it through the village of Kentheim. At bus stop 'Tanneneck' turn left towards

Note Careful on the steep downhill passage.

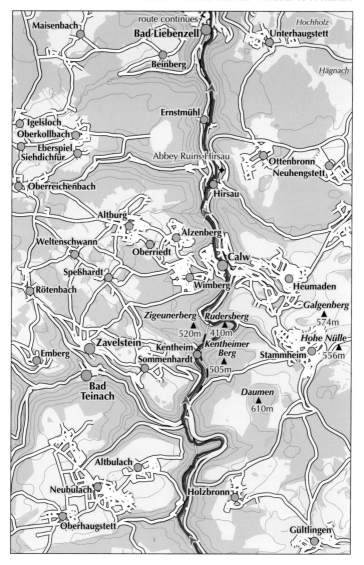

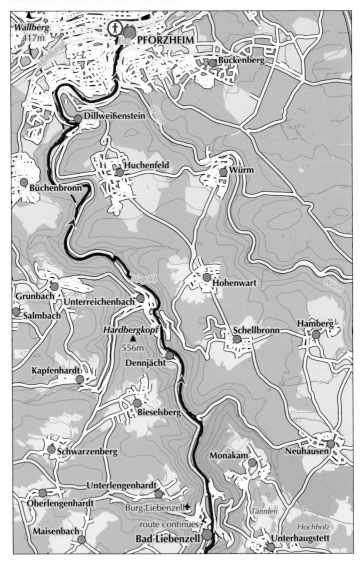

Senioren Residenz Schönblick, on the outskirts of Calw. Follow Badstraße into town, to Hermann Hesse Platz.

Nagold town

> Calw is the birthplace of Nobel Prize winning author **Herman Hesse** (1877–1962), famous for his classic novels *Steppenwolf, The Glass Bead Game, Narcissus and Goldmund* and many others.

Calw–Hirsau–Bad Liebenzell (7.5km)
Continue straight on to Marktplatz, briefly bear right and immediately turn left through the pedestrian precinct of Lederstraße. Cross another square and follow Inselgasse to the junction. Cross at the traffic light and continue on Hirsauer Wiesenweg by the fire station. Pass the sand and gravel depot and carry on straight past the barrier to the outskirts of Hirsau. By the small car park turn right, cross a footbridge and almost immediately cross another footbridge to the left to enter the Kurpark. Bear to the left through the park and at the end continue to

the left to pass below a bridge. Pass the playground and cross a car park up to the road. Cross the big road at the traffic light and continue up the hill on Erstmühlerweg. Bear left at the first fork. After the houses the trail runs between the train tracks and the river. In the next little village turn right, passing underneath the train tracks, and follow Liebenzeller Weg to the left to the outskirts of Bad Liebenzell. At the bottom of the hill turn left, cross the tracks and continue to the right on Regulastraße, past the station.

Bad Liebenzell–Pforzheim (21km)

At the bridge continue on the right side of the river on Ulmenweg. After passing a barrier continue straight through the bus-turning loop towards Monbachtal, along the river. Follow the path to the right to pass underneath the railway bridge, then immediately turn left across a bridge and left again to pass under the train tracks once more. Follow the idyllic path through the paddocks to Unterreichenbach. At the end, by the railway crossing, cross the road and continue straight on. Keep to the right

Trail near Unterreichenbach

Arrival in Pforzheim

without crossing the bridge. Bear right (uphill) after the water treatment facility and continue to the left. After passing the barrier cross the covered wooden bridge and head right, to pass underneath a concrete bridge.

After passing a picnic area and car park continue on Belremstraße, the upper street to the right, then turn left after the Youth Hostel, right before the bridge, on Mühlbergstraße, and continue along the river until the path comes up by a stone bridge. Continue straight ahead, then fork right on Friedenstraße. After about 150m follow the trail down to the right to continue along the river. At Kallhardbrücke cross the road and continue on Kallhardstraße, then bear right through the park to the bridge at Jahnstraße by the Jewellery Museum. Turn left and immediately right on Rennfeldstraße. Follow the street to the point where the Nagold flows into the Enz. Cross the little bridge and turn left along the Enz to Rossbrücke. Turn right, up the hill on Leopoldstraße and bear right on Bahnhofstraße to reach the station.

APPENDIX A

Route summary table

	Name	Distance	Height gain/loss	Time	Difficulty	Page
SOUTHERN BLACK FOREST						
Walk 1	Feldbergsteig	12km	570m/570m	4–5hr	Medium	49
Walk 2	Belchen	15km	630m/630m	5hr	Medium	53
Walk 3	High above Münstertal	19km	150m/1000m	5hr30min	Easy	58
Walk 4	Schönberg panorama trail	13km	510m/510m	4hr	Medium	65
Walk 5	Margrave's Land – Wiiwegli and Bettlerpfad	16km	380m/460m	4hr30min	Easy	69
Walk 6	Schluchtensteig	120km		6 days		75
Stage 1	Stühlingen to Blumberg	19.5km	580m/340m	5–6hr	Medium	77
Stage 2	Blumberg to Schattenmühle	20km	330m/380m	6hr30min	Easy	83
Stage 3	Schattenmühle to Aha	22km	780m/520m	7hr	Hard	90
Stage 4	Aha to St Blasien	17km	330m/490m	4–5hr	Easy	97
Stage 5	St Blasien to Todtmoos	18km	580m/540m	5hr30min–6hr	Easy	101
Stage 6	Todtmoos to Wehr	23.5km	430m/900m	7hr	Medium–hard	107
Ride 1	Southern Black Forest Cycle Trail	option 1 via Basle: 245.8km option 2 via Kandern: 235.8k		4–5 days		113
Stage 1	Hinterzarten to Bonndorf	38.5km	330m/340m	4hr	Easy	116

	Name	Distance	Height gain/loss	Time	Difficulty	Page
Stage 2	Bonndorf to Waldshut	51km	90m/650m	4hr	Easy	122
Stage 3	Waldshut to Rheinfelden	45.5km	180m/220m	4hr	Easy	129
Stage 4A	heinfelden to Steinenstadt via Basle and France	50km	180m/240m	4hr30min	Easy	137
Stage 4A	Rheinfelden to Steinenstadt via Kandern	45.5km	490m/550m	5hr	Hard	145
Stage 5	Bad Bellingen to Hinterzarten	61.5km	320m/180m	5hr	Medium	152
CENTRAL BLACK FOREST						
Walk 7	Kaiserstuhl rim route	21km	6010m/610m	6hr	Medium	165
Walk 8	Edelfrauengrab and Karlsruher Grat	11.3km	530m/530m	4–5hr	Medium–hard	170
Walk 9	Above Renchtal	24km	660m/590m	6hr30min	Medium	174
Walk 10	To the source of the Danube	21.5km	440m/440m	5hr	Easy	181
Walk 11	Zweribachfalls and Vosges chapel	18km	560m/560m	5hr	Medium–hard	186
Walk 12	Zweitälersteig	108km		5 days		191
Stage 1	Waldkirch to Kandel (or St Peter)	10km (19km to St Peter)	970m/30m (1090m/610m to St Peter)	4hr30min (6rh30min to St Peter)	Hard	193
Stage 2	Kandel to Simonswald	26km	530m/1380m	7–8hr	Hard	199
Stage 3	Simonswald to Oberprechtal	26km	1090m/950m	9hr	Hard	205
Stage 4	Oberprechtal and Höhenhäuser	25km	740m/520m	7hr30min–8hr	Medium	212
Stage 5	Höhenhäuser to Waldkirch	24.5km	390m/790m	6–7hr	Medium	217

	Name	Distance	Height gain/loss	Time	Difficulty	Page
Ride 2	Kaiserstuhl Radweg	64.5km	182m/182m	6hr	Easy	223
Ride 3	Kinzigtal Radweg – Alpirsbach to Offenburg	65km	210m/490m	4hr30min–5hr	Easy	232
NORTHERN BLACK FOREST						
Walk 13	Above Baden-Baden	11km	360m/360m	3hr30min	Easy	247
Walk 14	Sasbachwalden idyll	10.5km	530m/530m	3hr30min	Easy	252
Walk 15	Upland moors (Hornisgrinde)	14km	540m/340m	4hr	Medium	256
Walk 16	Kaltenbronn Moor	15km	96m/590m	3hr30min–4hr	Easy	261
Walk 17	Großes Loch and Teufelsmühle	17km	570m/570m	4hr30min	Medium	266
Walk 18	Seensteig	71km		4 days		270
Stage 1	Baiersbronn to Mitteltal	15.5km	450m/430m	4hr	Medium	273
Stage 2	Mitteltal to Schliffkopf	19km	790m/330m	5hr	Medium	278
Stage 3	Schliffkopf to Mummelsee	15.5km	400m/400m	4hr	Easy	283
Stage 4	Mummelsee to Schönmünzach	21km	410m/990m	5hr30min	Easy	288
Ride 4	Enztal Radweg – Gompelscheuer to Pforzheim	45km	180m/600m	3hr30min–4hr	Easy	293
Ride 5	Nagold Radweg – Nagold to Pforzheim	56.5km	250m/400m	4hr	Easy	300

APPENDIX B

Glossary of useful terms

Here is a selection of useful words while exploring the Black Forest, some too regional to find in the dictionary!

Almgasthof/Almgaststätte	mountain café/restaurant
Besenwirtschaft/Straußi	rustic farmhouse winery bistro, usually only open seasonally
Vesperstube	snack bar, eatery
Vesperkarte	snack menu

Unusual items you might find on the menu

Bärlauch	wild garlic (*Bärlauch* dishes are a seasonal speciality in spring)
Bibbeleskäs	smooth cottage cheese (like fromage blanc)
Brägele	fried potatoes
Brennerei	distillery
Flammkuchen	similar to pizza, but extremely thin and crispy, spread with crème fraîche and a variety of toppings
Gschwelldi	boiled potatoes (with skin)
Kartoffelsalat	potato salad
Knöpfle	similar to Spätzle, but comes as button-shaped pasta (*Knopf* = button)
Neuer Süßer	barely fermented grape juice, available only in September/October during the grape harvest
Obstler	mixed fruit brandy
Schäufele	pork shoulder on the bone, salted and smoked
Schupfnudeln	similar to gnocchi
Schwarzwälder Schinken	a cured, smoked ham (regional speciality)
Schwarzwälderkirschtorte	Black Forest gateau (chocolate-cherry gateau frequently laced with kirsch)
Spätzle	local pasta speciality, usually topped with melted cheese
Viertele	a quarter litre of wine
Wurstsalat	meat salad (sausage)
Zwiebelkuchen or Zwiebelwaie	onion pie, a seasonal dish usually served in the autumn with *Neuer Süßer*

More useful words to know

Allmend	community-owned pasture land
Alm	mountain pasture
Ausgang	exit
Auskunft	information
Aussicht	view (eg *Aussichtsplatform* = viewing platform, or *Schöne Aussicht* = nice views)
Bach/Bächle	stream
Bahnhof	train station
Bannwald	(in Baden-Württemberg) strict forest reserve
Bergwerk	mine
Besucherbergwerk	museum mine)
Bett & Bike	certification for cyclist-friendly hotels
Bildstock	wayside shrine
Brücke/Brückle	bridge
Brunnen/Brünnele	fountain
Buck	hillock
Bühl	small hill
Burg	fortress (theoretically a Burg has more of a defensive, fortified, character than a Schloss)
Dobel	ravine
Eingang	entrance
Etappe	stage (of a route)
Fachwerkstadt	a town dominated by old timber-framed buildings
Fachwerkstraße	a themed car route that passes through *Fachwerkstädte*
Fahrrad	bicycle
Fahrradverleih	bicycle rental
Fahrradweg	cycle trail
Fahrrad-Reparatur	bicycle repair shop
Fels/Felsen	rock
Fluss	river
Friedhof	cemetery
Fußgänger	pedestrian
Gastgeber	host (of accommodation)

Gasthaus	inn	*Schloss*	castle
Gemeinde	community	*Schlucht*	gorge
Gepäck	luggage	*See*	lake
Geschlossen	closed (a shop/restaurant)	*(Kinder)Spielplatz*	playground
Gesperrt/Sperrung	closed/closure (a trail)	*Sportplatz*	sports ground
Haltestelle	bus or train stop	*Sprungschanze*	ski-jumping ramp
Hauptbahnhof (Hbf)	main train station	*Staudamm*	weir
Hexe	witch	*Steg*	small bridge
Hock	a village party. These are jovial affairs mostly focused on local food, wine and crafts. There may be brass bands and various other local acts.	*Steig*	small, usually ascending trail (from *steigen*, to climb)
Hof	farm	*Straße*	street
Hütte	usually a basic shelter hut, often by a picnic and grill place	*Tal*	valley
		Teich	pond
		Turm	tower
Kapelle	chapel	*Umleitung*	diversion
Kirche	church	*Unterkunft*	accommodation
Kurhaus	the administrative centre of a spa town, but usually also has a café (and a public toilet)	*Wandern*	walking
		Wandern ohne Gepäck	walking without luggage
		Wanderbus	bus service that services popular walking routes
Kurgarten/Kurpark	landscaped park or garden with cafés and easy walking trails	*Wanderheim*	walkers' hostel
		Wanderparkplatz	car park with access to trails
Lebensgefahr	danger of death	*Wanderkarte*	(topo) map
Markt	farmers' market	*Wanderweg*	walking trail
Matten	pasture	*Wasserfall*	waterfall
Mühle	mill (*Wassermühle* = water mill)	*Weg*	way, trail
		Wegkreuz	crucifix often found at crossroads
NSG (Naturschutzgebiet)	nature reserve	*Weinberg*	vineyard
Pauschale	package deal (*Wanderpauschale* = package deals for walkers	*Winzer*	vintner
		Winzergenossenschaft	vintner cooperative
Pension	simple, private accommodation	*Wii*	local dialect for wine (pronounced 'vee')
		Vorsicht!	Attention!
Radeln	cycling (*Radler* = cyclist)	*Velobus*	Bus with a trailer for transporting bicycles
Radfahrer	cyclists	*ZOB (Zentraler Omnibus Bahnhof)*	central bus station
Radweg	cycle path		
Rathaus	town hall		

APPENDIX C
Further information

Unfortunately, there are no decent books specifically about the Black Forest published in English. To a limited extent it is covered in *Lonely Planet: Munich, Bavaria and the Black Forest*. A new edition was published in March 2013. There is a section dedicated to the Black Forest and Lake Constance in the Frommer's Guide to Germany.

The best source of information is the internet. The Black Forest Tourist Board (see below) has an excellent and very informative website that links to almost every little town's own pages for more detailed information about such things as accommodation and bike rental. This is probably the only website address that you will need to know.

When searching for information on the internet it is much better to check German pages with the help of Google translator or some similar device, than trying to glean information from English pages. Even if a German website does offer an English version, most of the time these only contain a fraction of the information that is available in German. This is particularly important when researching long-distance routes, which usually have their own websites that are kept current with information about the condition of the trail or any temporary closures.

Tourist information

The tourism infrastructure in the Black Forest is excellent. Most small towns have a tourist information office – look in the town hall (Rathaus), or Kurhaus – and quite a lot of information is also available in English, especially for the most popular places. Tourist offices also offer advice on walking routes and many sell their own maps of the immediate region.

Black Forest Tourist Board
www.schwarzwald-tourismus.info

Freiburg (Head Office)
Tourism Competence Center
Wiesentalstraße 5
79100 Freiburg
Tel +49 (0)761 896460
mail@schwarzwald-tourismus.info

Freiburg
Tourist Information am Rathausplatz
Tel: +49 (0)761 3881 880
info@visit.freiburg.de
https://visit.freiburg.de/

Breisach-Touristik/Kaiserstuhl-Tuniberg Tourismus eV
Marktplatz 16
79206 Breisach am Rhein
Tel: +49 (0)7667 940155
Fax: +49 (0)7667 940158
Breisach-touristik@breisach.de
https://tourismus.breisach.de/
www.naturgarten-kaiserstuhl.de/en

Hochschwarzwald (High Black Forest)
Hochschwarzwald Tourismus GmbH
Freiburger Straße 1
79856 Hinterzarten
Tel: +49 (0)7652-12060
info@hochschwarzwald.de
www.hochschwarzwald.de

Central Black Forest
Mittlerer Schwarzwald
Hauptstraße 17
77723 Gengenbach
Tel: +49 (0)7803930149
www.mittlererschwarzwald.de

Nördlicher Schwarzwald (northern Black Forest)
Tourismus GmbH Northern Black Forest
Sonnenweg 5, 75378 Bad Liebenzell
Tel: +49 (0)7052 8169770
Fax: +49 (0)7052 8169775

info@mein-schwarzwald.de
www.mein-schwarzwald.de

Nationalparkzentrum Ruhestein
Ruhestein 1
72270 Baiersbronn
Tel: +49 (0)7449-92998 0
Fax: +49 (0)7449-92998 499
info@nlp.bwl.de
www.nationalpark-schwarzwald.de/de

Pforzheim
Schloßberg 15-17
75175 Pforzheim
Tel +49 (0)7231 39 3700
Fax +49 (0)7231 39 3707
tourist-info@ws-pforzheim.de
www.stadt-land-enz.de

Villingen-Schwenningen
Rietgasse 2
78050 Villingen-Schwenningen
Tel +49 (0)7721 822340
Fax +49 (0)7721 822347
tourist-info@villingen-schwenningen.de

Transport
Deutsche Bahn (DB) www.bahn.com
Baden-Württemberg bus and train journey
planner www.efa-bw.de
Karlsruhe-Baden airport
www.baden-airpark.de/en/
Stuttgart airport www.flughafen-stuttgart.de
Friedrichshafen airport www.bodensee-
airport.eu/
Basle/Euroairport www.euroairport.com

Accommodation
Accommodation in all categories can be
booked conveniently at:
Buchungsservice Schwarzwald
c/o Lohospo GmbH
Tel: +49 (0)761154331-50
www.schwarzwald-tourismus.info
Bett & Bike
www.bettundbike.de
Wanderbares Deutschland
www.wanderbares-deutschland.de

Bike rental
Bike rental portal from Schwarzwald
Tourismus
www.schwarzwald-tourismus.info/erleben/
radfahren/fahrradverleih

Southern Black Forest Cycle Trail

Freiburg
Freiburg Aktiv
Wentzingerstr 15
D-79106 Freiburg
Tel +49 (0)176-54329898
info@freiburgbikes.de
www.freiburgbikes.de

Titsee-Neustadt
Intersport Ski Hirt
Titiseestr 26
D-79822 Neustadt
Tel +49 (0)7651 922 80
info@ski-hirt.de
www.ski-hirt.de

Ski Hirt
Seestr 37
D-79822 Titisee
Tel +49 (0)7651 936 16 33
titisee@ski-hirt.de
www.ski-hirt.de

Neuenburg
Fahrrad-Fachgeschäft Alfons Harwardt
Rebstr 12
D-79395 Neuenburg am Rhein
Tel +49 (0)7631 741 60

Kaiserstuhl

Vogtsburg
Fahrradverleih Kaiserstuhl
Unterholz 3
D-79235 Vogtsburg-Niederrotweil
Tel +49 (0)7662 6407
info@fahrradverleih-kaiserstuhl.de
www.fahrradverleih-kaiserstuhl.de

Breisacher Fahrradverleih
Fischerhalde 5a
79206 Breisach am Rhein
Tel +49 (0)7667 2871183

sid@fahrradverleih-breisach.de
www.fahrradverleih-breisach.de

Ihringen
Fahrzeughaus Schneider (no helmets)
Am Krebsbach 1
D-79241 Ihringen
Tel +49 (0)7668 6 55
https://fahrradverleih-ihringen.de/verleih

In Switzerland
www.rentabike.ch

Kinzigtal

Offenburg
The city of Offenburg operates a scheme that lets you use bicycles for free, for up to two days. All you have to do is show your passport and pay a deposit. Helmets are also available.
www.tbo-offenburg.de/dienstleistungen/liegenschaften/parken-auto/fahrradverleih

City-Parkhaus
Mon to Sat 07:00am – 8:00pm
Tel: +49 (0)781 76253

Kinzigstraße 3
77652 Offenburg
Mon to Sat 08am–12pm / 12:30pm-4pm
Fri 8am-1pm
Tel: +49 (0)781 92760
Fax: +49 (0)7819276236
info@tbo-offenburg.de

Enztal and Nagold Radweg
Due to the topography in the northern Black Forest, which is characterised by its narrow valleys and steep hills, cycling in the northern Black Forest with regular bicycles is a challenge (except along the routes described here). Thus, most places now only rent out e-bikes. The Alpstein Tourismus map (*E-biking in der Schwarzwaldregion Calw*) has a list of places where bicycles can be rented (mostly e-bikes), repaired or re-charged (e-bike).

The website of the northern Black Forest tourism association has a list of places where bikes can be rented, serviced or charged (e-bikes).

Tourismus GmbH Nördlicher Schwarzwald
Sonnenweg 5
75378 Bad Liebenzell
Tel +49 (0)7052 8169770
info@mein-schwarzwald.de
www.mein-schwarzwald.de

DOWNLOAD THE ROUTES
IN GPX FORMAT

All the routes in this guide are available for download from:

www.cicerone.co.uk/1021/GPX

as GPX files. You should be able to load them into most formats of mobile device, whether GPS or smartphone.

When you go to this link, you will be asked for your email address and where you purchased the guide, and have the option to subscribe to the Cicerone e-newsletter.

www.cicerone.co.uk

LISTING OF CICERONE GUIDES

BRITISH ISLES CHALLENGES, COLLECTIONS AND ACTIVITIES

Cycling Land's End to John o' Groats
Great Walks on the England Coast Path
The Big Rounds
The Book of the Bivvy
The Book of the Bothy
The Mountains of England & Wales:
  Vol 1 Wales
  Vol 2 England
The National Trails
Walking the End to End Trail

SHORT WALKS SERIES

Short Walks Hadrian's Wall
Short Walks in Arnside and Silverdale
Short Walks in Dumfries and Galloway
Short Walks in Nidderdale
Short Walks in the Lake District: Windermere Ambleside and Grasmere
Short Walks on the Malvern Hills
Short Walks in the Surrey Hills
Short Walks Winchester

SCOTLAND

Ben Nevis and Glen Coe
Cycle Touring in Northern Scotland
Cycling in the Hebrides
Great Mountain Days in Scotland
Mountain Biking in Southern and Central Scotland
Mountain Biking in West and North West Scotland
Not the West Highland Way Scotland
Scotland's Best Small Mountains
Scotland's Mountain Ridges
Scottish Wild Country Backpacking
Skye's Cuillin Ridge Traverse
The Borders Abbeys Way
The Great Glen Way
The Great Glen Way Map Booklet
The Hebridean Way
The Hebrides
The Isle of Mull
The Isle of Skye
The Skye Trail
The Southern Upland Way
The West Highland Way
The West Highland Way Map Booklet
Walking Ben Lawers, Rannoch and Atholl
Walking in the Cairngorms
Walking in the Pentland Hills
Walking in the Scottish Borders
Walking in the Southern Uplands

Walking in Torridon, Fisherfield, Fannichs and An Teallach
Walking Loch Lomond and the Trossachs
Walking on Arran
Walking on Harris and Lewis
Walking on Jura, Islay and Colonsay
Walking on Rum and the Small Isles
Walking on the Orkney and Shetland Isles
Walking on Uist and Barra
Walking the Cape Wrath Trail
Walking the Corbetts
  Vol 1 South of the Great Glen
  Vol 2 North of the Great Glen
Walking the Galloway Hills
Walking the John o' Groats Trail
Walking the Munros
  Vol 1 – Southern, Central and Western Highlands
  Vol 2 – Northern Highlands and the Cairngorms
Winter Climbs: Ben Nevis and Glen Coe

NORTHERN ENGLAND ROUTES

Cycling the Reivers Route
Cycling the Way of the Roses
Hadrian's Cycleway
Hadrian's Wall Path
Hadrian's Wall Path Map Booklet
The Coast to Coast Cycle Route
The Coast to Coast Walk
The Coast to Coast Walk Map Booklet
The Pennine Way
The Pennine Way Map Booklet
Walking the Dales Way
Walking the Dales Way Map Booklet

NORTH-EAST ENGLAND, YORKSHIRE DALES AND PENNINES

Cycling in the Yorkshire Dales
Great Mountain Days in the Pennines
Mountain Biking in the Yorkshire Dales
The Cleveland Way and the Yorkshire Wolds Way
The Cleveland Way Map Booklet
The North York Moors
The Reivers Way
Trail and Fell Running in the Yorkshire Dales
Walking in County Durham
Walking in Northumberland
Walking in the North Pennines
Walking in the Yorkshire Dales: North and East

Walking in the Yorkshire Dales: South and West
Walking St Cuthbert's Way
Walking St Oswald's Way and Northumberland Coast Path

NORTH-WEST ENGLAND AND THE ISLE OF MAN

Cycling the Pennine Bridleway
Isle of Man Coastal Path
The Lancashire Cycleway
The Lune Valley and Howgills
Walking in Cumbria's Eden Valley
Walking in Lancashire
Walking in the Forest of Bowland and Pendle
Walking on the Isle of Man
Walking on the West Pennine Moors
Walking the Ribble Way
Walks in Silverdale and Arnside

LAKE DISTRICT

Bikepacking in the Lake District
Cycling in the Lake District
Great Mountain Days in the Lake District
Joss Naylor's Lakes, Meres and Waters of the Lake District
Lake District Winter Climbs
Lake District: High Level and Fell Walks
Lake District: Low Level and Lake Walks
Mountain Biking in the Lake District
Outdoor Adventures with Children – Lake District
Scrambles in the Lake District – North
Scrambles in the Lake District – South
Trail and Fell Running in the Lake District
Walking The Cumbria Way
Walking the Lake District Fells –
  Borrowdale
  Buttermere
  Coniston
  Keswick
  Langdale
  Mardale and the Far East
  Patterdale
  Wasdale
Walking the Tour of the Lake District

DERBYSHIRE, PEAK DISTRICT AND MIDLANDS

Cycling in the Peak District
Dark Peak Walks
Scrambles in the Dark Peak
Walking in Derbyshire
Walking in the Peak District – White Peak East

Walking in the Peak District
– White Peak West

SOUTHERN ENGLAND

20 Classic Sportive Rides in
South East England
20 Classic Sportive Rides in
South West England
Cycling in the Cotswolds
Mountain Biking on the
North Downs
Mountain Biking on the
South Downs
Suffolk Coast and Heath Walks
The Cotswold Way
The Cotswold Way Map Booklet
The Kennet and Avon Canal
The Lea Valley Walk
The North Downs Way
The North Downs Way Map Booklet
The Peddars Way and
Norfolk Coast Path
The Pilgrims' Way
The Ridgeway National Trail
The Ridgeway National Trail
Map Booklet
The South Downs Way
The South Downs Way Map Booklet
The Thames Path
The Thames Path Map Booklet
The Two Moors Way
The Two Moors Way Map Booklet
Walking Hampshire's Test Way
Walking in Cornwall
Walking in Essex
Walking in Kent
Walking in London
Walking in Norfolk
Walking in the Chilterns
Walking in the Cotswolds
Walking in the Isles of Scilly
Walking in the New Forest
Walking in the North Wessex Downs
Walking on Dartmoor
Walking on Guernsey
Walking on Jersey
Walking on the Isle of Wight
Walking the Dartmoor Way
Walking the Jurassic Coast
Walking the South West Coast Path
Walking the South West Coast Path
Map Booklets
– Vol 1: Minehead to St Ives
– Vol 2: St Ives to Plymouth
– Vol 3: Plymouth to Poole
Walks in the South Downs
National Park

WALES AND WELSH BORDERS

Cycle Touring in Wales
Cycling Lon Las Cymru
Glyndwr's Way
Great Mountain Days in Snowdonia

Hillwalking in Shropshire
Mountain Walking in Snowdonia
Offa's Dyke Path
Offa's Dyke Path Map Booklet
Ridges of Snowdonia
Scrambles in Snowdonia
Snowdonia: 30 Low-level and
Easy Walks – North
Snowdonia: 30 Low-level and
Easy Walks – South
The Cambrian Way
The Pembrokeshire Coast Path
The Pembrokeshire Coast Path
Map Booklet
The Snowdonia Way
The Wye Valley Walk
Walking in Carmarthenshire
Walking in Pembrokeshire
Walking in the Brecon Beacons
Walking in the Forest of Dean
Walking in the Wye Valley
Walking on Gower
Walking the Severn Way
Walking the Shropshire Way
Walking the Wales Coast Path

INTERNATIONAL CHALLENGES, COLLECTIONS AND ACTIVITIES

Europe's High Points
Walking the Via Francigena
Pilgrim Route – Part 1

AFRICA

Kilimanjaro
Walking in the Drakensberg
Walks and Scrambles in the
Moroccan Anti-Atlas

ALPS CROSS-BORDER ROUTES

100 Hut Walks in the Alps
Alpine Ski Mountaineering
Vol 1 – Western Alps
The Karnischer Hohenweg
The Tour of the Bernina
Trail Running – Chamonix and
the Mont Blanc region
Trekking Chamonix to Zermatt
Trekking in the Alps
Trekking in the Silvretta and
Ratikon Alps
Trekking Munich to Venice
Trekking the Tour of Mont Blanc
Walking in the Alps

PYRENEES AND FRANCE/SPAIN CROSS-BORDER ROUTES

Shorter Treks in the Pyrenees
The GR11 Trail
The Pyrenean Haute Route
The Pyrenees
Walks and Climbs in the Pyrenees

AUSTRIA

Innsbruck Mountain Adventures

Trekking Austria's Adlerweg
Trekking in Austria's Hohe Tauern
Trekking in Austria's Zillertal Alps
Trekking in the Stubai Alps
Walking in Austria
Walking in the Salzkammergut:
the Austrian Lake District

EASTERN EUROPE

The Danube Cycleway Vol 2
The Elbe Cycle Route
The High Tatras
The Mountains of Romania
Walking in Hungary

FRANCE, BELGIUM AND LUXEMBOURG

Camino de Santiago – Via Podiensis
Chamonix Mountain Adventures
Cycle Touring in France
Cycling London to Paris
Cycling the Canal de la Garonne
Cycling the Canal du Midi
Cycling the Route des Grandes Alpes
Mont Blanc Walks
Mountain Adventures in
the Maurienne
Short Treks on Corsica
The GR5 Trail
The GR5 Trail – Benelux
and Lorraine
The GR5 Trail – Vosges and Jura
The Grand Traverse of the
Massif Central
The Moselle Cycle Route
The River Loire Cycle Route
The River Rhone Cycle Route
Trekking in the Vanoise
Trekking the Cathar Way
Trekking the GR10
Trekking the GR20 Corsica
Trekking the Robert Louis
Stevenson Trail
Via Ferratas of the French Alps
Walking in Provence – East
Walking in Provence – West
Walking in the Ardennes
Walking in the Auvergne
Walking in the Briançonnais
Walking in the Dordogne
Walking in the Haute Savoie: North
Walking in the Haute Savoie: South
Walking on Corsica
Walking the Brittany Coast Path

GERMANY

Hiking and Cycling in the
Black Forest
The Danube Cycleway Vol 1
The Rhine Cycle Route
The Westweg
Walking in the Bavarian Alps

For full information on all our
guides, and to order books and
eBooks, visit our website:
www.cicerone.co.uk.

CICERONE

Trust Cicerone to guide your next adventure,
wherever it may be around the world...

Discover guides for hiking, mountain walking, backpacking,
trekking, trail running, cycling and mountain biking, ski touring,
climbing and scrambling in Britain, Europe and worldwide.

Connect with Cicerone online and find inspiration.

- buy books and ebooks
- articles, advice and trip reports
- podcasts and live events
- GPX files and updates
- regular newsletter

cicerone.co.uk